NEWCASTLE

NEWCASTLE

A DUKE WITHOUT MONEY: THOMAS PELHAM-HOLLES
1693–1768

RAY A. KELCH

Professor of History,
San Francisco State University, California

ROUTLEDGE & KEGAN PAUL

LONDON

First published in 1974
by Routledge & Kegan Paul Ltd
Broadway House, 68–74 Carter Lane,
London EC4V 5EL
Printed in Great Britain by
Butler & Tanner Ltd,
Frome and London
© Ray A. Kelch 1974

ISBN 0 7100 7700 9

CONTENTS

At first glance it appears strange that no historian or biographer has completed a life of Thomas Pelham-Holles, Duke of Newcastle. He was active in the public life of the nation for nearly fifty years and the sources for a life are more abundant than for almost any other public figure of Georgian England. What is attempted here is a study of his economic resources and financial history rather than a full biography encompassing all areas of his activity, a work which we hope to see from the pen of Mr John Brooke. It is concerned with what is essentially the private man, with the economic reality behind the public façade so well known to his contemporaries. Indeed, Newcastle was so totally involved and committed to his public role that he might be said scarcely to have had a private life. No direct attention is paid to his official activities inherent in his great offices of Lord Chamberlain, Secretary of State or First Lord of the Treasury, or others, except where they impinge on his economic or financial interests.

This is the first attempt at a financial biography of a great public figure for the whole of his career as well as the first attempt to go behind the generalizations about Newcastle's finances made by generations of historians. The most surprising conclusion of this study for these historians will be that the extant manuscript sources do not provide evidence that political expenditures kept Newcastle on financial tenterhooks throughout his life. The sources demonstrate beyond reasonable doubt that it was primarily a grand ducal life style for over fifty years which was the main culprit and only secondarily his public and political charges. Although he was a paragon of economic irrationality in his own life, there is no evidence of any kind that he used the opportunities provided by his public offices to rebuild his private fortune, and even his contemporaries agreed on that.

The sources for the study are plentiful on one level and fairly scarce on another. The sources for his over-all financial history are plentiful.

First, among the hundreds of volumes of the Newcastle papers in the British Museum, there are many containing his personal and family correspondence, and that with the duchess, which provide large amounts of information relating to every aspect of his private life, his thoughts on his situation, advice he received from many sources, and actions contemplated or taken. Various special accounts, ledgers or abstracts for household expenditures, personal expenses, Sussex, etc., are also found there. Second, his private bank account survives in the ledgers of Hoare's Bank, as does that of the trustees of his estates. Third, the complete accounts of the trustees of the Newcastle estates from 1738 to 1770 survive among the Monson papers in the Lincoln-shire Archives Office, and, incompletely, from 1738 to 1752, among the Newcastle papers in the British Museum. Unfortunately, rentals and abstracts for the duke's estates have survived only for relatively brief periods, mainly the 1720s and 1730s, so a full reconstruction of his estates and landed income from this source is impossible. By bringing together data from all of these sources and accounts, as well as information from correspondence in various collections, it has been possible to reconstruct fairly completely and, hopefully, accurately, Newcastle's financial history.

It is hoped that this study will be a contribution to the economic and social history of the landed classes in eighteenth-century England and it may, as well, provide some possible explanations for New-castle's behavior at various points in his public career.

ACKNOWLEDGMENTS

The academic historian who enjoys teaching as well as research is often hard pressed for time to do both well. It is only when leave is earned that he may expend time in relatively undisturbed research which may, and often does, enrich his teaching. I would like to thank the Trustees of the California State University and College System for sabbatical and research leave during which time much of the research into Newcastle's life was completed.

For the use of manuscript sources in their care my thanks are owed to the Trustees of the British Museum, to the Public Record Office, to Lord Monson for permission to use his papers deposited in the Lincolnshire Archives Office; to the East Sussex Record Office for permission to use the Sayer Manuscripts; to the Chichester Estates Ltd for permission to use the Pelham papers in the custody of the Sussex Archaeological Society, Barbican House, Lewes; to the Duke of Newcastle for permission to use the Newcastle papers in the Manuscript Department of the University of Nottingham Library, to the India Office Library, to the Bank of England and to the National Register of Archives. My special thanks go to the ever-helpful archivists and librarians and their staffs in the record offices, libraries and other depositories where I have worked in the United Kingdom, as well as to those of the University of California, Berkeley, California State University, San Francisco, and the Henry E. Huntington Library, San Marino, California. Without the fine co-operation of Messrs C. Hoare and Co. in opening the bank's ledgers to me, and to their archivist Mr Reginald Winder, whose knowledge and uncommon courtesy made research there a pleasure, many areas of Newcastle's financial life could not have been known. Mr S. W. Shelton of Glyn Mills and Co. was most generous in giving help and guidance concerning eighteenth-century banking practices.

I would like to express my appreciation for help, suggestions, criticisms and encouragement to the following individuals, among the many to whom such acknowledgment is due: Professors Gordon E. Mingay of the University of Kent, H. J. Habakkuk of Oxford University, Ragnhild Hatton of the London School of Economics, D. J. Wenden, Bursar of All Souls College, Oxford, Clayton Roberts and John Rule of the Ohio State University, John Beattie of the University of Toronto, Henry Snyder of the University of Kansas, Henry Roseveare of the University of London, J. Jean Hecht of Columbia University, John L. Shover of the University of Pennsylvania, William L. Fisk of Muskingum College and William N. Bonds of California State University, San Francisco. Particular thanks are due to William P. Dunk for research assistance and to Lorraine Whittemore for editorial help. For typing and unusual patience I thank Mrs Dorothy Harvey and Mrs Diane Litchfield.

I would be ungrateful if I did not acknowledge the help and encouragement of members of my family: my late father Albert Robinson Kelch, who gave me a love of history, and my mother Clara Lindsey Kelch; my sister and her husband, Mr and Mrs David R. Canan, who helped make my university years pleasant ones, and Lawrence, James and Roy, my twin, good brothers all.

Professor-Emeritus Warner F. Woodring—scholar, teacher, friend and gentleman—deserves my entire thanks for introducing me to the pleasures and problems of England in the eighteenth century and I dedicate this book to him in sincere esteem.

These scholars and friends are not to be held responsible for the errors of commission and omission—which are my own.

INTRODUCTION

The Duke of Newcastle was an eighteenth-century Englishman attempting to function in politics. As a peer he had his place in the House of Lords and as a politician he served as a chief minister of the crown. Basic to both his political and ministerial careers was the landed wealth he had inherited and the political and social system into which he was born and which he never questioned. The elements which made Newcastle's public life possible were a product of the evolution of English society and institutions to his day, a concatenation of attitudes, beliefs and practices relating to political activity, landed wealth and social status which was uniquely English.

No greater error could be made than to assume from exalted social rank and daily life removed from the work-a-day world, that the English aristocracy in the eighteenth century was unconcerned about economic and financial matters. Underneath even the brightest ducal coronet was a head full of figures relating to accounts of income, debts, leases and the like, as well as the regular passions and prejudices of man. Any reading of family correspondence demonstrates their deep and lasting interest in things economic: marriage contracts, family settlements, wills, purchases and portions.

In Newcastle's day the aristocracy was the wealthiest section of the community, and titles roughly reflected degrees of wealth. An aristocracy without adequate funds was an anachronism, and status tended to erode when financial independence vanished. The aristocracy therefore attempted to create a system which would ensure continued financial stability for the family from generation to generation by means of the law of entail, by the strict family settlement, by carefully drawn marriage contracts and by the development of a system for the management of their landed estates.

The aristocracy was on the whole a consumer, not a producer, of wealth. Noblemen's incomes passed through their hands and ledgers

I

into those of the merchants and craftsmen who supplied their needs and desires. Only a few were investors in commercial or other ventures because they seldom possessed great liquid capital. If they had cash reserves or available credit they were likely to invest in land, which was the very symbol of their permanence.

The major source of income for the aristocracy was rents paid by tenants on their landed estates. The annual rents were supplemented from time to time by fines paid by tenants upon renewal of leases, and from sale of wood or other produce of the estates. The aristocrats did not as a rule engage in farming themselves, except for the home farm which produced some of the food and vegetables consumed by the family. Some fortunate ones received added income from leases granted for the exploitation of coal or mineral deposits on their lands, but the number of those who profited from this source is thought to have been relatively small. Still others had incomes arising from urban landholding, usually in London, which they leased or developed—such as the Bedfords—or from inherited leases—such as Newcastle's on Clare Market. An additional source of income for the aristocratic class was office-holding but this benefited relatively few. Some names stand out, such as James Brydges, Duke of Chandos, or Henry Fox, Lord Holland, each of whom profited greatly from holding the Paymaster's office. The importance of office-holding in aristocratic finance has been studied thoroughly in only a few cases, notably Professor Habakkuk's analysis of the estate and office income of Daniel Finch, second Earl of Nottingham.[1] Generalization is difficult, but it is likely that official salary and perquisites were only a supplement and not the mainstay in the incomes of those who held office. Office-holding might very well be an additional cause for expenditure and consume the profits of an office, as we will see in the case of Newcastle.

When annual income, savings, inheritance or marriage portions did not meet the costs of living, of improvements or emergencies, the aristocrats turned to borrowing. The sources of capital were few—goldsmiths, wealthy London merchants or even at times an affluent landowner—and finding the money posed a difficulty requiring the aid of one who knew the money market, usually a London scrivener or financial intermediary. Larger sums were usually borrowed by mortgage upon the security of the landed estates, while lesser sums were borrowed upon personal bond or promissory note. In dire need life annuities were sold but this was a very costly means of raising money. Debt was an ever-present companion for many families in the aristocratic class.

Restoration England, or more particularly London, saw the development of the goldsmith-bankers and the growth of the financial community. The aristocrats appear to have been fairly slow in making full use of the possibilities afforded by these developments. On the one hand the new banks could be used for the receipt and deposit of current income, for the easy transmission of money by bills of exchange to pay current charges, and on the other, as a source of funds for borrowing upon their estates or other security.

By the early eighteenth century several of the banking houses appear to have specialized in financial services to the aristocracy—among them Hoare's, Child's and Coutts. Newcastle's father, Lord Pelham, began using the service of Richard Hoare's bank and both Newcastle and Henry Pelham used it extensively, establishing what amounted to a tradition, just as the Bedfords consistently availed themselves of the facilities of Child's Bank. It would be difficult to overemphasize the role of Hoare's Bank in the duke's financial history during his active life. The duke appears to have had little personal contact with Sir Richard Hoare, his son or grandsons, nor does the bank appear to have profited in any unusual way from its involvement in Newcastle's personal financial life. In fact, when the bankers were calling in loans during the war-time credit crisis of 1759,[2] they treated Newcastle no differently from their other clients, for they called their mortgages on Claremont and Newcastle House and he had to turn to a non-banking source, Lord Clive, to hold his mortgage.

Since aristocratic income was largely derived from the ownership of land it was important for the continued solvency of the family that its estates be well managed or administered. Estate management had a long history going back to medieval monastic and collegiate usage and its problems were little changed in the eighteenth century. The hierarchy of management included the landowner himself, the land stewards on the individual estates, and a person variously known as a 'receiver-general,' 'overseer,' or 'man of business,' who stood between the owner and his stewards and who did the day-to-day work of supervising the financial affairs of the estate as a whole. On large estates an accountant was usually employed to check the accounts of the estate stewards, of receivers and of the household. As would be expected, some aristocrats found delight and reward in a careful interest in and supervision of their estate and financial affairs, especially the improving landlords, while others paid little attention to these matters until necessity demanded it. The land steward on the individual parts of the estate was the essential person, for he supervised bailiffs and had direct responsibility for tenants, leasing, improvements, repair and the like, as well as seeing that rents were regularly paid and forwarded to the estate office. Stewards were often local men of substance and the position was becoming somewhat professionalized by the eighteenth century, for we have textbooks appearing, such as Laurence's *The Duty of a Steward to his Lord* (1727), which detailed their duties and responsibilities.

The estate office from which the receiver-general worked was located at the principal seat of the family in the country or at its London residence. It appears that the affairs of the larger estates tended to be centred in London where accounts, records and correspondence were kept, and where all the services of the metropolis were at hand. It was the receiver-general who, naturally, received the income of the estate from whatever source, who issued money to the estate owner himself and to the heads of the departments of the household, and who paid charges of every kind.

In former times the income from the estate had been sent to the estate office in coin and was kept in a chest under lock and key. Although this practice continued well into the eighteenth century, with the more common use and acceptance of bills of exchange or drawn notes, and the development of deposit banking, it was much easier for the money to be diverted from the receiver's hands. At times the owner would order rents to be sent directly to him, or the stewards on their part would deposit their receipts directly in the bank. On other occasions the owner borrowed from his stewards in anticipation of the next rent collection. Such actions made the task of accounting much more bothersome and difficult and the receiver-general could not be at all certain of the financial condition of the estate much of the time. Newcastle's surviving estate accounts and his personal account at Hoare's Bank demonstrate that he and his stewards engaged in these practices.

Estate accounting was double-entry book-keeping, where the debit side was termed the 'charge' or all receipts of the receiver, while the credit side was called the 'discharge,' or all payments made, leaving a balance of cash either on hand or due.[3] This system underwent little change in the eighteenth century and it provided a check on the honesty of the staff as well as a rough over-view of the efficiency of the estate by comparing the rents, income, arrears, salaries, expenses, etc., year by year. However, the system was of no great value in testing the profitability of individual estates or the value of capital outlay, but its popularity demonstrates that it met the basic needs of the landed estates. Normally the annual accounts would be prepared by the receiver-general from information gained from the estate stewards' accounts, from the accounts maintained by the heads of the household departments and from his own receipts and disbursements. The whole was then checked by the accountant and finally submitted to the owner for his inspection and approval. The Duke of Newcastle followed this traditional pattern in all respects and in times of financial crisis paid very careful attention to his estate accounts.

It appears that the health of landed estates was seldom endangered by factors which were purely agricultural or administrative. The disease which threatened was usually over-spending and the consequent creation of debt which the produce of the estate could neither liquidate nor comfortably service. The remedy first recommended was reduction of current expenses. This meant retrenchment and it could be accomplished by closing houses, putting a temporary stop to building, retirement to the country, or even to the Continent, where expenses could be reduced without embarrassment. If these means were not effective, recourse could reluctantly be had to the sale of outlying parcels of the estate, if not entailed, or, if they were, by securing agreement to bar the entail. At other times a private Act of Parliament had to be obtained to effect a settlement of estate finances. Naturally the aristocrats placed the sale of landed estates last among possible options.

The creation of an estate trust, with the concurrence of the owner and of the major creditors, was a nearly final means of rescuing an estate and of possibly avoiding the sale of land. In such a case trustees took control of the estate and studied its financial condition—amounts and kinds of indebtedness, its income and possible improvement, and its full resources. Then they proposed a scheme for the reduction of expenses to fit an annual budget and provided a fixed but reduced income to be paid to the holder of the estate. The trustees used all sums remaining to pay off the most pressing creditors, to consolidate the remaining debt and to pay interest on it regularly and promptly, and to defray their own expenses. Thus a trust removed, partially or completely, the control of an estate from the hands of its legal owner for either a fixed or an indeterminate period. No full study has been made of eighteenth-century landed trusts but Professor Mingay has demonstrated that the trustees (strictly, guardians) for the second

Duke of Kingston, who was an orphan and a minor, did such a thorough and effective job during their six-year administration, 1726–1732, that they paid off most of the large debts, put the accounting system in order, improved estate management and increased the net yield of the properties by a third.[4] On the other hand, the Myddleton family of Chirk Castle, who had garnered large debts through extravagance and partly through electioneering costs, were not saved by a trust. The trustees were not able to prevent debts from growing and much of the estate had to be sold.[5] It can be said that trusts were unusual, for most sensible owners would not have endangered their estates to the degree where they would have lost control of their inheritance. We shall see that Newcastle's heedless spending and enormous debts necessitated the creation of an estate trust in 1738; this trust could not by itself save him without a new family settlement arranged in 1741, which made it possible to sell land to pay off great indebtedness. The trust and the settlement saved him from bankruptcy but sadly reduced his income in the process.

We have seen that the aristocracy was a consuming class, and by its very nature it consumed in a conspicuous manner in order to sustain its status in society. The great peaks of expenditure in building, in marriage portions, in provisions for children, or grand tours and the like, are easily noted but it appears that it was the day-to-day costs of maintaining one or more households in the country and in London which consumed the major part of aristocratic incomes. If extraordinary costs could not be met from current income or savings, then the aristocracy had no choice but to borrow and this they did.

The Duke of Newcastle was not a bourgeois. He lived in England's most aristocratic age and was a member of a select nobility and he reflected the values and ways of life of that world. He was not creative in his life style, in his political ideas, in the manner in which he conducted his economic affairs or in which he organized his household and family. Yet he was different; he spent almost his entire adult life in national politics as a holder of great offices of state and in the management of his own and the government's electoral interests. At the same time he lived on a truly grand and ducal scale which consumed the produce of his great estates, his offices, and many of the estates themselves.

The personalities, interests and activities of both the duke and the duchess had a direct bearing on their financial life and problems. First we will consider each as an individual personality and then proceed to recreate the structure of management of the estates, of their financial affairs and of their household.

THOMAS: THE DUKE

Newcastle has rarely been considered as a private individual and therefore usually appears as one-dimensional: as a politician-courtier-statesman, attired in court dress and bedecked with his blue ribbon, hustling about involved in affairs great and small. His contemporaries judged him severely, and usually ungenerously, as a man whose great wealth and connections gave him a station beyond his abilities, who was hampered in the use of the abilities he possessed by his own fears, insecurities and jealousies; as one who loved power for its own sake; as one who worked incessantly but accomplished little and did not see national policy needs clearly; but as an almost indispensable political manipulator and manager. Contemporary judgments on the man were usually political or politically coloured and related largely to his public life.

Personal comments concerning him usually dealt with his obvious eccentricities, which were always fine material for funny stories; with his busyness; or with his love of fine food, entertainment and the good things of life. It is worth noting that to a generation which loved gossip more than most and which retailed it with eagerness in correspondence, Newcastle's personal and private character is unblemished. He avoided the sins of the flesh, he gambled only socially, he drank moderately except at election entertainments or great celebrations and he consciously sought to avoid viciousness in his relationships with his fellow men. He was always ready to impute to his own folly all of his problems. Although his private financial problems were known to the political world they were seldom mentioned, except by Horace Walpole and some writers of doggerel verse.[6] He was surely the strangest man in public life in eighteenth-century England, and his eccentricities may well have helped him escape the added charge of dullness.

Newcastle was honest with himself about his own personality and abilities. In 1739 he wrote a very confidential letter to his friend and counsellor, Lord Hardwicke, which was transcribed by the duchess, in which his self-image was displayed. 'My dear Lord, I know myself as well as any of my friends know me, my Temper is such, that I am often uneasy and peevish, and perhaps, what may be called wrong headed, to my best Friends, but that allways goes down with the Sun, and passes off, as if nothing had happened.' In the same letter he recited his service as Secretary of State for fifteen years, the first seven of which he served with Lord Townshend, 'and then, never thought, myself, or could be thought by any body, but to act a Subordinate part in the House of Lords, but for eight successive Sessions, my Station has unavoidably brought me to be foremost in the Scene of action there, I shall say nothing to you one way or another of my qualifications, I am not vain of my abilities.'[7] A few discerning persons of his own time saw behind the hustle and bustle a man of ability and felt him commonly judged beneath his worth; and modern historians have been, on the whole, more generous in their judgments of him than the bulk of his contemporaries.[8]

What part did this man of admitted average ability, and who was eternally busy in political and public affairs, play in the management of his own financial interests? The answer to that query is one of the purposes of this study but any answer must be qualified by the duke's economic beliefs or understanding. First, the duke's economic values had been internalized by his early training and environment. His position was not that of a middle-class citizen but rather that of an aristocrat who looked upon money or capital as an item to be used or expended to sustain a public station and to meet private need. He did not look upon capital as an instrument for the creation of additional wealth; he did not invest it in company stock of any kind nor did he invest it in land to add to his annual income. He spent it. Second, the duke possessed a basic financial honesty which was a matter of conscience with him. This honesty covered public funds as well as private financial interests. This attitude was probably inculcated by his father, but it was repeated constantly by his mentor, Bishop Bowers, who pointed out to him the importance of financial probity in maintaining a good family name, reputation and interest. Newcastle was fearful of defrauding people and stated that he wanted no one but himself to suffer from his folly in spending too much. Further, Newcastle had strong guilt-feelings about his inability to oversee adequately his own estate affairs, as a noble in his station should. He was eternally promising to change and to improve his ways, and upon occasions of real crisis in his financial affairs he did so for a few months. He could not and would not change his habits and life-style and become an ordinary landed gentleman whose primary concern was the welfare of his estates.

8

The duke did not spend money solely for his own needs; he was also very generous to his aides, staff and family, whether he had the money in hand or not. He also was generous with sinecures for those who served him, as was expected, but there was never enough to go round and some solicitations bore no fruit. Owing to his public activities, the duke depended to an unusual degree on his higher servants, and his frequent inattention to his personal financial interests, an inattention which in at least one instance continued for over half a year, invited abuse. However, on the whole, the surviving evidence suggests that he was ably and faithfully served by those he employed.

Newcastle realized that he alone was responsible for his financial condition and never attempted to blame anyone else. No one could control him in the use of his own wealth, and his expenditures were directly related to his various roles in life. None the less, he was forever seeking advice, both personal and professional. All of the duke's major political protégés were also involved at one time or another in seeking to help him save himself from a financial crisis or collapse: Philip Yorke, Lord Hardwicke; Andrew Stone; and William Murray, Lord Mansfield.

Is there a key to understanding this man and his personal and public roles? In every outward way he was a man of his own time and class: in life style, in appearance and dress, and in political ambition and service. Yet dozens of contemporary evaluations and descriptions of him and his actions picture a strange, almost unbelievable person, who none the less held important posts in practically every ministry.

It has been suggested by no less a person than Namier, and by others since, that any attempted explanation of Newcastle must be in part psychological. It appears to me that it was his child-like insecurity, as evidenced by his overweening need for recognition, appreciation, indeed love, which is the basic factor most useful in explaining his life-long patterns of behavior. We know little of his childhood: his mother died when he was about seven years of age and the shock of this loss may have some significance in the formation of his personality. His father did not marry again. He attended Westminster School, for which he retained a fondness, and later matriculated at Clare Hall, Cambridge, which fixed a love of that university in his heart forever.

One can see in so many of the duke's actions an almost pathetic demand for affection, approbation or for concern for his situation. He was afraid to anger, affront or disappoint anyone high or low, for he did not know when he might need these 'friends.' In the Pelham family his affection for his only brother Henry was deep and his dependency real. The affection was reciprocated by Henry; but the duke personalized any political or family disagreement as a lack of love for him or lack of understanding of his predicament of the moment, as we shall see. The duke was close to his sister Lucy, who married Henry Clinton, Earl of Lincoln, but was not particularly so with his other sisters. The extended eighteenth-century family was nearly always a large one, for kinship was claimed on all sides even when blood relationship was slight. This custom was helpful in the political life of the century but was of small value in meeting emotional needs. Newcastle was close to some nephews, nieces and Pelham cousins, but other relatives do not appear to have played a major role in his existence. They were useful politically.

Even in the case of his personal staff, the duke's need for service was mixed with his own need for a close social and affectional relationship. This was demonstrated clearly in his association with Andrew Stone, who had been in his service from about 1734 as his private secretary and who was M.P. for Hastings, as well as Undersecretary of State. In the summer of 1743 Stone was about to be married and the duke was apprehensive that his secretary would no longer have the time or inclination to come to Claremont. In writing to Stone, rather than speaking to him directly, the duke displayed his emotional dependence upon him: [9]

> I am persuaded you know too well my real affection & friendship
> for you, to doubt the satisfaction I have in the prospect of your
> happiness. . . . You know the confidence I have for many years
> had in you & you cannot be ignorant of the satisfaction I have
> had in your conversation which I have always found agreeable,
> & in many respects useful to me. You must know also my way of
> life, & my Inclinations, make it necessary for me, to have one
> with me in whom I can spend my leisure hours with pleasure,
> such a one I have ever found in you, but I am not so unreason-
> able as to think that can be the case hereafter to the degree that
> it has been, . . . [if you cannot go on] I will be looking for some
> other person, to pass my private hours with, and who may be
> of some use to me also in the dispatching of necessary business.

Stone replied from Whitehall, assuring Newcastle that his marriage would not lessen his ability or desire to serve him after the summer, when perhaps he could 'by some small Relaxation of my office-attendance in Town, when not called by particular business' have plenty of time to spend with him at Claremont.[10] Personal and private attendance, as well as competence, were required by Newcastle from his personal staff, for the dependence was both professional and emotional.

Newcastle's need for affection and approbation is one explanation for his activities on the patronage side of political life, an area which required infinite attention, vast amounts of work and much worry on his part. He used patronage not only for the obvious and known purpose of stabilizing the Whig or government position but also to bind people to him by personal obligation—politicians, clergy and family. When writing he naturally gave the accepted and expected public reasons for his incessant electoral activity, that he was serving 'the Good Old Cause,' the tradition of the Revolution, or 'the Present Royal Family,' as he usually termed it. He would have been incapable of writing of the satisfaction of his emotional needs through the use of patronage even if he sensed it. Contemporaries remarked repeatedly on his inability to say no to supplicants for his recommendation; he eternally promised to intercede for everyone; and when the impossibility of his promises became obvious he was charged with untruthfulness, insensitivity or double-dealing. Thus by his behavior he added endlessly to his ample list of real or imagined 'enemies.' His personal need made him a willing slave to the minutiae of the eighteenth-century arts of political patronage in church and state.

Many of Newcastle's personal eccentricities, his fear of offending, his restlessness, his jealousy, his peevishness at times and his general timorousness were a result of his psychological makeup. His contemporaries made particular point of noting mannerisms which were not expected to be found in an aristocrat conscious of his station. Charles Hanbury-Williams noted 'his disagreeable manner, his affronting vivacity,' in a letter to Henry Fox in 1754,[11] while Richard Glover commented on his qualities 'of notorious insincerity . . . and servility to the highest and the lowest.'[12] Lord Chesterfield, who at least attempted to be fair, carefully made note of those characteristics which should not be a part of a nobleman's behavior at his levees: 'he accosted, hugged, embrased, and promised every body, with a seeming cordiality, but at the same time with an illiberal and degrading familiarity.'[13] Horace Walpole made repeated statements about his psychology which show insights into the man, such as 'he had no pride,' that he served and caressed both friends and enemies until they were beyond needing his aid, 'then he would suspect they did not love him enough,' and finally, 'always inquisitive to know what was said of him, he wasted in curiosity the time in which he might have earned praise.'[14] Walpole, although a very sharp and mean critic of the duke, whom he did not actually know well, saw clearly the point under discussion: Newcastle's constant need for affection, for reassurance and for praise. He could never get enough of it for him to feel that it was meant or perhaps deserved. His basic insecurity always defeated him and the next day he needed to be reassured all over again, for neither ducal rank in the peerage, nor vast wealth, nor high office gave him defenses against his fears.

Tobias Smollett must have been present at some of Newcastle's levees, for his humorous descriptions of them compare favorably with the serious comments of Lord Chesterfield. In one description, in *The History and Adventures of an Atom*, he pictured Newcastle's manner at these gatherings as 'grinning, giggling, laughing, and prating, except when fear intervened' and that he promised all to those who solicited his aid. 'He shook one by the hand; another he hugged; a third he kissed on both sides of the face; with a fourth he whispered; a fifth he honored with a familiar horse laugh.' Most tellingly Smollett noted, 'He never had courage to refuse even that which he could not possibly grant: and at last his tongue actually forgot how to pronounce the negative particle.'[15] Smollett was building his tale on fact and although he wrote it for humor, which it certainly contains, it is not to be wondered at that some of his contemporaries thought the duke but little above a buffoon.

The constancy of Newcastle's spending habits throughout his life-time supports the contention that he was driven to spend by an inner compulsion or need as well as by the normal demands of his social and political station. Other noblemen of great wealth held positions of high trust, but did not ruin their estates as a result, while still others greatly improved their estates thereby. We shall demonstrate that the duke's problems came not from direct political expenditures but from his style of life and open-handed generosity to one and all. He could not stop spending in spite of repeated promises made at every stage of his life, from as early as 1715 to as late as the 1760s. He built or re-built Claremont, he improved Newcastle House, he added to Halland and to Bishopstone in Sussex and refurbished Nottingham Castle—all places where he could receive his 'friends' and feast and entertain them, as he did from kings down to tenants. His parks and gardens provided the frequent gifts of venison and melons, etc., which he sent to individuals and to corporations. The entertainment and the feasts at his various seats, as well as the gifts, all showed his generosity, his station, and were Newcastle's means of earning personal praise, as well as binding persons to his election interest.

The reckless use of his wealth, the willingness to accumulate vast debts, the heedlessness of warnings of the verge of insolvency, and the disregard of expert financial advice are so irrational that the duke's emotional need to spend or give away his substance appears to be the best explanation of his behavior. He realized his limited ability and probably undersold himself, but he could compensate for lack of great gifts of mind by his gifts of substance. Even his great estate and great salary could not produce enough substance to sustain the generosity, generated in part by his insecurities.

The person most intimately involved in his emotional and financial life was the Duchess of Newcastle. Historians have ignored her for the good reason that she did not actively participate in his public life. However, in this study her activities and interests are of consequence, and it is important to consider her place in her husband's life and actions.

HENRIETTA: THE DUCHESS

Henrietta Godolphin, or Harriot as she was familiarly called, shared Newcastle's life for over fifty years; yet she remains a somewhat shadowy figure. She lived at Claremont or in London and engaged in the expected pursuits of her class, visited her aristocratic friends in their great homes and entertained in return, took the waters at Bath, enjoyed music, the theatre and gambling. She did not like the constant round of political activity in which her husband engaged and evidently took little part in his public life. She did not, like the strong-willed Gertrude, Duchess of Bedford, intrude herself into her husband's political interests. After all, politics was a man's world.

The duke and duchess were apart a great deal of the time, as witness the volumes of correspondence, for the duke wrote to her frequently even if it were only what he termed 'a little Dabb' dashed off during a break in his busy routine. He was in London much of the time and she was at Claremont; when he was at Claremont he was likely to be surrounded by his personal staff or advisers and engaged in office or political discussions. It is obvious that the duke's passion for politics, and the business of his offices, left him little time for regular domestic enjoyments with his wife.

The duchess was intimately involved in the financial welfare of her husband but she was protected to a degree by her marriage settlement which provided for her jointure and for her pin money. However, her husband's constant financial difficulties affected her directly, and he often called upon her to be his surrogate in looking into the condition of affairs in the family with the accountant, since he was unable to do so adequately himself.

Their marriage was a typical arranged one for their class, as we will see, but they apparently came to love each other very much. Although they were hopeful, during the early years of marriage, for children, it became obvious that there would be none. About six months after their marriage it was rumored in Bath that the young duchess was dying. Vanbrugh wrote to his friend Newcastle, 'My business now, is only to congratulate Yr Grace ten thousand times on the falseness of that Story tho' I find there was enough of it true, to give you a round Allarm. I am extremely glad to hear your danger is over, of Losing a Wife, whose place you can never Supply.'[16] Vanbrugh's solicitude may well imply that the duchess had suffered a miscarriage. The duchess was apparently frequently ill but much of her illness appears to have been psychosomatic. Some references to her personality and activities make it appear that she was neurotic—she was surrounded by doctors, and the duke had an apothecary among his regular staff. Both appear to have been hypochondriacs of the first order.

The correspondence provides glimpses of their personal relationship; it is obvious from them that the duke came to love his wife and that he depended upon her greatly. Newcastle left his duchess shortly after Christmas 1718 to go north to look over Nottingham Castle, which was being refurbished. He wrote to describe the castle and their apartments and told her, 'Dear Harriot believe me I will come the first Moment I can, for I long prodigiously to be with you, but am now preparing everything for our pleasure in the summer.'[17] He wrote again two days later and ended by saying, 'I long to see My Dearest, Dearest Girl, & am & always shall be Most Affect'ly My Dear Harriot,' and signed his letter, as eighteenth-century husbands often did, with his formal signature, 'Holles-Newcastle.'[18]

We know that she refused to go to Sussex with the duke when he was canvassing and electioneering. She was concerned about the amount of drinking he did upon these occasions. When he was in

Sussex in 1721 on such a mission, she wrote regularly to him and expressed her concern, but he replied on March 8 that he had 'spent all day Burgessing att Hastings & hardly drank a drop.'[19] However, his abstinence could not last and in spite of his promises he had to tell her, 'we had a great deal of Company att Haland, where I transgressed for the first time since I came into the country. I was a little sick this morning, & wanted prodigiously My Dear Nurse. I am mighty well this evening.'[20] The hangover he suffered from his transgressions evidently had taken the pleasure out of his visit to his home county, for he wrote later from East Grinstead that the receipt of her letters 'is the only pleasure I have in the Country, for I must own I am thoroughly tired with all these diversions, I used to love in Elections.'[21]

The duke depended on the duchess for security at home and for a haven from the tensions of his public life, but upon occasion, as in all relationships, disagreements took place. For example, in 1759, after forty-two years of marriage, they had a major tiff. Guests had come to Claremont and during their visit some disagreement had caused the duke to lose his temper; his remarks had angered the duchess. The duke, perhaps unwilling to risk a face-to-face scene, wrote to ask his wife's forgiveness and pardon:[22]

Be the same to me, you ever was. For Godsake My Dear, consider the many Happy years we have by the Mercy of God had together; how much our Mutual Happiness depends upon each other; you know, you must know, how much, how sincerely I love & esteem you; you must also know, that if once your affection, your dear Warm Heart is altered to me, I shall never have a Happy Moment afterwards, all other uneasiness, & affliction I can get over, from that I never can, & this is *the Most Solemn Truth.*

What were the abilities of this granddaughter of the great Marlborough and his strong-willed duchess? Did she inherit any of the financial acumen of her grandparents? There is no doubt of her ability to keep her private accounts, for two of them in her own hand survive, one for the period 1737 to 1750 and the other for 1757 to 1776, the year of her death. They were very carefully done and her expenditures categorized over a long period of time. These accounts are the best available evidence of her activities and interests in life. Perhaps most obvious from them is her serious interest in music. She studied the harpsichord with Dr Maurice Greene, a well-known London organist of St Paul's and professor of music at Cambridge, as well as a composer of harpsichord and organ music. She noted in her accounts, 'paid Dr. Greene 6 mos. learning 18 guineas,' and for composing, 'Dr. Greene for his anthem, Jan. 1743, £21.0.0.' She also paid a great sum to 'Signr Adams for writing music, £366.'[23]

The accounts show her various charities to persons and institutions, such as her annual subscription of ten guineas to Hyde Park Hospital, payment of wages to her personal servants, medical bills, vials when visiting, and books, 'For a French play of Volterre's [sic] 2.6.' She kept strict account of her gains and losses at gaming and maintained a separate column for each game played: bragg, quadrille, tridrille, whist, cribbegge [sic] and piquet. She seems to have been a consistent loser year by year; in 1738 she noted, 'Lost at play in the whole year £35.0.0.' which is close to an average figure, but in the year 1744–5 she lost £162.[24] At least the duchess knew the annual cost for this form of recreation and her figures mean that she noted her good or ill fortune each day she played. She also kept very careful accounts of the money she spent for clothes and lumped these expenditures together with her pocket-money expenses each year. These two expenses fluctuated between two and three hundred pounds a year in her account book for 1757–76, when she was, of course, well along in years. In 1757 she spent £207; in 1759 it rose to its highest, £393; but by 1764, it was to a low of £189. It is also instructive to note some of the uses for her pocket money: 'Boardwages for three dogs for 3 months, £1.19.1' and 'A set of strings for my guittar [sic] £0.5.0.'[25] It is obvious from these accounts that she had had some training or instruction in account-keeping and was able to work with her husband's accountant and with household officials, as she was so often requested to do by her husband.

From the correspondence and from the various accounts, we have been able to make the duchess a bit more distinct as a person and to reconstruct the domestic scene of the Newcastles. It seems obvious that they were emotionally close and that the duke depended on her greatly in all domestic concerns, but that she had little interest or concern with his passion for public affairs, although she had a normal interest in her husband's political welfare. She seems to have lived a life more typical of her class than did the duke, in that she was forever visiting, buying christening presents, concerned as much as her husband, or even more so, with matters of health, buying fabrics for clothes, and gambling. She evidently was unlike her husband in that she did not write as many letters; or at least few have survived. Often the duke's correspondents sent their greetings to the duchess, and she no doubt knew most of the important political and diplomatic persons who figured so prominently in her husband's life. She is rarely mentioned as being present at the duke's great entertainments or dinners, but she may have been. However, her husband's life was largely with men in politics and not with their wives. There can be little doubt that they were separated much of the time, owing to the duke's incessant activity in the political and diplomatic world, as we have noted.

Thus two wealthy individuals, married by the needs of their aristocratic class, and each strange or a bit neurotic, were apparently well matched. The one followed the aristocratic ideal of state service, in which he found ample reason for his existence; and the other followed interests which reflect clearly the accepted activities for women of her class. There is no evidence at hand which would indicate that the duchess's particular needs, desires or demands caused the duke to live beyond his means. There is much evidence which indicates that she was active in the process of management, and that she attempted to aid her husband in restraining the costs of their establishment. How was the establishment managed which sustained these two persons in their personal and political lives? We will attempt to reconstruct the management of the Newcastle interests and to discover the part played by each of them in this endeavor.

THE MANAGEMENT OF DUCAL AFFAIRS: ESTATE, HOUSEHOLD AND FINANCES

The Duke of Newcastle held freehold or leasehold estates in eleven counties of the kingdom, stretching from his ancestral county of Sussex in the south, to Dorset in the west, and to Yorkshire in the north. His most extensive estates were in Lincolnshire and Nottinghamshire, but all, whether large or small in extent, required constant management and attention. He usually referred to 'my Estate' or to 'my Estate in Notts,' or some other county, and rarely mentioned individual manors or farms. However, many of them are named in surviving rentals and in the Deed of Trust of 1738. The duke was primarily interested in the produce of the estates and secondarily in the political influence of which they were the foundation.

Newcastle was in essence a London man, or perhaps more correctly, a court man, that is, one whose life was largely spent at the center of public affairs. He lacked a personal, intimate knowlege of his estates, except for Sussex, and evidently had no interest in agricultural matters as such. The only estate he visited frequently and regularly was Sussex; he visited Nottingham a few times as a young man for political purposes but appears never to have visited his other estates. The duke had neither the time nor the knowledge for a general overview of his properties. He was constantly busy with the affairs of his offices and with the electoral interests of the government, to say nothing of his personal passion for patronage matters; he had to rely on others, hopefully more expert than himself, to manage his estates. The duke's political role, which was his primary one, limited his freedom to do as he pleased with his estates. He was always reluctant to consider increasing rents or taking any other action which might give umbrage to his tenants, who were often voters in the county or principal borough. The diverse geographical location of his estates and the size of the holdings in the various counties, as well as the duke's political interests in many of them, made their management extremely complex.

In attempting to reconstruct the manner in which the duke's affairs were managed, we will begin with the basic unit first—that is, with the land steward and the specific area for whose collection and management he was responsible—and then proceed to a consideration of the problems of central supervision and control.

The parts of the estate under the supervision of a land steward were grouped together for ease of collection and supervision; that is, contiguous areas were collected by one person for, within a county, estates were sometimes divided between collections. Nottinghamshire, for example, was divided into three collections, one of which also collected all of the Derby estate. Dorset and Wiltshire leaseholds were separately collected; Lincolnshire, Sussex and Yorkshire each had its own collector, as did the Clare Market estate in London; while lands in Dorset, Wilshire, Hertfordshire, Kent, Suffolk and Middlesex were grouped together for no reason that is apparent.

We come now to the problem of terminology in the study of management. The trouble lies in the fact that there was no consistency in the use of terms to describe areas of responsibility. 'Land steward' is the term most generally used for an individual responsible for the general supervision of an estate, including the leasing of lands and the collection of rents and profits. Newcastle used such terms as 'Inspector of my Estate' in various counties, as well as 'Collector' and 'Receiver.'[26] These land stewards, who had direct relationships with the duke, were often important local men, and men of substance as well. They were well paid for their efforts on the duke's behalf and served him in political affairs, also, in their areas. Two of the duke's stewards served in Parliament as his nominees.

The land steward had the authority to appoint and to pay persons to help him with his many responsibilities. A great many terms were used for these helpers and the terms usually indicate the work done, such as 'under receiver' or 'deputy receiver' of rents; 'gamekeepers,' 'park keepers,' 'wood reeves' and 'housekeepers' leave no doubt as to function, but such a term as 'beadle,' used in many connections, does not clearly indicate function.

The collection of rent would appear, on the surface at least, to be a very simple matter; but an example chosen from the very early part of Newcastle's life will serve to indicate its complexity. Newcastle held the Manor and Royalty of Hastings; in 1715 its collector, a Mr Austen, died, and his son applied for his father's position. He applied through Anthony Trumble, one of the Pelhams' Sussex agents and a Hastings attorney, who sent his proposal to Newcastle and to the Reverend Mr Bowers. Mr Austen's description of the work involved is most revealing. He stated that there were, in all, 667 tenants in the collection and that they were scattered over 37 parishes, which meant a ride of 25 miles in length and 12 miles in breadth. However, the annual rents paid by these tenants amounted to only £21.18s.2d., for some cottagers and other tenants paid only 4d. or 6d. per annum. Young Austen offered to undertake the collection for a fixed salary of £30 p.a., plus small perquisites. He indicated that his father had collected on poundage, that is, at 4s. in the pound, but that arrearages had made his salary come to less than £30. Mr Bowers wanted to refuse to pay £30 a year because of the smallness of the collection. However, Austen pointed out that, although the annual rents were very low, some tenants had paid fines of £20 to £40 on the last renewal of their leases, which were now worth from £60 to £100, and that at the next expiration the duke could advance the fines as he pleased.[27] It is clear from this one example that a land steward had to have considerable help to carry out his duties and that there had to be constant communication between his deputy receivers and himself, and between himself and the owner or his agent.

The collection of the rents and profits was the simplest of the land steward's functions. He was also responsible for overseeing the condition of the buildings on the estate and for approving necessary repairs. When a survey was called for, he usually employed a land surveyor for the purpose. When leases came due, it was a major responsibility of the steward to negotiate the new terms of the lease, to draw it up and to submit it, if called upon to do so, to his employer for approval. The steward received an extra fee, usually a guinea, from the owner for preparing each lease and counterpart. Above all he had to keep full records of his activities; vouchers had to be produced at audit times to prove his expenditures, and receipts had to be carefully noted for the sale of timber or underwood or for other produce of the estate. At times of election, stewards were often called upon to provide public entertainment for the tenants, to note their political proclivities, and to carefully record all moneys 'spent or gave away' for elections. The accounts were submitted annually for examination and audit, either at Michaelmas (September 29) or at Lady Day (March 25).[28]

The central office for conducting the business of the estates was located at Newcastle House in Lincoln's Inn Fields. Here copies of the leases, rent rolls, correspondence and other necessary materials were kept. Normally the stewards sent their annual accounts to be audited, but at other times they appear to have brought them to London in person. Upon other occasions the auditor examined the accounts and signed them wherever he happened to be, in Westminster, at Claremont, or, rarely, when he travelled to Nottingham or Newark. When the accountant had compared the estate rental with the account of rent collections and had checked the vouchers for various payments or 'outgoings' for correctness, he would sign the accounts. When he had signed them it was said that he had 'passed' them. The next step in the procedure was for them to be submitted to the duke, who glanced at them and had his questions answered. Upon rare occasions he would not accept certain expenditures made by his stewards and allowed by his accountant. When satisfied, the duke would sign the last page of the accounts, indicating his final acceptance. This procedure was called 'allowing' the accounts; and often two years would elapse before the steward's accounts were given their final quietus. Thus the Newcastle estates had the rents collected by the stewards or their agents, the stewards' accounts were audited and passed by the accountant; and they were finally allowed by the duke himself.

Rents of the estates were collected twice a year even though the accounting for the funds was done annually. When the rents had been collected, and current bills, taxes, repairs and so on paid, the stewards remitted the money directly to Hoare's Bank in London, evidently in cash, for the stewards regularly noted in their accounts the cost of the carriage of the money, which was not an insignificant item. At times they would remit money directly to the duke or to his chief man of business when either was particularly pressed. When in dire need the duke would anticipate his rents by borrowing from his stewards against their next collection and would ask them to 'get their rents in' at the earliest possible date. On the other hand, the stewards often held fairly large sums of the duke's money in their hands for considerable periods of time, which gave them ample opportunity to make private use of the funds.

The central figure in the functioning of the duke's interests was the individual often termed a 'Man of Business,' at times 'Supervisor of the Whole,' or occasionally simply 'Secretary,' but for whose functions no really adequate eighteenth-century term exists. Perhaps the modern term 'business manager' would most accurately describe his duties. Every great estate had such a functionary, for he was essential. He had a necessary interest in every aspect of the financial affairs of his employer, and whatever his salary it was inadequate to his responsibilities.

Newcastle's first man of business was Peter Forbes. He had been first employed by Newcastle's father, but by 1713 he was a settled member of the household. Later he lived at Newcastle House and remained active in the duke's affairs until about 1755, although with reduced responsibilities after about 1737, when James Waller began to act as auditor. He apparently performed all of the work of central administration for the great estate, no doubt with some staff; he served, in a sense, as a clearing-house for the thousand and one matters, large and small, which were created by the necessities of a great estate and a large household. He received money from stewards and from the duke, he deposited funds with Hoare's and drew drafts on them, he negotiated purchases for the household, he paid for purchases made by the duke, he corresponded with stewards and other agents about financial, political and personal matters for Newcastle and transmitted his directions, but, above all, he had the awful task of attempting to find enough money to satisfy a veritable army of ducal creditors who often came to badger him for payment face to face.

Forbes seems to have had a salary of £200 p.a. and to have held two small sinecures from Newcastle as Lord Lieutenant of Middlesex, that is, as Treasurer of the Trophy Money and Treasurer to the Lieutenancy of Middlesex. The duke provided for him in old age too, for he was Clerk of the Peace of Westminster in 1760 and died in 1762. The myriad duties which Forbes performed in the day-to-day supervision of the Newcastle interests for so many years more than earned him whatever rewards he gained.

The appointment of James Waller about 1737, evidently to take over some of the burden of work performed by Forbes, marks a turn to more professional aid in the management of the estate. Waller served Newcastle until 1753, with varying degrees of efficiency as chief accountant. In that year the duke's anger over the condition of the accounts, which came to light during an effort to create a new budget, caused him to discharge Waller. The duke hated change, and this action was a rare one for him.

The year 1753 appears to mark a definite change in the management of the duke's affairs. The change was probably precipitated by the detailed study of Newcastle's tangled finances made by William Murray, who was Solicitor General at the time and a protégé of the duke. He appears to have been responsible for the discharge of Waller, perhaps for the semi-retirement of Forbes, and for the hiring of new talent to oversee the duke's affairs. It was probably upon his recommendation that Mr John Sharpe was employed to have general supervision. Sharpe was a well-known solicitor, an agent for several colonies, and, as Solicitor to the Treasury, was at the center of much government business. He lived in Lincoln's Inn Fields and was returned to Parliament in 1754 for a Walpole family borough.[29] In place of Waller, Newcastle employed, probably on the recommendation of Sharpe, Mr James Postlethwayt. He was no doubt well known to Sharpe at the Treasury, for he was a close student of public finance and published in 1759 *The History of the Public Revenue from the Revolution in 1688 to Christmas, 1758*.[30] Sharpe had a very high respect for his abilities but did complain that upon occasion he had too much business, meaning, no doubt, that he had several clients besides Newcastle. Unfortunately Mr Sharpe did not serve long, for he died in 1756 and was followed to the grave by Mr Postlethwayt in 1761. Mr Edward Woodcock apparently replaced Sharpe as one of the duke's principal solicitors. Mr John Twells, who had served in the family as apothecary since 1746 and whose father had served as land steward in Nottinghamshire, came into added responsibilities following Postlethwayt's death. He seems to have taken over the job of checking or 'passing' the accounts before they were presented to the duke. He was well paid for his varied responsibilities, for he held a sinecure in the Customs worth over £500 p.a.[31]

The Steward of the Household was the official of greatest importance after the man of business. This man had over-all responsibility for the functioning of the household or 'family'; his duties were manifold, and he had to account for the spending of great sums of money. In general, it can be said that he was responsible for all that went on indoors, whether the duke was in residence at Newcastle House, at Claremont, or at Halland or Bishopstone in Sussex. The local agent or the housekeeper was in charge when the duke was not in residence, but all of the staff came under the house steward's control. Nottingham Castle, which the duke refurbished as his northern seat when he was quite young, never in fact served as a residence for him and was occupied by various agents and housekeepers. The functions of the Steward of the Household for Newcastle were often more extensive than those which are usually associated with such a position.

The role of Steward of the Household was apparently performed from 1715 to 1741 by Mr Robert Burnett, but he was a principal agent of the duke in Sussex as well. It is almost impossible to classify Burnett, for he performed so many services for the duke. The steward upon whom Newcastle depended greatly and for whom he had a real affection was Samuel Burt, who followed Burnett. He was efficient, honest and dependable; Newcastle was greatly saddened by his death in 1752. Newcastle asked the aid of 'Dear Jemmy,' his cousin, Colonel James Pelham, in finding a replacement for Burt, for 'my Family is in the Greatest Confusion' and, as if Burt's death was not enough of a blow, his cook had gone off to work for the Duke of Marlborough! Newcastle described the type of individual needed, together with his duties: 'He should have some acquaintance with Sussex, have a Spirit to govern a Family; and a Turn to the Kitchen, and Table—at least enough to know and understand Provisions, and to keep accounts.'[32] Colonel Pelham found no one, and eventually the duke promoted one of his own staff at Claremont, John Greening, to this responsible and essential post, where he served for many years.

The Master of the Horse was responsible for the functioning of the only department 'out of doors,' the Stables. For many years the duke employed Mr Seymour as Master of the Horse and later a Mr Creswell. The department expended large sums each year for food for the horses, for equipment, repairs and liveries, as well as for hounds and harriers, and was a constant drain on the duke's finances. From his early days the duke took delight in his carriages and equipage as evidence of his station. One of the great court days of any year was 'The Birthday,' that is, the celebration of the king's birthday, during which the courtiers and others vied with one another in the magnificence of their dress and display as they came to offer their congratulations to their sovereign at Kensington Palace. On May 28, 1718, Newcastle, who was now Lord Chamberlain, came to the palace for the birthday, and it was said that he exceeded 'all ye nobility for the magnificence and splendour of his equipage' and that 'his coach was preceded by all his Domestics and also by 12 watermen in new cloathes, who also walked on foot 2 and 2.'[33] Such display by the new Lord Chamberlain must have given some fillip to the rather dull court of George I, but the duke's display was aiding the development of the deficit in his stables account.

A rather shadowy official was the Steward of the Home Farm at Claremont, who had charge of all the gardens and greenhouses. He had a staff of gardeners to perform assorted tasks in the kitchen garden, herb garden and the greenhouses, and to take care of the fruit trees. The only area even remotely connected to agriculture in which Newcastle took a personal interest was his gardens and greenhouses, especially the latter. He spent large sums on greenhouses in which to grow the melons and 'pine-apples' in which he delighted. He sent them as gifts to his personal and political friends, as well as enjoying them himself. The farm also produced grain, hay and meat for the duke's establishment.

An estate of such magnitude and an owner of such expensive tastes created constant problems above and beyond the day-to-day burdens of the man of business to keep it all going, and to supervise the household, stables and farms. The major problem was financing, for the duke's continual over-spending made the need for long-term credit inevitable. Very little work has been done by historians on the subject of money management in the eighteenth century, and much is needed. Newcastle was an aristocrat and not a bourgeois; he had little detailed knowledge of financing, although he later knew many of the prominent financial leaders of the city of London and regularly sought their advice when in the Treasury.[34] Naturally he turned to his bankers, Hoare and Arnold, who specialized in financial services for many nobles and aristocrats, but when that source was used to the limit others had to be found. Next he, or his man of business, would seek out those who were termed 'friends,' who were willing to take his bond or note for varying amounts. However, a specialist in money, or one who knew where ready money was available, was actually needed, a scrivener or agent. One of the leading scriveners of London was the attorney and adviser, Peter Walter, and Newcastle depended upon his advice for many years in meeting his need for financing. At one time or another nearly every political protégé or personal agent was involved in the search for additional credit for the duke.

Hoare's Bank was central to the financial functioning of the New-castle interests during most of the duke's lifetime. His primary account there was usually termed a 'drawing account,' that is, one into which deposits were made and upon which drafts were drawn day by day. Deposits were made by the duke, by his man of business, by the land stewards and by officials from the Secretary of State's office or from the Treasury for the duke's salary. Drafts were drawn mainly by the man of business to pay myriads of bills, to send money to land stewards or household officials and to creditors in general. Of course, the duke himself drew from his own account from time to time. These bank drafts were sometimes termed 'circulating notes' or bills and were sometimes not paid for months. It also appears that interest was paid upon them from time to time, perhaps to keep them from being honored in times of financial stress for the estate. Newcastle's accounts at the bank were balanced only nine times during his life. When this was done the great ledgers were taken by officials of the bank to Newcastle House, where they could be examined by the duke and by his accountant; when satisfied, the duke would 'allow' the balances by signing the ledger. The bankers also kept a separate account of money borrowed of them, which they termed the 'Money Account.' Here were recorded the sums borrowed by their clients, the pay-ments of interest, and the repayment of principal. Newcastle's name appeared in this volume for many years, as we will see.

We have outlined the structure of management of Newcastle's estate, household and finances to the degree that they become apparent from the sources. Such structure as did exist was in part inherited from the past and in part created by the duke's men of business and other advisers; it is doubtful if the duke himself had a significant part in building it. Newcastle would probably have thought in the sense of the eighteenth-century usage of the term 'method' rather than the modern term 'structure,' that is, whether estates in individual counties were 'in a proper Method,' that is, things done and accounted for in a tradi-tional way. The duke probably did not see his interests as an entity;

the idea of the structure of a whole estate is the creation of the modern historian for his own convenience in attempting to understand the economic life of the landed classes.

Having considered the persons and personalities of the duke and duchess, their interests and activities, as well as having attempted to reconstruct the way in which their affairs were managed by their various servants, we are ready to begin a detailed examination of the Newcastle financial and economic interests over a period of nearly sixty years, from his original inheritance in 1711 to his death in 1768.

NOTES

1 H. J. Habakkuk, 'Daniel Finch, 2nd Earl of Nottingham: his house and estate,' in *Studies in Social History*, ed. J. H. Plumb (London, 1955), p. 139 ff.

2 See D. M. Joslin, 'London bankers in wartime, 1739–84,' in *Studies in the Industrial Revolution*, ed. L. S. Presnell (London, 1960), pp. 167–9.

3 For a general discussion of practices, see Sidney Pollard, *The Genesis of Modern Management* (London, 1965), pp. 209–15.

4 G. E. Mingay, *English Landed Society in the Eighteenth Century* (London, 1963), pp. 67–71.

5 *Ibid.*, pp. 125–30.

6 Stebelton H. Nulle, *Thomas Pelham-Holles, Duke of Newcastle: His Early Political Career, 1693–1724* (Philadelphia, 1931), Appendix B, pp. 171–8. Example: 'A Tale of Two Tubs . . .' (1749) 'When all was past, & Peace Restor'd/ He found himself a needy Lord./ His lands were mortgaged, Rents diminish'd;/ From splendid Grandeur almost finish'd,/ Most melancholy Prospects rise,/ Some far, some near, to blast his Eyes.'

7 Add. MSS. 35046, f. 165v, Claremont, October 14, 1739.

8 See Turberville, *House of Lords in the XVIIIth Century*, and Owen, *Rise of the Pelhams, passim.*

9 Add. MSS. 32700, ff. 211–13, Claremont, June 13, 1743.

10 *Ibid.*, ff. 232–3, June 22, 1743.

11 Earl of Ilchester and Mrs Longford-Brooke, *The Life of Sir Charles Hanbury-Williams, Poet, Wit and Diplomatist* (London, 1928), p. 285.

12 [Richard Glover], *Memoirs by a Celebrated Literary and Political Character, . . .* (London, 1814), pp. 151–2.

13 [Philip Dormer Stanhope], *Characters by Lord Chesterfield . . .* (London, 1778), p. 49.

14 Horace Walpole, *Memoirs of the Reign of King George the Second* (London, 1847), I, 165–6.

15 Tobias Smollett, *The Adventures of Sir Launcelot Greaves together with The History & Adventures of an Atom* (Oxford, 1926), pp. 318–19.

16 Bonamy Dobrée and Geoffrey Webb (eds), *The Complete Works of Sir John Vanbrugh* (London, 1928), IV, 94. To Newcastle, Bath, October 9, 1717.
17 Add. MSS. 33073, ff. 3–4, Nottingham Castle, December 29, 1718.
18 *Ibid.*, f. 5.
19 Add. MSS. 33073, f. 7.
20 *Ibid.*, f. 11, Lewes, March 17, 1721.
21 *Ibid.*, f. 10, March 19, 1721.
22 Add. MSS. 33076, f. 77, Newcastle House, October 18, 1759.
23 Add. MSS. 33627, *passim*, 1737–50; James D. Brown, *British Musical Biography* (Birmingham, 1897), p. 172.
24 *Ibid.*
25 Add. MSS. 33628, *passim*, 1757–76.
26 Add. MSS. 33060, f. 138.
27 Add. MSS. 33064, f. 80, F. Austen to Anthony Trumble, Hastings, June 27, 1715.
28 Gordon E. Mingay, 'The eighteenth-century land steward,' in E. L. Jones and G. E. Mingay (eds), *Land, Labour and Population in the Industrial Revolution* (London, 1967), pp. 3–27.
29 L. B. Namier and John Brooke, *The History of Parliament. The House of Commons, 1754–1790* (London, 1964), III, 428.
30 *Dictionary of National Biography*, XVI, 205.
31 L. B. Namier, *The Structure of Politics at the Accession of George III* (London, 1929), p. 231, n. 1; Add. MSS. 32946, Newcastle to Hardwicke, Claremont, January 5, 1763.
32 Add. MSS. 33066, f. 328, Hanover, September 29, 1752.
33 Lady E. Newton, *Lyme Letters: 1660–1760* (London, 1925), p. 268.
34 See Reed Browning, 'The Duke of Newcastle and the Financing of the Seven Years' War,' *Journal of Economic History* (June, 1971), XXXI, 344–77.

CHAPTER 1

THE EARLY FINANCIAL
HISTORY TO 1724:
INHERITANCE,
LIFE AND DEBTS

Thomas Pelham was born into the security and privilege of a Sussex family which for centuries had held broad acres there, which had always played an important role in local affairs, and which had, at times, acted on the larger national stage. His father, Thomas, Lord Pelham, inherited a large and profitable estate and invested significant amounts of his capital in government securities, Exchequer bills, and tallies, as well as in Bank, East India Company and other stocks. He opened his London bank account with Henry Hoare, goldsmith, in 1696; he and his sons after him maintained their accounts there throughout their lives. Lord Pelham's annual income late in life from his land rents and from his investments was nearly £12,000, which made him a very wealthy man.[1] Young Pelham's mother was Grace Holles, sister to John Holles, Duke of Newcastle and one of the richest men in the kingdom. Through wealth and wide connections, Pelham would have been a man of some importance if he had never left the county of his ancestors.

The national prominence which the Pelham brothers achieved was due largely to a decision made by their uncle in the disposition of his estates. He decided to make his nephews in turn his heirs. When Earl of Clare, Holles had married Margaret Cavendish, daughter and sole heir of Henry, second Duke of Newcastle. When Margaret inherited her father's estates, they were found to be encumbered with debts of £80,000, and her husband agreed to assume the responsibility for discharging the debts; in return, by formal indenture dated January 17, 1693, he obtained his wife's rights over the property she had inherited.[2] Later Holles was created Duke of Newcastle in his own right. He and his wife had only one child, a daughter named Henrietta Cavendish Holles. This girl would be heir to the great Holles estates, as well as to those of her Cavendish grandfather in the north of England, in London and in many other areas. Her parents do not appear to have been the ideal married couple; each was strong-willed and difficult to get along with.

Welbeck Abbey in Nottinghamshire was the major seat of the Duke of Newcastle, and it was here that he took the decision which was to have such a profound effect on the life of his nephews. What precipitated the action will probably never be known, but it was evidently the product of much thought and concern. Late in August of 1707, the duke called Peter Walter to his study, told him in strict secrecy that he wished to make his will, and talked at length with him about its provisions. Walter was ordered to draw up the will, which he did in a few days, and then presented it to the duke for his approbation. Finally on August 29, 1707, the document was signed by Newcastle and witnessed by Peter Walter and a servant.[3] The executors were to be the duke's brother-in-law, Lord Pelham; Henry, later Lord Paget; and the Duchess of Newcastle.

Four years later, on July 15, 1711, Newcastle died, following a riding accident, and great must have been the shock to his wife and daughter when the will was opened and its contents became known. In the will the duke left the newly purchased Orton House and lands, as well as lands in the county of Huntington, to his wife, to do with as she pleased. To his daughter he gave lands and properties in Staffordshire, Yorkshire and Northumberland, with certain exceptions, as well as a £20,000 portion promised for her marriage settlement. The remainder of his real estate and hereditaments he left to his nephew, Thomas Pelham, eldest son of Lord Pelham and of his wife, Grace. Thus, while a young man of seventeen and still a student at Clare Hall, Cambridge, Thomas found himself possessed of an estate entailed upon him and his heirs male and, failing his own line, to his younger brother Henry Pelham, and failing that line, to his cousins William and Gilbert Vane and their issue male. Anyone inheriting the lands was required under the will to assume the Holles name. To his wife the duke left only the family jewels in fee simple; the family gold and silver plate she had for life only, and upon her death that was to go to Pelham in tail. The duke did not forget his financial and political aides, Peter Walter and William Jessop, M.P., who were each left £1,000.[4]

Duchess Margaret, not unexpectedly, decided at once to fight to break the 'pretended' will which partially disinherited her daughter of her father's lands and of some of her maternal grandfather's. For advice she turned to Robert Harley, Earl of Oxford. He and his brother, Mr Auditor Harley, acted as her chief advisers and suggested that she retain counsel at once so that the 'pretended settlement on Mr. Pelham' might be challenged.[5] Lord Pelham retained the services of the attorney general and of Mr Jessop, the late duke's chief agent in the north, to help him in his defense.[6] It is clear that Lord Pelham was preparing to take all that had been left to his son, and he so informed Harley, who gave a copy of the letter to the duchess and remarked to her, 'I must confess that I cannot but be a little moved to think that anyone should set up the least pretense to disturb you in the possession of your estate which is not only your own inheritance, but that and the Clare Estate are due to your merit.'[7] Lord Pelham was indeed making every effort to ensure his son's claim; and sentiment for the duchess who had been treated ungenerously, or for Cavendish family feeling, had no place in his thinking.

The duchess attempted to delay proceedings in the Prerogative Court and began action in the Court of Chancery; on his part, Lord Pelham began his action in Chancery against the duchess and Lady Henrietta during the Michaelmas Term, 1711. When the case was argued before Lord Keeper Harcourt and two other judges on March 10, 1711, the duchess refused any accommodation and would not produce the deed of 1693 settling the Cavendish estates; when she was ordered to do so and refused, the court ordered her estates sequestered, on December 9, 1712.

Up to this point, the Earl of Oxford had supported the duchess in her battle and his interest was not unbiased, for he and the duchess hoped for a marriage between Lady Henrietta and Edward Harley, the earl's eldest son. After she had lost her case in Chancery, the duchess insisted upon appealing to the House of Lords and naturally expected Oxford to support her. This was an action which Oxford could not take, for the world knew of his personal interest in the case; his high position in the ministry would have made it politically unwise as well. Upon his refusal the duchess ended all contact with him and turned against the proposed marriage. She carried her case to the Lords against all advice, and lost when it was heard and dismissed on May 19, 1713. As Robert Molesworth reported to his wife, 'The Duchess of Newcastle has lost her cause in the House of Lords. It was so bad a one that not one lord, Whig or Tory, opened his lips for her. . . .'[8] Following this appeal the sequestration was ordered, but Lady Henrietta begged exception, for some of the property covered by the order was hers.

Lord Pelham had made speedy efforts to aid his son in securing his inheritance not only because of his natural desire to aggrandize his family, but also because of his own failing health. It is likely that Lord Pelham as an executor knew at least the general intention of Newcastle to make his son his heir, for he proceeded directly to establish his son's rights. He wrote in September, 1711, to various collectors or receivers of rents in Nottinghamshire and Lincolnshire informing them of the duchess's claim to all of her late husband's estate and stating that several persons had 'attuned' to her. He advised the receivers for the estates, which by the late duke's will belonged to his son, not to pay any money by direction of the duchess.[9] In spite of his illness he kept up his efforts, for in October, 1711, he wrote to his son from Halland and carefully addressed the letter to 'Mr. Holles,' but in his salutation called him 'Dear Tommy.' He told him of his letters to the receivers and advised the young man not to meddle with the duchess. He had secured the support at Welbeck of Mr Jessop, who knew all of the late duke's affairs, and hoped he was certain of Walter's adherence to the cause. Pelham was willing to pay Mr Walter his £1,000 legacy as counsel should direct him, a none-too-subtle way of engaging his fidelity. Lord Pelham urged his son to write to the receivers at once, telling them of the change himself.[10]

The undetermined nature of the disputes within the family and his own illness, plus the fact that his son was a minor, made it essential for Lord Pelham to provide protection for his son's interests. He established a guardianship for him in the persons of William Monson, an old family friend, and his son-in-law, George Naylor. The death of Lord Pelham on February 23, 1712, compounded the problems of estate management. No extensive landed estate could be managed by the owner alone, for the responsibility required talents and knowledge not only in agriculture but also in finance, law, politics, and human relations. Around the Pelham interest in Sussex a good number of knowledgeable, experienced and trusted persons revolved. The new Lord Pelham had first his legal guardians to depend upon until he reached his majority, and they in turn could call upon those who had intimate knowledge of the estate, financial and political interests of the late Lord Pelham.

Standing ahead of others in service to the Pelham family and to the young man was the Reverend Mr Thomas Bowers. As early as 1707 he was intimate enough with the family land problems to be engaged to help settle a controversy over an exchange of lands between the late lord and his brother, Henry.[11] Bowers had lived at Halland part of the time and probably served as family chaplain and as tutor. Some of his time was spent in helping to keep up the Pelham political interest in Sussex, as well as in acting as receiver of rents. It is not surprising that the guardians of 'the Right Honourable Thomas Holles, Lord Pelham' soon appointed Bowers, who is described as living in Hellingly in Sussex, as their collector and receiver of rents for the young lord. Bowers's appointment was duly signed on June 23, 1712, by the guardians and witnessed by two men who had also been of importance in the estate and financial affairs of the boy's father, Peter Forbes and John Waller.

The Sussex affairs of the young Lord Pelham were in good hands. Mr Bowers remained a close confidant and adviser, in fact almost a second father to Pelham, until his death. He was aided by Peter Forbes, who remained as chief man of business for many years and did a prodigious amount of work in trying to keep abreast of the financial concerns of his master. John Waller, and later his son James A. Waller, served the Pelhams in financial matters, and as auditors, for years. The Monsons, the father who became William, Lord Monson, and his son Charles, were eventually named as trustees of the Newcastle estates.[12]

The Pelham interests in Sussex were in competent hands during the minority, but the matter of the inheritance of the young lord from his uncle was at a virtual impasse. The Duchess of Newcastle had lost her battle to invalidate her husband's will, but she would in no way co-operate with the legal talent arrayed either on her side or on that of her opponents. The Court of Chancery might sequester her property, but the question of what property was justly Henrietta's and what was legally bequeathed to Thomas, now Lord Pelham, had not been determined. At a very early point in the controversy it had been proposed by Edward Harley, Auditor of the Exchequer, by Lord Cheyne, and by others, that an accommodation be negotiated, but the duchess stoutly refused such a move. Yet an agreed settlement through the good offices of a mutually satisfactory mediator gave promise to save countless pounds in legal costs and perhaps be a surer way of securing an equitable settlement.[13]

It was finally agreed by the Harleys and the Pelhams that William, Lord Cowper, a highly respected barrister and Q.C., who had been Lord Chancellor and who would be so again, should be asked to undertake the job. Cowper wrote to Pelham in December, 1713, telling him that he had been asked to undertake the heavy task of mediating the family quarrel over Duke John's will and to make an accommodation.[14] In spite of his reluctance Cowper agreed to attempt a settlement and told Lord Pelham the method of operation, i.e. to set aside that which plainly belonged to one side or the other, and then the mediator would determine from each side secretly the lowest it would go for an accommodation for the remainder.[15] The making of an accommodation was not quite that simple, for Duchess Margaret would not agree to a division of the property; the Vanes had an interest, for they were remaindermen under the will; and, during the whole period since the duke's death, rents which were actually Lord Pelham's had been regularly paid to the duchess and to Henrietta, so that he, not unnaturally, demanded his money. Also, the young lord demanded a residence to match his great wealth, and sought both Bolsover and Welbeck Abbey; and since he could get neither, demanded Nottingham Castle.

In spite of the duchess's intransigence, the negotiations were undertaken and made steady progress. The duchess lost another battle when her only child married Edward Harley against her mother's will on August 31, 1713, at Wimpole. The daughter was nearly as strong-willed as her mother. Lord Cowper's work appears to have gone forward fairly smoothly and general agreement was reached in the summer of 1714, shortly before Pelham became of age in July.[16] Further progress was at a standstill as long as the duchess lived, for she would not be a party to the division of the property and it was understood that all concerned would have to agree before an Act of Parliament could be secured to ratify the accommodation.

The 'Treaty of Accommodation' was signed on July 13, 1714, by the Harleys and Lord Pelham, and by the remaindermen, Henry Pelham and the Vane cousins; but the Vanes refused to tie themselves to its provisions in case they should ever inherit. The extensive estates, the great families enmeshed in the disputes, and the various cases in law and equity, in addition to the appeal to the House of Lords, made the dispute public property. It was reported in the *Newsletter* of London on July 15, 1714, that a settlement had been reached, and fairly accurate details were given:[17]

> The Lord Harley and the Lord Pelham have referred their affairs
> to arbitration, they have agreed the matter, and by that
> arbitration £20,000 a year comes to my Lord Harley and
> £25,000 a year to the other. My Lord Harley had with his lady
> £10,000 besides undisputed.

Thus two days after the actual signing the news was published to the town and country, a coup of eighteenth-century journalism.

Throughout his life, Pelham enjoyed celebrating his birthday; in 1714, he had double reason to celebrate, for not only had the family agreement been signed but he also achieved a goal of every young man by turning twenty-one. He celebrated the event as a rich and powerful Sussex magnate ought to, by entertaining the county lavishly. Again the London *Newsletter* reported the great affair:[18]

> 27 July 1714, London
> On Wednesday last came of age the Lord Pelham, and at his seat in Sussex [Halland] he made them a noble entertainment, where were dressed seven oxen, fifteen sheep, six calves, eight bucks, and so proportionable of fowls, etc. There were eighty stand of sweetmeats on the first table, . . . forty-nine hogsheads of strong beer, seven hogsheads of claret, besides champagne, burgundy, etc. . . . the aforesaid feast cost two thousand pounds.

This grand entertainment is an example of a style of living and a custom of costly hospitality which would continue to his life's end, providing a support for his political life and giving him great personal satisfaction. It was also to be one of the major contributing factors of his continual financial distress.

Pelham and the Harleys had reached their agreement, but the duchess remained not only adamant in her refusal to join in, but estranged as well from her daughter and son-in-law. The situation remained static almost as long as the duchess lived, except that a reconciliation took place between the Harleys and the duchess shortly before her death, which occurred on December 24, 1716. Although the one remaining obstacle to securing the needed Act of Parliament had been removed, it was a full year before final understanding had been reached. In April, 1718, Pelham, now Duke of Newcastle, demanded in a 'Memorandum of Agreement' between himself and Lord Harley that certain conditions be met, most particularly, 'That Lord Harley shall discharge all the late duke's debts, so that none of them shall charge, or in any wise affect the present duke's estates or lands.'[19] Newcastle also insisted that he be paid the moneys which had been kept from him, for he added in his own hand, 'It being evident that the Duke of Newcastle has been kept out of great Sums of Money legally belonging to him for near seven years, & even since the late Agreements for near four—he is justly entitled to some consideration.'[20] He also insisted that he must have Nottingham Castle, even though his opponents told him it was in great disrepair. It is evident that these final demands had to be agreed to before the solicitors could finish their work on the details of the proposed Act. The remarkable patience shown by Newcastle and his advisers in the long disputes would pay off, for they would win on every point.

The private Act, 5 George I, cap. 3, entitled 'An Act to render more Effectual the Agreements that have been made . . .' between the contending parties, received the royal assent on February 18, 1719. It was a comprehensive document, for it recited not only the will of the late Duke of Newcastle, the various suits at law, and the treaty of accommodation but the specific detail of the estates and financial arrangements as well, and ran to sixteen pages in its printed form.

In essence the Act provided that Henrietta Cavendish Holles Harley, to give her her full name, was to receive all lands which were once held by her grandfather, Henry Cavendish, Duke of Newcastle, but not including some timber standing on part of it. She was also to receive what was promised to her in her father's will, as well as any and all lands purchased or conveyed to her father from the date of his will, that is, August 29, 1707, to the date of his death in 1711. For his part, Newcastle agreed to pay the Harleys for all of their property in Powis, or Newcastle House in Lincoln's Inn Fields. All the rest of the property belonged to the new Duke of Newcastle, and he was relieved of paying all manner of encumbrances under Duke John's will. This was accomplished by establishing a trust in which were settled and vested the lands of the late Henry Cavendish, Henrietta's grandfather, and all estates of her father purchased after his will in 1707, with certain exceptions. The trustees, William, Lord Cheyne, Peter Walter and John Morley, were empowered to sell land to pay any and all debts. They were to pay Newcastle £7,805.8s.0d. due for rents and profits of the estates which should have gone to him during the period since his uncle's death; he was to have timber worth £10,700 from the woods at Welbeck Abbey or interest on that sum at 5 per cent until delivery, as well as the additional sum of £2,800 or interest at 5 per cent. Specific sums of money were to be paid by the trustees on behalf of the Harleys as well, and Newcastle made promises relative to the improvement of buildings and lands and their leasing. The trustees were to pay all debts and legacies of Duke John or of Margaret, the late duchess, 'so that Thomas Duke of Newcastle and the remaindermen, may therefrom and from every part thereof, be absolutely freed and Discharged.' When the trustees had discharged their responsibilities, all of the remaining lands of the late Henry Cavendish, Duke of Newcastle, which had been vested in them, or the equity of redemption of the mortgaged lands, were to become the property of Henrietta.

Thomas Pelham-Holles (as he was now styled both by will and Act of Parliament), Duke of Newcastle, in the peerage of Great Britain, received free of encumbrances the lands which had been the clear property of his uncle, while the Cavendish lands were made by sale to pay all and every debt and legacy of either the late duke or the duchess. Young Holles-Newcastle, as he always signed himself, was free to enjoy the profits of his uncle's wide Holles properties. It is also quite clear that he inherited indebtedness neither from his father nor from his uncle and that his future, indeed present, burden of debt would be of his own making.

The Harleys, or the Earl and Countess of Oxford as they later became, spent their money in maintaining the good aristocratic life of the eighteenth century, and in gathering one of the great collections of manuscripts and books of the century. Their income was insufficient to meet the costs of their endeavors, just as their adversary's was inadequate to sustain his social and political roles, so they were plagued by debt. Evidently the animosity between the Whig Pelhams and the Tory-oriented Harleys never abated. Many years later, following the Rebellion of 1745, when the government was attempting to secure loyal M.P.s from the north, Newcastle's agent, James West, wrote to Henrietta, Countess of Oxford, asking her support for the government. Her reply gave a picture of her attitude: 'You know I have never ask'd or received any favor from the Duke of Newcastle or Mr. Pelham but I believe I shall be inclined to oblige them in this particular.' She wanted to be informed if opposition was to be expected so that she could give proper orders. She had inherited her father's interest in politics, and her comments give a vivid picture of aristocratic electoral concepts for the century, as well as of her own financial acumen: 'For altho I shall resent it from every tenant who disobeys me yet I will not permit Mr. Tyler or anybody on any account to bring me Election Bills.'[21] Thus, if her disobedient tenants had to be bribed, the government would have to foot the bill.

The Duke of Newcastle possessed by inheritance one of the great estates of the realm, an estate unencumbered by debt and charged with only modest provisions for his brother and sister. He held land in freehold and leasehold tenure in eleven counties of the kingdom. His most extensive estates lay in Lincolnshire, Nottinghamshire, Sussex and Yorkshire, with smaller holdings in Middlesex, Dorsetshire and Wiltshire, and the smallest inheritance in Hertfordshire, Suffolk, Derby-shire and Kent. Besides these lands, he held the very profitable Clare Market estate in London, which lay to the south of Newcastle House and Lincoln's Inn Fields.

What was the Duke of Newcastle's income early in life? What was the gross annual income produced by his great estates? It is possible to establish Newcastle's landed income with fair exactness, largely because of the necessity for bringing together such information for the purposes of establishing a trust to pay his debts in 1738. The Deed of Trust of 1738 gave the gross annual rental and incidental income for the trust estate as £24,421.[22] To this must be added the income of the Sussex estate, which was not a part of the trust and which produced roughly £2,500 p.a. in the early part of the duke's career.[23] There may have been other small sums coming to the duke from lands excluded from the trust, but with the totals which are available (and there are no full runs of estate rentals or other accounts for this early period) we can say that his gross landed income from all sources was nearly £27,000. Naturally it might fluctuate widely when copyhold fines fell due. The Newcastle papers give no evidence of added income from the leasing of coal- or mineral-bearing lands at any time. Obviously this income is calculated from evidence from the late 1730s, except in the case of Sussex, and may be open to question. However, the size of the estate appears to have been stable for there is no evidence in the papers for the buying or selling of lands, except in Sussex, for income from that source was materially reduced through the gift and sale of lands to his brother Henry.

Although his estates provided the major portion of Newcastle's income throughout his life, it is necessary to investigate and to consider other possible sources of financial gain in order to ascertain his total income. Most obviously these sources include, first, the salary and profits of public office and, second, the income from investments in government securities or dividends from stock in various chartered or other companies. (See Figure 2, p. 133.)

The duke held public offices of honor or profit for over fifty years. He received patents of appointment early in life to the lord lieutenancies of Middlesex, Westminster and Nottingham, as well as appointments as Vice-Admiral of Sussex and Steward of Sherwood Forest. These offices of honor were marks of royal favor, but were actually based on his local power or influence and could hardly be denied him. These offices, although evidence of great local influence and sources of some small sinecures, were causes of expenditure rather than sources of much profit.

Early in 1717, Newcastle received his first appointment at the center of affairs when he was made Lord Chamberlain of the Household and began his tutelage in the ways of courts, experiences which would cause him to be termed 'an old and cunning courtier' years later.[24] The duke held this position for seven years. Often it entailed constant attendance at court, and the ceremonial and administrative duties could be onerous. However, George I kept his public role to a minimum during most of his reign, and part of the duties of Newcastle's office could be performed by the Vice-Chamberlain, Thomas Coke.[25] The traditional salary for the position was only £100 plus £1,100 board wages per annum.[26] There is no evidence of an added pension to supplement his salary. Each Lord Chamberlain also received upon his appointment 1,000 ounces of white plate (silver), and Newcastle's was estimated to cost the Treasury £400.[27] It appears doubtful if this position, although of greatest honor and dignity at court, was a profitable one for the young duke. Indeed he was at the time in need of cash to clear his debts at court; the office could have contributed relatively little to his gross income early in life and may well have helped him build a burden of debt.

Many of the landed gentlemen of Great Britain invested part of their capital resources in securities of various kinds, which added materially to their annual incomes, as we saw in the case of Newcastle's father. It could be assumed that with an income of the magnitude of Newcastle's there would be a surplus for such investment. However, a search of the records of the Bank of England can provide no evidence of the duke's ownership of Bank, South Sea Company or East India stock. This negative evidence is fully supported by the absence of any indication of the purchase, transfer or payment of dividends of such stock in his personal account at Hoare's Bank, 1714–30.[28] We are therefore safe in assuming a gross income of between £26,000 and £27,000 for the early years of the duke's life before he assumed the highly profitable public employment as Secretary of State in 1724.

The most familiar word encountered in a study of Newcastle's finances is 'debt.' For that reason we have gone to great lengths to demonstrate that he inherited his estates free of debt from either father or uncle. It is just as certain that at least from his majority he did not enjoy a single debt-free moment for the remainder of his long life. The most intriguing, perplexing and difficult question for the historian studying his economic and financial condition is the origin and cause of Newcastle's vast and continued indebtedness. There has been conjecture in plenty by contemporaries and by historians, as we will see later, but little effort has been made by the latter to go into the Newcastle papers to secure enlightenment. In spite of the bulk of these papers, relatively few account books have survived for estate, personal and household affairs. There are none for purely political expenditures. Those which have survived are of great value, however, and can be supplemented from correspondence, from Newcastle's accounts at Hoare's Bank, and from the accounts kept by his trustees from 1738 forward.

The evidence is overwhelming that shortly after reaching his majority he was already under serious pressure of debt. It can be conjectured that he borrowed money on his credit in anticipation of his control of the estates but we know in fact that in the two-year period 1715–16 he borrowed £21,000 upon mortgage and bond. He mortgaged his Sussex estates for £10,000 to William Guido of Lincoln's Inn Fields,[29] and to John Morrice, London merchant, for an additional £6,000.[30] In addition, he borrowed of Hoare a total of £5,000 on bond, making in all the £21,000.[31] The mortgages were paid off following his marriage and Hoare had been repaid by 1725 but the duke had borrowed from others on his bond, up to 1721, the great sum of at least £14,700, which remained unpaid in either principal or interest at the beginning of the trust in 1738.[32]

How were his vast debts accumulated and why was he unable to stop building new debt? In answer to the question we must see Newcastle not as a free and independent landed gentleman but as an individual whose role was determined for him to an unusual degree by the political and social expectations of the society in which he lived. His freedom of choice was severely limited by the inheritance from both father and uncle of economic and political power and responsibility, and by the concomitant demands of his peerage rank, which reflected this power and influence, as well as by his status and prestige as a chief minister of the crown. Many of the duke's expenditures followed of necessity from his role in eighteenth-century society and government, but the need to spend was reinforced by his own psychological insecurities. His role was great and his areas of influence were extensive. His style was grand in every area; his income was insufficient to support the style.

It is in the area of political expenditure that historians have always maintained that Newcastle spent prodigiously. Yet it is difficult to explain political expenditure adequately. No one would argue that such costs as buying votes at elections, election treats of food and drink, transporting voters to the polls, and the expenses of canvassing, paying local corporation costs and maintaining political clubs, were non-political. Such costs, however, came largely only at election times, which were infrequent.

The really difficult area of expenditure to categorize is that involved in 'keeping up one's interest' in local areas, a county or a corporation. Eighteenth-century expectations for a great landed magnate were fairly well acknowledged: he should make annual contributions to charities such as schools, hospitals and the like, as well as providing special help in times of distress; he should take the lead in celebrating national events, royal birthdays or anniversaries, and great victories in war; he should entertain the local nobility and gentry; he should provide appropriate cups or plates for races and other local contests, as well as using his influence at the center of power for local economic advantage or for the advancement of local persons. Take, for example, a great entertainment given for hundreds of guests at Halland or Bishopstone in Sussex, to celebrate a victory on land or sea, a celebration costing tremendous amounts for food and drink, for bonfires, for bell ringing, for cannon-firing, and the like—was the purpose of such huge expenditures political or social or patriotic? Obviously it was partly all of these, for it demonstrated the Pelham wealth and leadership as well as their concern for, and pride in, national achievement. The costs of most such entertainments appear in the accounts under household expenditures and not in a special category. The maintenance of one's interest in an area was a family expenditure.

It cannot be doubted that Newcastle spent much money in keeping up the Pelham interest in Sussex and elsewhere. It is very difficult, if not impossible, to determine the extent and amount of his payments for strictly political purposes, as here defined. If any account books ever existed for such expenditures, and none is mentioned in agents' correspondence, they have disappeared or have been destroyed. Newcastle's local land stewards and collectors or receivers of rents often acted as election agents as well, and reported to him on local conditions and problems. The accounts which have survived seldom indicate expenses which were political or electoral; usually they indicated the ordinary expenses of an estate, that is, repair of buildings, fencing, ditching and the like.

We have seen the debt which the young man accumulated, and there can be no doubt at all that part of it came from political expenditures;

but unless new material should become available we shall never be able to say with full authority where the money went. It would be difficult to sustain Namier's admittedly inexact statement that Newcastle 'had sacrificed a large part of his fortune to electioneering' by the end of his life.[33] The duke's income was large and he spent for political purposes as was expected; Namier demonstrated that the seats to which he could nominate unaided by the Treasury were fewer than once thought; the period of heaviest political spending was in the early part of his career, probably in Nottinghamshire; some boroughs took little nursing, apparently Yorkshire ones, while others, like Lewes, required constant attention; and still others were of no great trouble or expense, due to compounding for one seat with local Tory families. The general elections of 1715 and 1722 were difficult in terms of costs and were directly related to Newcastle's financial problems; each was held before he had direct Treasury aid available, it will be noted. There is no direct relationship between his later financial crises and the general elections held while he was in high ministerial office. Direct and indirect electoral expenditures were only a part of the cause of his lifetime of financial concern and probably a smaller part; the real culprit was his expenditures in maintaining his particular style of life year after year. These expenditures may have made it impossible for him to pay off youthful debts which were contracted, in part, for political purposes, and led eventually to the trust of 1738.

Newcastle was active in the Whig cause before and during the election of 1715. In fact, the first contemporary estimate of him was made in connection with political activity. Lady Mary Wortley Montagu, in August, 1714, was attempting to convince her husband that Newcastle, then Lord Pelham, should nominate him for Aldborough in Yorkshire and termed Pelham in her judgment as 'very silly but very good natured.'[34] Montagu and Mr Jessop, Newcastle's agent, had been nominated for the borough in 1713; and Montagu had evidently spent much of his own money in the contest which ensued between them and the dowager Duchess of Newcastle's nominees, who won.[35] In the following election Newcastle nominated Richard Steele to one of his seats at Boroughbridge in Yorkshire, probably upon the advice of Mr Jessop, who knew the politics of the northern area.[36] Newcastle's bank account shows that Jessop received a £400 draft in 1714.

There is some clear evidence of Newcastle's expenditure in this first election of the Hanoverian period. In Nottinghamshire, where the duke held estates worth over £7,000 per annum and where his interest in the city was very great, his candidates were Mr Gregory and Mr Plumptre. To help in the electioneering and in the election Mr Plumptre was paid £200 in 1715 from the duke's account at Hoare's, but much more than that was spent. The two candidates submitted their abstract of election expenses, which showed that they had expended £864.19s.8d. The candidates had given a bribe, or inducement, of one shilling to each man in the town of Nottingham; had spent various sums in meat and drink as treats to the voters; and had expended £20 for transporting voters from London to Nottingham.[37] It is doubtful whether the candidates received immediate reimbursement except for the above-mentioned £200, for it became a Newcastle custom to give a personal bond to cover such unpaid debts, usually payable two years after date, with interest.

Newcastle, with his wide political interests, had several agents about the country, and his personal bank account shows payments to them which were, in all probability, largely political. In Sussex, for example, he used several persons, friends and relatives, to help maintain his interest. Among these at this time were Brigadier Watkins, Sir William Ashburnham, Anthony Trumble, Sir John Shelley and Francis Pelham. During the 1714-15 period Brigadier Watkins received £350; and £700 in all went to Ashburnham, Shelley and Pelham. Mr Trumble, a Hastings attorney, presented a bill for £173.8s.0d. for carrying voters to Chichester for the county election.[38] It might also be noted that Robert Walpole received a draft for £1,000 late in 1714 from the young man's account.

If we total all the known and probable direct political expenses for this crucial campaign, we get £3,688. Of course, this may be too low a figure for we have no way of knowing if all of the bills for this election have survived. Obviously this is a very large sum of money, but his estate should have been able to sustain it. There can be little doubt, however, that such expenditures helped to build his current debt. Perhaps his debt was growing at this juncture because he did not have the full income from the estates he had inherited from his uncle. He might have borrowed in anticipation of this additional income. In his current account at Hoare's Bank, he was doing well when it was balanced on February 1, 1716. A total of £28,351.6s.5d. had passed through his hands since the account had been opened in July, 1714, and the account balanced £30 in his favor; this would become a most unusual event.[39] Although his drawing account was in balance, we know from Bowers that he had large and continuing indebtedness and we can conjecture that this was due not only to these large political expenditures but also to the multitude of charges arising from living and improving his homes. The wilder contemporary estimate that he spent £100,000 in political activity in 1714–15 can be dismissed out of hand as Tory propaganda put forth by Bishop Atterbury.[40]

We have seen, first, that Newcastle had experienced financial advisers in the persons of his guardians before he became of age, the Reverend Thomas Bowers until Bowers's death in 1724, and others who had served the family faithfully. At the same time it is obvious that the duke did not heed the advice given him in financial matters. Second, we have noted that there can be little doubt that he had accumulated debts or commitments before he came of age. The best evidence we have for his financial condition during that period comes from the letters of Bowers, who had the closest knowledge of his affairs. As early as May, 1715, Bowers wrote to Newcastle:[41]

> By inquiring into ye state of your Ldsp. affairs here [Sussex], I find (yt tho a great deal has been lately pd off) yet there are some debts still remaining yt must be immediately discharged, and knowing ye state of your Finances at London, I have been contriving to ease your Ldsp. at present by borrowing £200 at 5% until Michaelmas.

Bowers could borrow the sum only if he had a promise under the duke's own hand that it would be repaid on time. This is a certain indication of the early weakness of Newcastle's financial position and reputation, at least in Sussex.

Evidently Newcastle had promised his mentor repeatedly that he would pay attention to his own affairs and that he would retrench his expenses. This he failed to do, and Bowers was not at all fearful of giving the young duke plain admonitions upon every opportunity, explaining to him, 'Your Lordship will be witness to the tender affection I have had for you almost since your infancy, and now that sincere friendship I have after you have grown up forces me to do my utmost to preserve you from ruin,' a condition Bowers felt was very near. He was sorry to see Newcastle 'still retain an aversion to business' in spite of his promises to retrench his expenses and to manage his own affairs, 'but I must put your Lordship in mind that the resolution is not yet put in Execution, and every day's delay is very dangerous.' This letter was written on the very day Newcastle had borrowed the £10,000 of William Guidot, and Bowers begged Newcastle 'to consider that after the Sum is rec'd and paid away, there will still be vast debts remaining unpaid and there is no other way to pay them but by frugal management.' Finally Bowers gave the young duke a bit of political and economic philosophy to muse upon. 'It is certainly [*sic*] that the reputation and interest of a great man ... require riches and good management for his support, and if those be wanting the building will fall of course.'[42] This was sound advice for Newcastle, and it was repeated to him often. At times in his career the duke attempted to follow it, and he always retained a nagging guilt that he was not doing what he should be doing in his estates and financial affairs.

One of the time-honored means of relieving the pressure of debt or of rebuilding the fortunes of a noble family was to marry an heiress or a woman who could bring a large portion. Newcastle was at this time twenty-three years of age and was a most eligible bachelor, for he had much to recommend him: one of the great estates of the realm, a dukedom, wide family connections, a not unbecoming personality and figure, and a good moral character. It was financially impossible for him to marry for love alone; and romantic love was not a necessary ingredient in aristocratic eighteenth-century marriages, as all prospective fathers-in-law knew. Marriage was a bargain to be struck to the advantage of each family. Although Newcastle had offered to marry his cousin Henrietta in order to facilitate a family settlement, it can be doubted whether this offer was very seriously intended; it was, at all events, rejected. The correspondence gives no evidence of an extended or extensive search for a suitable bride for the young duke; we can conclude that only one girl was seriously considered—Henrietta Godolphin, granddaughter of John Churchill, Duke of Marlborough. Newcastle had decided to marry, and the pressure of debt was probably a factor in the timing of his decision.

In all probability the initiative for this particular match came from Sarah, Duchess of Marlborough, who took a lively interest in the affairs of her grandchildren. The instrument used by Sarah in her endeavor was Sir John Vanbrugh, who related that he had been asked by her to incline Newcastle to favor Henrietta, or Harriot, as she was usually called. Vanbrugh reported the whole story in a letter, probably to the girl's father, Lord Godolphin, and added, 'Her Grace did not *seem inclined to think* of giving *Such a Fortune as should* [*sic*] be any great inducement *to the Dukes preferring this Match, to others* which might probably be offered;' but that the duchess stressed, instead, the

fine personal qualities of the girl. When the possibility of such a
marriage alliance was mentioned to the young duke, he was very
interested and 'the Hopes of having a Posterity descend from the
Duke of Marlborough, had an extraordinary weight with him.' However, Vanbrugh was struck by Newcastle's seriousness in regard to
the qualities he wanted in a wife, for the young duke had noted the
bad education and bad manners of many of the ladies of the town and
the court.[43]

Vanbrugh had probably begun his commission in 1715, but matters
became serious late in 1716. Sir John visited Newcastle at Claremont
and spoke at length of Harriot's qualities and how they matched what
he wanted. Newcastle was fearful of being deceived and that he might
'find himself ty'd for life to a Woman not Capable of being a usefull and
faithfull Friend, as well as being an Agreeable Companion.' Vanbrugh
reported to Sarah that the duke had made many 'nice' inquiries as to
Harriot's temper, person, sense, behavior and other qualities, and
that he felt that he had left him disposed to her above all other women.[44]

Although Sarah had given Vanbrugh the commission to help
arrange the match, when success was about to be achieved she turned to
Peter Walter for aid, a decision which angered Vanbrugh. Peter Walter
evidently was to handle the financial side of the affair, and Vanbrugh
thought himself ill-used. 'I don't say this Madam, to Court being
farther employ'd in this matter; for a Matchmakers is a Damn'd Trade,
And I never was fond of Meddling with Other Peoples Affairs.'[45] Thus
Vanbrugh's efforts in this affair added fuel to his famous feud with
Sarah. At this time Newcastle was at Bishopstone in Sussex, and
Vanbrugh in his usual colorful way reported the treatment he had
received:[46]

> I need make no remarks to your Grace Upon this Abominable
> Womans proceeding Which shall not however lessen my regard
> to my Lord Duke, nor good Opinion of his Grand Daughter,
> who I do not think has one grain of this Wicked Womans
> Temper in her; if I did, I wou'd not advise you to take her, tho'
> with the Allay of a Million.

Upon receipt of this letter Newcastle wrote immediately to Bowers,
who was in Canterbury, for his advice. Bowers replied on November
13 that the letter had made him happy, and then went immediately to
the financial implications. The clergyman implied that a 'treaty' had
been generally agreed upon except for the portion, and that he felt that

'we' should get as much as possible since it could be had without hurting anyone:[47]

> As far as I can consider the case in this short time I cannot see how your Grace can dispense with less than £30,000. At present besides presents to the lady, jewells & charges of the marriage vous sauvez bien qu'il faut avoir vingt mille livres sterling pour mettre les Terres de Sussex en liberte & dix mille livres sterling seront necessaires pour les autres occasions qui touchent votre honneur et votre interest apres cela il restera une somme aussi large. mais se vous faites le bon manager (comme j'espere vous voules) vous pouvez payer tout cela fort [illegible] peu a peu.

The practical Reverend Mr Bowers, although he changed to French to do so, after giving the young man the figure to aim towards in the negotiations for a bride, advised him to follow through so that he might be relieved of some of the burden of debt.

The haggling over the amount of the portion continued throughout the fall of 1716 and the early spring of 1717. Vanbrugh reported to Newcastle the state of the contest with the strong-willed and economically wise Duchess of Marlborough. Sarah claimed that she had to persuade her husband to part with the money, and Vanbrugh felt that the duke's money could not be better used 'than to compass the best match in England, for the only Daughter of his Next Heir.' Vanbrugh's common-sense attitude towards the use of wealth was neatly summed up in his comment to Sarah, 'And if Riches are not to be employ'd, on such Occasions; I know no difference between him that has them, and him that has them not.'[48] Sir John is here quoting to Newcastle his letter to Sarah, but then he goes on to characterize the old duchess: 'I don't at all believe however, she's indifferent in the Matter, for she is not a Fool, tho she's a [illegible] worse thing. But, as in all her other Traffic, so in a husband for her Grand Daughter, she would fain have him good, and cheap; and she certainly fancys she can wheddle Peter Walter to play the Knaves part, and bring her business about with you, alone, without meddling much with your Friends & Relations.'[49] It appears that Newcastle's side was asking for at least £30,000 and perhaps more, but that Sarah was offering considerably less.

Newcastle wrote frequently to Vanbrugh, who continued to be his chief middle-man, concerning the portion. Vanbrugh told him that he had been to see Lord Godolphin, that he was well disposed to the match, and that if it had been in Godolphin's power, he would not have disputed Newcastle's financial demands. Sir John had also spoken with Robert Walpole and Lord Townshend about the matter, and they had advised Newcastle that it was 'best to ly by a little, and not seem to her Grace too forward.'[50]

Perhaps Newcastle and his advisers did not press the matter, for it was not until March 30, 1717, that the indenture was finally signed which provided for the financial arrangement which preceded the wedding. The haggling had ended when £20,000 was accepted as the portion which Lady Henrietta Godolphin should bring with her. The sum was to be paid in full by John, Duke of Marlborough, at or before the ensealing of the document.[51] Newcastle for his part assigned, with the approval of his late father's executors, the Bank stock, Exchequer annuities, etc., which they were holding, to James Craggs and Peter Walter in trust for the use of his wife to secure an annuity of £1,400 for a part of her jointure.

Thomas Pelham-Holles and Henrietta Godolphin were married on April 2, 1717, just three days after the indentures were signed; Newcastle got a wife of whom he became very fond, and was relieved of some of his most pressing debts. There is no evidence that the marriage portion passed through his account at Hoare's Bank. It can be assumed that the duke received cash from Marlborough, for Bowers used the term 'paid away' when writing on the subject of the portion. It is most probable that Bowers's advice was followed, and that the £20,000 was used to lift the mortgages upon the Sussex estate held by William Guidot and John Morrice of London, totaling £16,000 and perhaps a bond held by Hoare for £2,000, which was cleared in July, 1717. We know that the Sussex estate was free of major encumbrances in 1723, for at that time Peter Walter suggested borrowing £10,000 on it.

It was within two weeks after his marriage that Newcastle was made Lord Chamberlain of the Household on April 14, 1717. The appointment was part of the rearrangements necessitated by the Whig schism of 1717, which brought Sunderland and Stanhope to the helm.[52] It is quite evident from the sources which have survived that neither the marriage nor the office relieved Newcastle of continual financial pressure.

If the pressure of debt was constant, so was the advice from his old friend and mentor, the Reverend Mr Bowers, now a prebend of Canterbury Cathedral. Bowers wrote lengthy letters to Newcastle, which contain much information about the state of the duke's finances and about eighteenth-century economic philosophy, showing keen psychological insight. Bowers told Newcastle that he was responsible for his own personal situation, 'it not being in anyone's power to control you.' The clergyman recognized what today would be called a 'self-destructive urge' and told Newcastle that, although no one would admit to such an intention, if 'his manner of Living shews it,' it would be looked upon by observers as proof of his intention. Most importantly, Bowers stressed style of life as the major cause for the duke's financial problems, as well as noting the essential freedom and responsibility of a rich aristocrat.

The economic aphorisms of the old prebend should have been full of instruction for Newcastle:

> Tis certain no man can be easy and happy in this world till he has ye command of money: for proportionable riches are necessary to support ye reputation & power of every great man: so yt what ease a great man has yt runs in debt is forced and preternatural, & is owing to his being in a continual hurry, & banishing ye thought of his [condition?]; this is divesting a man's self of his reason for awhile & keeping his mind continually intoxicated.

Perhaps Bowers noted here a characteristic of Newcastle—his continual scurrying about—which observers of later years would often record. To Bowers it was evidence of the duke's refusal to stop to consider his real situation.

In marshalling his reasons why Newcastle should retrench and watch his expenses, Bowers did not forget the costs of elections. He asked the duke to consider, 'yt four years hence (or sooner if ye King please) there will be a new Parliament, & then tho we should be better managers than we were the last time, yet a considerable sum must be expended in a just and honorable way, for I know your Grace would not let your interest sink.' Bowers was reminding him of the expenses of the 1715 election, probably in Sussex, and noting the young man's determination to succeed in politics. This most interesting letter leaves no doubt of Bowers's various roles in Newcastle's life: priest, probably tutor, friend, admirer, election agent and financial adviser. We have also seen that he served as a collector of rents upon occasion.[53]

Newcastle had repeatedly promised his old friend that he would retrench, and Bowers complimented him on his resolution:[54]

> You never said a truer or juster thing in your life, for all honest and wise men will commend you for it, your friends will rejoice and your enemies be mortified: for if you are steady in your

management, 6 or 7 years will produce wonderful good effects, and these are nothing in the life of one so young. God has given you a good understanding and if you will make use of it for your own benefit, you cannot fail of being happy.

After these compliments, Bowers, although fearful of being tedious, hoped the duchess would present him with children which 'will be visible moving arguments for consideration, and make even your care pleasing to you.'[55] Rarely has a letter of advice marshalled so many arguments from so many points of view to support a course of action; rarely has one had less effect. It is certain that neither the receipt of a £20,000 marriage portion nor high office at court eliminated for long the financial distress of the Duke of Newcastle.

The aristocrats of Georgian England expended large sums on building seats in the country and town houses in London to reflect their social and political positions. The capital outlay in building, remodeling and repairing these homes, and their constant operating costs, were a cause of financial embarrassment to many of the leaders of the great world. Newcastle maintained five homes to meet his personal, social and political needs. In Sussex he inherited Halland, an old Elizabethan manor house which was the true Pelham seat, that he loved and where he entertained often. His second Sussex seat was Bishopstone, near the coast, which was his favorite hunting lodge. In London, he inherited Powis, or Newcastle House, from his uncle; it still stands in Lincoln's Inn Fields. In the family settlement he received Nottingham Castle, in the town of Nottingham, as his northern seat. What the young man lacked, and felt he had to have, was a seat conveniently located near London and the court, where he might entertain and find recreation. His old friend, Sir John Vanbrugh, had a building in Surrey, not far from Hampton Court, which he offered to sell to Newcastle shortly after he came of age, either in 1715 or 1716. This building would form the core of Newcastle's beloved Claremont, where the great and near-great would be entertained for over fifty years.

The five ducal homes were a constant but varying source of expense, naturally greater when the duke was in residence. Directly related to the existence and use of these buildings was the continuing cost of maintaining the 'household' or 'family.' The term 'family' or 'our family' was used constantly by the duke and duchess; it denoted all of their servants and retainers, from the highest to the lowest, and, indeed, seemed at times to include the Newcastles themselves. Upon the basis of surviving evidence of a statistical nature, as well as from repeated assertions in the correspondence, it seems clear that the related costs of building, maintaining and operating these establishments, together with the costs of the stables, formed the major category of expense to the Duke of Newcastle and were the prime cause of his financial difficulty. It was not strictly political expenditures which caused Newcastle a lifetime of financial worry, but rather his manner or style of life in maintaining his ducal estate.

Sir John Vanbrugh had general supervision of the building and remodeling of several of Newcastle's properties. Much of the work was undertaken by a contractor or carpenter named Mr John Smallwell. His accounts demonstrate that Newcastle was involved in the modernization of Newcastle House, that is, in fitting new windows, adding new wainscoting, etc., as early as the spring of 1715. Smallwell and his partner, Thomas Keynarston, were also involved in building additions to Claremont; their day or 'measured' accounts submitted in November, 1717, show that they had expended over £1,500 in 1716–17, although they had been paid only £500.[56] Vanbrugh told Newcastle in the same month that he was working hard to get the building at Claremont under cover, that the work at Newcastle House was nearly finished and that the house would soon be ready for him.[57] Smallwell died in the summer of 1718 and was still owed £500, but the family was willing to take a two-year bond for the amount.[58]

Newcastle requested that Vanbrugh survey Nottingham Castle in order to see if it would be adequate for the duke's needs, and to report on its structural condition. Late in November, 1718, Vanbrugh set out for Nottingham to undertake his commission for his friend. He reported to the duke that 'twas [as] horrible a day, as Storms, hail, Snow and the Divil [sic] can make it, I have been over your Castle, inside and out,' and that he had found it much better than it had been represented to him. 'And so upon the Whole I think I may reasonably congratulate your Grace upon being Master of this Noble Dwelling.'[59] Newcastle was so interested in the castle that he decided to form a party and to make a trip there in the middle of the winter to see it for himself, as we noted earlier. Vanbrugh wrote to urge him to stay in London and to come in the spring. However, the duke was probably at Nottingham before Vanbrugh's letter was sent, for it had been written on Christmas Day, 1718, and Vanbrugh wrote again on January 4, 1719, saying that he had learned from a letter from London that Newcastle had been to the castle. Now, at least, Newcastle could tell Vanbrugh what he wanted done 'to make it a more compleat dwelling' and informed him that he would soon return to London, where, as Vanbrugh put it, 'I shall be very glad to find your Grace, less frightened with the Nottingham Storms and Precipices than I apprehend.'[60]

If the young duke was in any way disenchanted with his northern seat, he did not indicate it to his wife. Newcastle and members of his party reported to their wives at each post; and the duke wrote that in spite of the need for repairs, sashes and windows, it was 'in the main very Noble and pretty convenient.' Although he missed his wife he was planning for their future there, and in his final letter he gave her some details of the arrangements. 'I have taken better care of my Dearest in her absence than you could expect, for we shall have the best and Snuggest Bed Chamber yt I ever saw. Besides there will be to our Apartment a large waiting Room for ye Servants & you will have a Dressing Room very pleasant with Two large windows & twenty foot square.'[61] Although Newcastle did spend money refurbishing the castle, there is little evidence that he made any great use of it personally. His official positions kept him close to London most of the time except for occasional excursions for personal or political reasons.

Throughout 1719 and 1720, Vanbrugh continued to superintend the buildings at Claremont, reporting his progress to the duke. He also adduced that he was sorry that he could not be at Claremont 'to get drunk upon your Birthday' but that he had eaten his venison in London and had wished him long life 'and that you may not repent of laying out more money in Building at Claremont.'[62] It is doubtful if the duke ever resented such expenditures, for he loved Claremont deeply. Even James Brydges, Duke of Chandos, whose seat, Cannons, at Stanmore, was an architectural showplace, had heard of Vanbrugh's work at Claremont, and wanted a room of similar design and workmanship in the London house he was building. Chandos wanted to visit Claremont to view the new room under discussion, but Vanbrugh asked him to wait until it was fully completed, 'that it may Stair [sic] in his face, And knock him downe at Once.'[63] Vanbrugh was perfectly willing to show his confidence in his own work, and was a bit put out that Chandos had not employed him as his architect. The account books for the building of Claremont have not survived, but the building and improvements which continued for years would probably have accounted for a sizeable portion of Newcastle's debts in the early part of his career.

Vanbrugh does not appear to have been involved directly in changes which Newcastle initiated in Sussex, but the accounts make clear that Newcastle was modernizing or improving both at Halland and at Bishopstone. Newcastle loved his ancestral county of Sussex; and he liked to spend time at these seats where he was a great man, among old county friends or political, legal and ecclesiastical acquaintances he brought down from London as guests. The duke went to Sussex fairly often to ride, hunt and relax, but he never ceased to nurse the Pelham interest. He always attempted a visit in August for the Lewes races and he sometimes spent Christmas in the south. On each of these occasions Newcastle was the politician. In a letter to Charles Stanhope, who was in Paris on a diplomatic mission, he reported on the local political situation and gave a nutshell description of his political mission: 'By what I have hitherto seen, the county seems in a very good disposition. My business is to fix 'em against the time we may want them.'[64]

Ready money was very short in Sussex early in 1718, for Mr Digby, one of Newcastle's agents, wrote to Peter Forbes that he not only had no money to pay bills but could not even buy necessities, and requested a bank draft for funds. He also noted Newcastle's changed attitude towards expenses and gave an early example of the duke's resolve to retrench, 'when h.g. [his Grace] was pleased to say, in a manner very different from what I had ever seen from h.g. before, that the expenses of keeping the hounds and horses was so great, that he could not think of keeping them any longer than the time he had promised the Duke of Kingston, which is, I suppose, the end of the next hunting season.'[65] It is doubtful whether the duke kept this resolution any better than he kept ones made later in his career.

One area of expense which has been neglected in the story of Newcastle's financial woes in his early life is that of legal costs. He and his advisers were involved in long and complex efforts to validate his inheritance from his uncle through suits in the common law courts, in Chancery, in the ecclesiastical courts, through negotiations undertaken by Lord Cowper, and finally by Act of Parliament. In all of these contests, the best legal talent available was secured; and although no accounts survive to demonstrate the costs of these efforts, they were no doubt very expensive.

Newcastle was fond of most of his family and was eager to ensure their welfare and comfort. The late Lord Pelham had left in the hands of his executors the sum of £5,000 for his younger son Henry and a marriage portion of a like sum for his daughter Lucy. However, when

it came time for Lucy to seek a suitable match, the £5,000 was insufficient to secure the desired alliance with the Earl of Lincoln. Evidently
these negotiations were taking place at the same time as Newcastle's
own with the Duchess of Marlborough. To end the negotiations with
the mother of the Earl of Lincoln, Newcastle agreed to augment the
portion provided by their father's will by an additional £7,000. We
know that Newcastle received £20,000 at his marriage on April 2,
1717, and that the sum was needed to free the Sussex estate from mortgage. Henry, Earl of Lincoln, and Lucy Pelham were married just over
a month later, on May 16, 1717, and Lincoln received £12,000 or at
least the original £5,000 and the interest on the £7,000.[66] We know
that Newcastle did not have £7,000 cash to pay the Earl of Lincoln, and
it appears that he was not paid at this time. For many years Newcastle
paid interest on an unsecured debt of £10,000 to Lady Lincoln, and this
probably represents part of the portion. He borrowed £3,000 from
Hoare's Bank in November, 1717, perhaps in connection with this
settlement, but more likely to pay pressing debts.

The duke was not without resources, but much of his wealth was not
readily convertible to cash. An example of this wealth was the family
silver, which would have represented a fortune to the ordinary gentleman. In 1717, the duke possessed 8,332 ounces of silver in dishes,
plates, salvers, ladles, saltcellars, and candlesticks, as well as in knives,
forks and spoons and a chamber pot.[67] He received 15,944 ounces
additional from the estate of his uncle, silver which was sent by Lady
Harley in ten boxes, making in all 19,704 ounces in his hands in May,
1726. The discrepancy in the figures is due to the fact that over 6,500
ounces were pledged or sold to Hoare in 1716.[68] Such resources as
could not easily be liquidated were of little use for meeting day-to-day
emergencies; and much of the silver being entailed, it therefore could
not have been sold in any case. The duke had for current income the
produce of his estates and the salary of his office as Lord Chamberlain;
but he was also receiving moneys due him as a result of the family
settlement, which had just received the royal assent as a private bill.
Peter Walter, one of the trustees under a provision of the settlement,
paid Newcastle over £6,843 from his account in a five-month period,
June–November, 1719.[69]

It would have been most unusual if the duke had not had visions of a
debtless state from profits to be made by speculation in South Sea
stock. Newcastle tried to secure the right to buy shares through the
influence of his friend, Charles Stanhope, to whom he made it clear

that he hoped to rescue himself from his burden by South Sea profits and then rationalized his need by reference to the Whig cause. 'I should not be so pressing but I know you will forgive it, I really believe I shall by this gett quite clear & by that means, I shall be better able to serve my friends, & the good old cause, neither of which will I forsake while I live.'[70] Stanhope could be of no help, so Newcastle turned to James Craggs, a friend of many years. Craggs informed him that the South Sea directors' method for the new subscription 'has quite demolished ye Court Lists. . . . I am sorry I cannot do wt you desire for your friends, they must be contented to fare like the rest of the world.'[71] Thus the duke could secure stock neither for himself nor for those court figures among whom he moved from day to day. There is no evidence that he purchased a single share of stock, for his name does not appear in the lists of South Sea Company stockholders at the Bank of England. He could possibly have purchased in another name but neither, at this time, is there evidence of his borrowing money which might have been used to purchase stock, nor evidence of the payment of dividends to his account at Hoare's Bank.

While Newcastle was attempting to secure the option to buy South Sea stock for himself and his friends, he was engaged in a furious political battle in Nottingham, a strongly Tory town. He set out for Nottingham at the end of July and informed Stanhope, 'Tomorrow I sett out for Nottingham Castle determined to get the best of all opposition & not to choose one bad man.'[72] Newcastle had success in his efforts in Nottingham but the cost must have been very high, for he entertained lavishly.[73] He remained in the county for two months, which led Craggs to remark, 'The Duke of Newcastle is undoing himself at Nottingham, & seems to stay because he likes the life he leads.'[74] Although no accounts have survived for the costs of the Whig victory there, Craggs must have had adequate sources of information upon which to base his remarks, for he was correct. Newcastle's credit, evidently for the first time, was being seriously questioned; and the public spending of great sums in the campaign was a factor in the concern of creditors for their money. No doubt an additional factor for the timing of this crisis in the duke's personal finances was the bursting of the South Sea Bubble in August, 1720, while he was in Nottingham. Everyone either needed money to cover losses or was fearful for moneys they had out at interest, and hence they pressed for repayment.

It was essential that something be done immediately to restore confidence in the ability of the Newcastle estate to pay its outstanding debts. The establishment of a trust for the estate, whose major function would be the payment of interest and the principal of the debt, would give the needed assurance to creditors. Negotiations for a trust were evidently begun early in 1721 but the deed was not signed until July. Newcastle, in a letter to the Reverend Dr George Jordon, one of his clerks and the son-in-law of Bishop Bowers, reported 'the Deed of Trust was after many difficulties executed last week [July 7]. Not one Penny of Money yett paid, I know not when it will be.' The duke needed Jordon's help and insisted that he come to London for a few days. Mr Shelley, one of the duke's creditors, 'continues as impertinent as ever & I am afraid will show others the way to be so.'[75]

The Deed of Trust, which was dated July 7, 1721, has not survived. It may have been created for a two-year period only; or perhaps its inadequacy led to a study of its functioning at the end of that period of time. At any rate nothing is heard of it after 1724. The purpose of the trust was two-fold: to pay the duke's debts, as contained in a schedule or book of debts, and to provide a 'regulation' or budget for the duke's family in order to stop the debt-building process. Neither the schedule of debts nor the accounts of the trustees have come down to us.

However, Peter Walter recorded the total indebtedness in 1721 as £88,572 in a survey of the duke's affairs made in 1734.[76] It appears that approximately £9,500 of this was secured by the deed of trust, £3,296 on the Sussex estate and £30,000 on the Lincolnshire estate.[77] The trustees were required to pay Newcastle £6,500 p.a., and a budget was devised for that amount to cover the costs of his household and stables. The duke was so fearful for his financial condition that he was determined to live upon the budget proposed for him; he reported to Jordon, 'I have not in one instance exceeded my Scheme nor ever will for I am thoroughly convinced of ye necessity of sticking to it.'[78] He may have been convinced of the necessity for limiting his expenditures, but the proposed budget was unrealistic considering the size and complexity of his establishments. Newcastle found it impossible to effectively limit his expenditures; his resolutions to retrench were always overcome by more pressing needs.

In November, 1723, Newcastle asked Peter Walter to make a study of his financial situation since his marriage in order, as Walter stated it, to find a 'way of answering the present Emergencies.' Walter's study showed that the £3,000 jointure of the duchess, secured at this time half on the Sussex and half on the Lincolnshire estates, as well as the provision for the younger children, had been mortgaged in 1721 to Henry

Shelley for £2,746, and again to Robert Shelley in 1723 for an additional £1,300. Only £750 had been repaid on these two mortgages—leaving £3,296 outstanding.

The duke had evidently proposed as a question to Walter whether or not the trust of 1721 might be voided and £30,000 borrowed upon the estates in order that the debts on the trust, the mortgages on the Sussex estate, and many of the scheduled debts, be paid off. Walter considered this idea 'totally unpracticable and what nobody whatever will come into.' He advised that there was only one way to do it: to let the £9,500 remain a charge on the deed of trust and to borrow £10,000 on the Sussex estate; pay off the Shelleys their £3,296; and 'the residue to apply to such of ye Schedule of creditors as are most in need, and are most likely to give an uneasiness.'[79] It appears obvious from the figures and from the tone of Walter's report that the trust had not been able to provide the necessary sums to rescue the duke's credit. Perhaps the duke was creating new debt and thereby defeating the aim of the trust.

Since his financial condition was not improving and he was again in an emergency, Newcastle needed to know how closely he had been able to adhere to his budget, so he requested that Walter make a study of the household and stable accounts for the two-year life of the trust to date, July 7, 1721, to July 7, 1723, and that he compare them with the budget. Walter's report to the duke was ready on March 12, 1724.[80] The general accounts of the trust had been kept by Peter Forbes; the Household accounts, both ordinary and extraordinary, were kept by Mr Burnett, the Steward of the Household; and the Stable accounts, both ordinary and extraordinary, by Mr Seymour, the duke's Gentleman of the Horse. The distinction in their accounts between ordinary and extra-ordinary is by no means clear.

The income of the trust handled by Mr Forbes came from the rents and profits of the major part of the duke's landed estates in Lincoln-shire, Nottinghamshire, Derby and York, as well as from the Clare Market estate in London. During the two-year period, the various stewards had paid in to Forbes £30,597. From this sum Forbes had paid the duke his annual £6,500, capital and interest to creditors, and other charges, totaling in all £30,218, leaving a balance of £379 in his hands.

Walter then turned to a detailed study of the working of the budget for the Newcastle establishment. In doing so, he noted that the duke's servants were of undoubted probity, that they made purchases at good prices, and that they were in general careful of the duke's interests. Mr

Burnett had received for both of his Household accounts £5,812, but had overspent by £542. Mr Seymour had received for both of his Stable accounts £3,018, but had overspent by £107. So far so good, for over-spending of only about £650 for the two-year period was not too unreasonable. However, the bills actually paid did not tell the full story, for Walter discovered that the over-spending was only a very small part of the problem: there were unpaid debts as well, in both Burnett's and Seymour's areas, and 'several Extraordinary and contingent expenses unpaid,' which brought the total excess for household and stable costs to £5,312 for the two-year period. Mr Forbes's accounts showed that he had paid out in this period £8,830 to maintain his master's family; but if we add the debt accumulated in these two accounts, we find the true total to be £14,142, which is obviously above the annual budgeted amount. One of the major purposes of the trust was to aid Newcastle in reducing his costs of living so that he might have an excess or surplus, which could be used to reduce further the burden of indebtedness. Mr Walter reminded the duke that since the income from his Sussex estate 'are brought in ayd & contribution to those Expenses, I cannot but with great sorrow of Minde observe, that the aforesaid Extraordinarys of £5,312 is such a Sume of money wch if not restrained for the future, must unavoydably very much embarass your Affairs, and render your scheme of retrenchment ineffectuall.'[81]

The second object of the trust was to pay debts in order to rescue the duke's credit. We saw the total trust income to be £30,597; and if we subtract from this the total annual payments to the duke, i.e. £13,000, and the balance remaining in Mr Forbes's hands, we have left a total of £17,217, which should have been available for its major purpose. We have seen that while one debt was presumably being reduced, another was being built—in fact, defeating the purpose of the trust. Since the trust records have not survived, it is impossible to say by how much the debt was actually reduced. However, the Schedule of Debt prepared for the second trust of 1738 gives undoubted proof that the debt was not cleared, for the duke owed in principal for the category of indebtedness, termed 'Bonds before Midsummer, 1721,' a total of £14,700 as well as great sums of accumulated interest.[82]

The £6,500 proposed in the Scheme of Regulation of 1721 was for household and stable costs only. Naturally, the duke had many other charges besides these major ones, and provision would have to have been made to cover them. Income which would have been available to meet his other obligations or needs was probably as follows: roughly

£3,600 from the rentals collected by Peter Walter; £2,500 from the Sussex estate (which Walter had reminded him he had used to cover family expenses); and his official salary of £1,200. It appears likely that he should have had approximately £7,300 to meet his other costs: pocket money, the duchess's pin money, clothing and many other personal costs for necessities, luxuries, and political or capital expenditures. Thus the duke had a total spendable income of approximately £15,000 at this time, and the remainder of his estate income was presumably going for debt-reduction.

At the same time as feeble efforts were being made to live on a restricted income, Newcastle, always appreciative of the faithful service of Dr Bowers to his family, looked for opportunities to further his friend's career in the church. Bowers had been named a prebend of Canterbury in 1715 and had been made archdeacon in 1721, no doubt upon Newcastle's recommendation. This is an early example of the duke's concern for ecclesiastical patronage, which would continue throughout his public career until the church was 'pure Whig.' But a bishopric was the capstone of such preferment, and Newcastle worked tirelessly to secure one for his old friend and adviser. The duke had approached Carteret for Bowers and had received the promise of a bishopric for him eventually. Carteret reported to Newcastle in 1721 that Bowers had been thought of 'for ye Bishopric of Bangor once, but since we have thought it not worth his acceptance & turned to some dean or other.'[83] A clearer statement of the use of the church could scarcely be found: the Bishopric of Bangor was the poorest see in the church and not a fit reward for the dependent of a great family. Newcastle continued his efforts on behalf of Bowers to both Carteret and Townshend. The health of incumbents was a matter of vital importance, and Newcastle informed Bowers in August, 1722, that the newspapers said the Bishop of Chichester was very ill and that one newspaper said he was dead. 'I have upon this alarm renewed my application to Lord Townshend for you, who has promised me you should have it.'[84] The diocese of Chichester would be perfect for Bowers; for he knew the area well from years of residence and service there, and his appointment would demonstrate the Pelham power and influence. Bowers was duly nominated and elected Bishop of Chichester, but he continued to hold the archdeaconry of Canterbury *in commendam* until his death in 1724, a good example of eighteenth-century pluralism.

Newcastle needed all the help and advice he could receive from the new Bishop of Chichester. The resolve and pledge not to exceed his budget were not kept, and the phrase 'new contracted debt' begins to recur with tiresome regularity. His gross income from the trust, from non-trust sources, and from his salary was insufficient to meet the needs of a ducal establishment of such magnitude. By concentrating too much upon the costs of maintaining his establishment year by year, we may lose sight of special or periodic costs. It seems that it was the unusual costs which, in this instance, brought on 'the present Emergencies,' as Walter termed them.

The year 1722 saw the second general election of the Hanoverian period, and once again Newcastle was active in areas of his major influence in Nottingham and in Sussex, where he actively campaigned and from which he wrote regularly to the duchess and told her, 'I am thoroughly tired wth all these diversions I used to love in Elections.'[85] Newcastle was successful in all of his election endeavors and was quite exhilarated in spite of his exhaustion.[86] However, very little direct information regarding his expenses in this great contest has come down to us. John Bristowe, one of his Nottingham stewards, put in a claim in 1726 for £820, which he maintained was owed him for expenses in this election,[87] but this is about all the documentation we have left. Regardless of the absence of direct data regarding the duke's costs, we have indirect evidence in plenty which demonstrates that it was the election of 1722 which brought on the crisis in Newcastle's financial affairs.

In this post-election year crisis of 1723, Bishop Bowers took it upon himself, without Newcastle's knowledge, to approach the government for help to relieve Newcastle's pressure of debt. The duke soon learned of Bowers's action from Townshend himself, who spoke kindly to him about his problem, and requested that he and Walpole be permitted to procure from the king the money needed to relieve him. Bowers had informed Lord Townshend that the duke's new debt was £4,000. Newcastle thanked Townshend and said that he would speak with Walpole but that he had not come to any conclusion as to what course he ought to take. It was not long before he did so, for the thirty-year-old duke, burdened with debt, wrote to Bowers and delineated a policy which he kept for the rest of his life, a policy which was rare indeed in the politics of that century:[88]

You know very well my Dear Lord, the great backwardness I have always had, to ask or secure any Summ of money of ye king, how I detest it in others & consequently how unwilling I shall be to do ye like myself but however if no other way can be found out (wch I still hope may) rather than ye Innocent should suffer by long want of their money, I must overcome my own Temper & submit to those things by Necessity, wch other people have done by Inclination, but in that case, I think it much more honorable, as well as adviseable for me, to ask an Encrease of Salary, than accept of a present Summ of Money.

Newcastle's sense of public honesty is evidenced strongly in this statement to the man who probably knew him more intimately than did any other. The duke disliked those who used state service as a means of becoming crown pensioners, and he had a great fear of becoming a defaulter because of his folly and thus defrauding innocent creditors. It is indeed a paradox that this man who spent so much of his life dispensing positions in church and state to thousands of supplicants should have had such an aversion to helping himself.

Newcastle also informed Bowers in the same letter that he had 'some prospects for exchanging my Place for one infinitely more profitable.'[89] Undoubtedly the duke had discussed his financial needs with Walpole and Townshend and must have been told that he could expect more profitable employment when a position opened up. Indeed the office might have been mentioned: Secretary of State for the Southern Department. Newcastle was named to this position on April 6, 1724, ten months to the day after the letter quoted above, following Carteret's removal. The motivations for this appointment were many: primarily, the need of the brothers-in-law for an able and dependable person who would carry out policy, and second, the financial distress of the young duke incurred because of his political service to the Whig cause. The appointment recognized Newcastle's single-minded devotion to public service, his willingness to work and his political ability.

Bishop Bowers replied to Newcastle's letter on June 12, admitted that he had indeed gone to Lord Townshend about the financial problems, and gave quite plainly his own conclusions, that 'one reason for the distress was the vast expenditures in the service of the government, so in necessity, some relief might justly be expected from thence.' Bowers had also told Townshend of the trust and the budget, and 'that you had unhappily exceeded the allowance your grace had reserved to live upon' and that he could not see how the 'new contracted debts' could be paid because so much of the estate was already settled to pay old debts. Townshend asked what the new debt was and Bowers guessed that it was about £4,000, but later discovered that it was greater.[90] Bowers boldly suggested a more profitable place for Newcastle, 'for I knew your aversion to anything that should be called a Pension & just named the Groom of the Stole ... his lordship made no particular reply.' Townshend did say, however, 'that you had indeed deserved well of the government and that he believed the sum I mentioned might be procured without anybodys knowing it but a few particular friends that might be relyd upon' and that he would speak with Walpole about it.[91] There is no evidence that Newcastle was in fact offered the £4,000, or that he took it if it were. It would appear most unlikely that he would take a sum of money, and we do know that he received an increase in salary of over £4,000 per year, since his new salary would be £5,680, as against the £1,200 which he received as Lord Chamberlain.

In his perilous financial situation, Newcastle's mind turned to other possible palliatives, traditional ones for members of his class, but ones which demonstrate his basic financial honesty, his concern for his family and a personal disappointment. As usual, Newcastle tried out his idea on the long-suffering bishop and gave his rationale for the proposal. First, his disappointment was that he had been married six years and it was unlikely he would have any children to whom to leave his estates, although he had not given up all hope. Second, since he loved and esteemed his brother Henry equal to himself, he would like to see him married and settled; and he would consider Henry's children as his own.[92] However, Henry Pelham's income was too small to enable him to marry, but Newcastle had the answer to his problem ready at hand. The answer was a rich marriage for Henry. If Henry could get a bride with a fortune of '50 or 3 score Thousand pounds,' Newcastle would make over all of his Lincolnshire estate, 'which is over £6,000 p.a.' In return Henry would give Newcastle £30,000 to pay off the debt charged to those estates, and the estates would be released from the trust.[93] By Newcastle's scheme, both brothers would profit. Henry would get a wife and a fortune; Thomas would be partially relieved of debt; Henry's children would inherit their uncle's property. Newcastle saw these advantages, and said that Henry would thereby have an estate of near £8,000, 'equal almost to any Commoners, and if he should desire (wch I should be sorry for) he might be called up to the House of Peers.'[94]

Bowers received this long letter from the hands of a special messenger, for he alone had been told of this scheme and the duke needed his opinion on it. It is almost humorous that, after dealing in tens of thousands of pounds, Newcastle ended by saying that he needed immediately £600 to pay laborers, servants and others.

The bishop, who had had a lifetime of experience in financial matters, considered the points in Newcastle's letter and replied on June 12. His reply must have considerably cooled Newcastle's hopes in the scheme. The first cold, hard fact the bishop noted was the duke's total indebtedness: 'when you have received and payed £30,000 there will be still remaining a debt of £40,000 at least.'[95] There remained the problem of reducing the remaining debt while at the same time paying the expenses of living. 'Now pray consider whether, when so great a branch of your income is taken off, there will be sufficient to maintain you handsomely, and to discharge the principal & pay the interest of the debt so fast as it will be expected by the creditors: this cannot be done without a very frugal management; and therefore if this plot or scheme about Mr. P's marriage should take effect' it would mean an additional income of only £2,000 or £3,000, presumably largely interest saved by clearing the Lincolnshire estate.[96]

Here is an opportunity to calculate the amount of money Newcastle had borrowed by his thirtieth year: it was at least £100,000. We can correctly assume that £20,000 of indebtedness on the Sussex estate had been cleared by the marriage portion he had received from Marlborough. The trust of 1721 would have paid off at least £10,000 with its resources, and now Bowers indicated that the remaining old debt and the 'new contracted debt' totaled at least £70,000. This vast figure seems incredible, but the bishop had a close and detailed knowledge of the duke's financial affairs over a period of many years, as we have seen from his constant appeals to the young man to live within his means. Even if the faithful bishop exaggerated a bit for effect on his slow-learning pupil, the overstatement probably would not have been very great.

Interesting and instructive as Newcastle's thoughts may be in regard to eighteenth-century marriage practices and the importance of landed wealth in fixing great family connections, his scheme did not provide a way out from under his load of debt. Henry Pelham did not marry until October 29, 1726, when he took to the altar Lady Katherine Manners, the eldest daughter of John, second Duke of Rutland, with whom he apparently had been living for some years.[97] Katherine's marriage portion was not £30,000 but rather £10,000. Yet the duke entailed on Pelham certain lands in Sussex, as he had promised. In return Pelham undertook to pay off certain debts which Newcastle had incurred as early as 1715, presumably in Sussex.[98] It is interesting and unusual that this marriage contract was dated more than a month after the wedding itself took place, which may suggest that haste was in order.

In October, 1723, Bishop Bowers once again had a serious look at Newcastle's financial condition; and the view was appalling. The duke's debt was so high that additional sums had to be raised to pay part of them or the duke's credit would be gone. Bowers even warned Newcastle that he found his affairs had reached such a state that he might be haled into Westminster Hall by some of his creditors. The bishop remonstrated with the duke that in spite of his financial crisis new works had been undertaken at Halland, and the bishop asked why. He pointed out to the duke that if his creditors were not paid he would be guilty of an injustice. He begged Newcastle not to let his fancy carry him away, for unnecessary expenses must not be incurred.[99]

Newcastle's old friend, adviser and alter-conscience was in the final year of his life, but in spite of weariness and illness continued a special care for his affairs. Tired from his attendance at the House of Lords and from a visitation of his diocese, the bishop was resting in Burwash, Sussex, at the home of his son-in-law, the Reverend George Jordan. He was kept fully informed of the state of things by Mr Forbes, the duke's man of business. Newcastle had been able to borrow £2,000 from a Mr Whey and hoped to be able to borrow more, up to the total of £10,000, which Mr Walter had noted earlier was needed. Yet the bishop warned him:[100]

> Pray my good Lord give me leave to say, yt will be an Expedient only for a short time, & ye evil will quickly be upon us again, neither will it be in our power to put a stop to it, unless your Grace will be pleased timely to prevent it, in whose power providence has once more put it, to preserve your reputation, power & interest: & therefore I must beg your Grace would be a good manager, & not think of extraordinary Expenses, nor buildings, nor unnecessary or chargeable alterations: for if people see expensive schemes continued, they will despair of being relieved . . . & will take such means to save themselves, as will be of fatal consequences to us.

The bishop ended by appealing from private to public good in urging Newcastle to maintain his position: 'If your Grace will not be steady in right resolutions for your own sake, I hope you will do it for ye sake of ye Public, wch must suffer by your declension.'

The decline in Bowers's health continued and a visit to Bath did not have the desired effect. The duke was worried about his old friend's health and wrote to him about it; the bishop replied, thanking him for his concern but at the same time returning to his major charge: Newcastle must stick to his resolution to retrench.[101] Bowers returned to his cathedral city, and although Newcastle offered to send his own physician, Sir Hans Sloan, to Chichester to attend him, Bowers declined. He must have known that his end was near, for he asked Newcastle to mind his own health, 'that you may be always capable of doing good to ye public & your friends.'[102] In less than a month, on August 22, 1724, the Bishop of Chichester was dead.

In several ways the year 1724 is an important one in Newcastle's life, for it marks both an end and a beginning. The death of Bishop Bowers ended a period of dependence upon one who had known Newcastle since his childhood and who could speak to him almost like a father, even though the duke rarely followed his old friend's sage advice for long. From this period until firm confidence was built up with such persons as Hardwicke, Stone and Murray, Newcastle sought the advice of professionally interested persons. The year was an end and a beginning in his public and political life also. It was the end of his tutelage at the center of power and the beginning of his long career as a holder of such major cabinet offices as Secretary of State. Newcastle was already recognized as a major force in Whig politics after his great exertions in both the election of 1715 and that of 1722. This role would be expanded when he became a major government election manager.

Beneath the grandeur of Newcastle's public and private life was the nagging concern for his financial stability. His resolutions, repeated through the years, to retrench, to manage his own affairs, to control his whims and to live within his means, are certain evidence of this. His financial problems were in part caused by his psychological need to spend in order to gain approbation and reward, and in part by the conflicts he created between his public and private roles, all of which added to his already heavy burden of psychic fears and insecurities.

On the other hand it is doubtful if this great aristocrat, courtier and politician was very often fearful of bankruptcy: his annual income was large and his total landed wealth was enormous. The duke had no sons to provide for by settlement, and no daughters who needed portions. He and the duchess could spend as their personal, social and political needs dictated. The rub came as a moral question to Newcastle: he must not defraud or be the source of unjust treatment to his creditors. Here is a legacy of Bishop Bowers; this concern followed Newcastle to the end of his life. His last will and testament, made forty-four years later, provided first that all of his debts be paid. For Newcastle this was more than a formal insertion; at long last it would mark the quietus to a lifetime of financial concern.

NOTES

1 Add. MSS. 33137, ff. 222–5, Abstract of Lord Pelham's Account; Hoare's Bank, Ledger E 1, f. 63 *et seq.*

2 A. S. Turberville, *A History of Welbeck Abbey and its Owners* (London, 1938), I, 225.

3 Add. MSS. 33137, ff. 220–20v.

4 Private Act, 5 George I, cap. 3.

5 British Museum Loan, Cavendish papers, 29/238, f. 466, Earl of Oxford to Duchess of Newcastle, August 11, 1711.

6 H. M. C., *Portland II*, 231–2, Oxford to Duchess of Newcastle, August 16, 1711.

7 *Ibid.*, p. 232, Oxford to Duchess of Newcastle, August 25, 1711.

8 H. M. C., *Manuscripts in Various Collections MSS of M. L. S. Clements*, VIII, 262, May 21, 1713.

9 H. M. C., *Portland V*, 92, Lord Pelham to Thomas Hewet, September 17, 1711.

10 Add. MSS. 33064, ff. 1 and 1*v*, Lord Pelham to Thomas Pelham-Holles, Halland, October 17, 1711.

11 Add. MSS. 33084, ff. 183–4, Thomas Bowers to Henry Pelham, Halland, February 12, 1707.

12 Add. MSS. 33137, f. 226, Bowers's appointment, June 23, 1712.

13 H. M. C., *Portland V*, Appendix, 658, 'Memoir of the Harley Family... by Edward Harley.'

14 Add. MSS. 32686, ff. 12–13, Lord Cowper to Lord Pelham, December 12, 1713.

15 *Ibid.*, ff. 14–15, same to same, January 9, 1714.

16 Add. MSS. 33054, f. 70, Newcastle Memorandum, April 2, 1718.

17 H. M. C., *Portland V*, 472.

18 *Ibid.*, 476.

19 Add. MSS. 33054, f. 69, April 2, 1718.

20 *Ibid.*, f. 70.

21 British Museum Loan, Harley papers, 29/117, Countess of Oxford to James West, Welbeck, January 17, 1746.

22 Lincolnshire Archives Office, Monson papers, 288/13/1, ff. 4–5; hereafter cited as L.A.O.
23 Add. MSS. 33064, f. 250.
24 [Richard Glover], *Memoirs by a Celebrated Literary and Political Character* ... (London, 1814), p. 145 ff.
25 John M. Beattie, *The English Court in the Reign of George I* (Cambridge, 1967), pp. 23–9, 52.
26 Robert Beatson, *A Political Index to the Histories of Great Britain and Ireland:* ... (London, 1806), I, 419.
27 Calendar of State Papers: Treasury Books, vol. 32 (2), p. 300 (1717).
28 Hoare's Bank, Current Accounts, Ledger F, *passim*.
29 Sussex Archaeological Society MSS., Indenture P. 168, July 30, 1715.
30 *Ibid.*, Indenture P. 172, May 1, 1716.
31 Hoare's Bank, Money Ledger, 1696–1718, f. 153.
32 L.A.O., Monson papers, 283/13/2 Trustee Accounts.
33 L. B. Namier, *Structure of Politics at the Accession of George III* (London, 1930), 2nd ed., p. 9.
34 Robert Halsband (ed.), *The Complete Letters of Lady Mary Wortley Montagu* (Oxford, 1965–7), I, 216–17, to Wortley, *c.* August 11, 1714.
35 *Ibid.*, p. 200, Note 1.
36 Rae Blanchard (ed.), *The Correspondence of Richard Steele* (London, 1941), Letter 101, Steele to Thomas Pelham-Holles, Earl of Clare, December 14, 1714, 'From Mr. Jessop's Essex-Street.'
37 Add. MSS. 33060, f. 18.
38 Add. MSS. 33058, f. 225. This bill is reproduced in Stebelton H. Nulle, *Thomas Pelham-Holles, Duke of Newcastle: His Early Political Career, 1693–1724* (Philadelphia, 1931), pp. 61–2; hereafter cited as Nulle.
39 Hoare's Bank, Current Accounts, Ledger F, 227.
40 Historical Manuscripts Commission, *Stuart papers* V, 611; see also D. G. Barnes, 'Henry Pelham and the Duke of Newcastle,' *Journal of British Studies*, No. 2 (May, 1965), p. 65.
41 Add. MSS. 33064, f. 75, Bowers to Newcastle, May 21, 1715.
42 *Ibid.*, f. 81, Bowers to Newcastle, July 30, 1715.
43 Bonamy Dobrée and Geoffrey Webb (eds), *The Complete Works of Sir John Vanbrugh* (London, 1928), IV, 91, Vanbrugh to [Lord Godolphin?], [1717?].
44 *Ibid.*, IV, 83–4, Vanbrugh to Duchess of Marlborough, November 6, 1716.
45 *Ibid.*
46 Add. MSS. 33064, f. 110, Vanbrugh to Newcastle, London, November 10, 1716.
47 Add. MSS. 33064, f. 112, Bowers to Newcastle, Canterbury, November 13, 1716.
48 Vanbrugh, *Works*, IV, 87, Vanbrugh to Newcastle, Whitehall, November 15, 1716; Add. MSS. 33064, f. 114.
49 *Ibid.*
50 Add. MSS. 33064, f. 122, Vanbrugh to Newcastle, Whitehall, November 27, 1716.

51 Sussex Archaeological Society MSS., Indenture P. 178, March 30, 1717.
52 See Nulle, pp. 89–98.
53 Add. MSS. 33064, ff. 131–2, Bowers to Newcastle, October 30, 1717.
54 *Ibid.*, f. 133.
55 *Ibid.*
56 Add. MSS. 33422, f. 62.
57 Vanbrugh, *Works*, IV, 68, Vanbrugh to Newcastle, Whitehall, November 27, 1716.
58 *Ibid.*, IV, 99, Vanbrugh to Peter Forbes, Greenwich, July 4, 1718.
59 *Ibid.*, IV, 105–6, Vanbrugh to Newcastle, Nottingham, December 17, 1718.
60 *Ibid.*, IV, 108, Vanbrugh to Newcastle, Castle Howard, January 4, 1719.
61 Add. MSS. 33073, ff. 3–4, 5, Newcastle to duchess, Nottingham Castle, December 29 and 31, 1718.
62 Vanbrugh, *Works*, IV, 113, Vanbrugh to Newcastle, London, July 23, 1719.
63 *Ibid.*, IV, 126, Vanbrugh to Newcastle, London, September 15, 1720.
64 Add. MSS. 9149, f. 158, Newcastle to Stanhope, Bishopstone, December 29, 1719.
65 Add. MSS. 32686, ff. 112–13, J. Digby to Peter Forbes, March 15, 1718.
66 Nottingham University Library, Newcastle papers Ne 9/97, Marriage Settlement.
67 Add. MSS. 33137, ff. 272–3, Inventory of Newcastle Plate 1717.
68 Add. MSS. 33137, f. 320.
69 Childs Bank [Glyn Mills], Current Accounts, 1719.
70 Add. MSS. 9149, f. 179, Newcastle to Charles Stanhope, Claremont, July 9, 1720.
71 Add. MSS. 32686, f. 166, J. Craggs to Newcastle, Cockpit, August 2, 1720.
72 Add. MSS. 9149, f. 179.
73 Nulle, pp. 49–51.
74 Add. MSS. 9149, f. 187, James Craggs to Lord Stanhope, Cockpit, September 6, 1720.
75 Add. MSS. 32686, ff. 176–6v, Newcastle to Jordon, Newcastle House, July 18, 1721.
76 Add. MSS. 33137, ff. 431–2v, Peter Walter to Newcastle, November 28, 1734.
77 Add. MSS. 33137, ff. 304–4v; Add. MSS. 32686, f. 256.
78 Add. MSS 32686, f. 176, Newcastle to Jordon, Newcastle House, July 18, 1721.
79 Add. MSS. 33137, f. 304v.
80 Add. MSS. 33064, ff. 249–50.
81 *Ibid.*
82 L.A.O., Monson papers 28B/13/2 Trustee Accounts.
83 Add. MSS. 32686, f. 198, Carteret to Newcastle, Whitehall, September 9, 1721.
84 Add. MSS. 32686, ff. 236–6v, Newcastle to Bowers, Newcastle House, August 25, 1722.
85 Add. MSS. 33075, f. 18, April 6, 1722.

86 See Nulle, pp. 138–46.
87 Add. MSS. 33320, f. 5.
88 Add. MSS. 32686, ff. 254v–5, Newcastle to Bowers, Claremont, June 6, 1723.
89 *Ibid.*, ff. 255–5v.
90 Add. MSS. 33064, ff. 218–19, Bowers to Newcastle, June 12, 1723.
91 *Ibid.*
92 Add. MSS. 32686, f. 255v, June 6, 1723.
93 *Ibid.*, f. 256.
94 *Ibid.*, f. 256v.
95 Add. MSS. 33064, ff. 222–3, June 12, 1723.
96 *Ibid.*
97 *Dictionary of National Biography*, vol. 44, p. 247.
98 Nottingham University Library, Newcastle papers, Ne D/103 Marriage Settlement, December 7, 1726.
99 Add. MSS. 33064, ff. 234–5, Bowers to Newcastle, October 12, 1723.
100 Add. MSS. 32687, ff. 42–3, May 24, 1724.
101 *Ibid.*, f. 44, June 3, 1724.
102 *Ibid.*, f. 48, July 24, 1724.

CHAPTER 2

DEBTS AND MANAGEMENT: THE NEW ESTABLISHMENT AND THE TRUST, 1724–38

As Secretary of State for the Southern Department, Newcastle now held one of the high offices of state, which carried great responsibilities and made major demands on his time and energy. Even a cursory perusal of the volumes of despatches and memoranda which Newcastle penned would substantiate this statement; but along with his official work went his continuing, and indeed increasing, unofficial role of recommending or dispensing patronage. It is easy to believe Newcastle when he stated so often that he had inadequate time to look into his own affairs. Therefore he was dependent to an unusual degree upon the advice of others for his personal financial interests and their day-to-day supervision. In essence, he was never able to live up to his promise to the late Bishop Bowers to manage his own affairs; he repeatedly asked the duchess to oversee the work of his professional financial employees.

During this fourteen-year period, the administration or management of the affairs of Newcastle was largely under the direction of Peter Forbes. As we have noted, Forbes had a multitude of duties to perform from Newcastle House or elsewhere. The major department heads, the Steward of the Household and the Gentleman of the Horse, received money from him for their areas, as he was their immediate superior and auditor. Forbes had come into the family service under the late Lord Pelham and had known Newcastle since he was small. He, along with Bowers, knew more of his affairs than anyone else. Forbes opened a drawing account at Hoare's Bank in 1713, from which he paid many bills; he continued to be active in the duke's affairs, although with reduced responsibilities later, until he was an old man, when he was called (in 1756), 'Overseer of the Clare Market Estate.' Thus this one man gave over forty years' service to the family.

We have repeatedly mentioned Peter Walter and have noted his relationship to the duke. His role was unusual in that he served as a collector for scattered estates, as well as being a financial consultant or analyst for Newcastle. Walter had a regular business in the financial areas of London life, perhaps analogous to a modern accounting firm in that he advised clients in their monetary affairs, audited their accounts and had ties to the money market. It will be remembered that Walter drew up Duke John's will, which made young Pelham his heir in 1707, and that he was in some way involved in the negotiations relative to Newcastle's marriage. Walter made a fortune from his various activities, purchased Stalbridge Park near Sherborne, Dorset, and did not die until 1745, at the great age of eighty-two.[1]

We have also noted that the duke employed in the 1730s Mr James A. Waller as accountant or auditor, perhaps to relieve Mr Forbes of some of his pressures and eventually to replace him. Waller served with varying degrees of efficiency until the early 1750s; the duke relieved him of his duties in 1754. It is interesting to note that this man was the son of John Waller, who had served the duke's father. It seems that three other father-and-son pairs worked for Newcastle: the Greenings and the Twells, who held high responsibilities in the family, and the Wilkinsons, who were collectors for Yorkshire.

No date prior to 1725 appears on the eighteenth-century estate accounts to be found in the Newcastle papers in the British Museum. There is not a full run of accounts for any single portion of the estate, but partial ones for each part. The local land stewards seem to have been men of substance; were undoubtedly solid Whigs who were aware of the necessity of keeping up Newcastle's interest; and apparently served as conduits for election money upon occasion. These men were central to the management of the estate on a local level, and their judgment had a direct bearing on the profitability of the whole.

What was the actual income which Newcastle derived from his landed estates and from his official salary during this period? First, let us look at the various collections in some detail (see Table 1).

It is difficult to determine with much exactness the administrative and other costs of the Newcastle estates. The problem is compounded for lack of full runs of estate records and vouchers. However, the discrepancy between gross rental value of the estates and the apparent net income is so great that an effort must be made to explain it.

We have seen above that it is relatively simple to determine *fixed* costs. The stewards received £765 p.a. for collecting the estate rents. Yet we know that both Walter and Burnett's salaries are out of proportion to the rents they collected; Walter served as adviser to the duke and Burnett was Steward of the Household. We must also note at once that neither the salary of Peter Forbes nor that of James Waller has been taken into consideration; each appears to have received £200 p.a. at

TABLE I

Sources of the Duke of Newcastle's income

Estate	Steward	Gross receipt	Salary
		£	£
Middlesex and Clare			
Market	Thomas Bedwell	5,000	65
Lincoln	John Dobbs	6,000	120
Nottingham	John Bristowe	4,500	90
As Keeper of Clumber Park he			
received free housing and £20.			20
Nottingham	Richard Twells	2,000	50
York	Andrew Wilkinson, M.P.	1,000	40
Derby and part of			
Nottingham	John Clay	1,800	50
As Keeper of Nottingham Castle, free			
housing and £20.			20
As Park Keeper he received an			
additional £10.			10
Sussex	Robert Burnett	850 (approx.)	100
Dorset, Wilts., Herts.,			
Suffolk and Kent	Peter Walter	3,800	200
		24,950	765

this time. If we are close to being correct in our information and in our surmises, then the fixed salary costs for managing the estates would have been £1,165 p.a.

It is in the area of *changeable* costs of estate administration that the real difficulty appears. First, taxes: the land tax varied from 2*s.* to 4*s.* in the pound, the local poor rate changed from year to year, or could do so, and the tithes varied. Second, the normal but varying costs of keeping the estate from deteriorating in value: that is, costs of repairs, rebuilding, fencing, ditching, etc. A third category of changeable expenses concerned the administrative costs over and above salaries: the cost of drawing up leases, usually a guinea per lease, cost of account books and of copying accounts, postage, carriage of money to London, and various costs the stewards lumped together in their accounts as 'out of pocket expenses.' A final changeable category was arrears of rent. There was almost always some arrearage, but it was not large. However, the stewards carried forward the arrearages year after year, long after they were beyond hope of collection.

In the absence of full estate accounts, there is happily one way of making an approximate assessment of Newcastle's net annual landed income. Since we have available the duke's personal account at Hoare's Bank in which the stewards deposited their net collections, we should be able to calculate from it what money was actually received. We must note immediately, however, that not all net money received by the collectors was deposited, for some of it was expended directly by the collector on the duke's order. This is noted most particularly in the collection of Peter Walter, who paid interest charges on outstanding mortgages directly from his collection, and paid other costs as well. For example, his collection for 1730–1 totaled £3,795, but he expended on the duke's behalf £2,494—he was paying interest on £22,000 at 5 per cent among other costs—so Mr Forbes received not a penny from him that year. A second example of the difficulty of using direct deposits in calculating the duke's annual estate income is seen in the accounts of Thomas Bedwell, collector of the highly profitable and low-cost Clare Market Estate. Ordinarily he sent his money to Mr Forbes, but in 1735–6 he deposited £3,050 at Hoare's; he sent Forbes £932; he paid Mr Chalie in the duke's household £615; and he gave Newcastle £600 direct. It is only in these two collections that such usage is found and it will be noted that each is centered on London, each profitable and close at hand.

Bearing these cautions in mind we find that in a test year, November 1, 1735, to November 1, 1736, the stewards deposited a total of £15,306.[2] Some additional deposits by Mr Forbes could have originated in landed income. We do know, as noted above, that Bedwell paid out directly to individuals that year £2,147, which would make the total net income from land £17,453. We will test our reconstruction after we have taken note of the other major source of his income, his official salary.

We are fortunate in having an account of the income and the out-goings of Newcastle's office as Secretary of State from 1725 to 1744. The salary affixed to the position was £5,680 per annum, but certain other small profits were part of the perquisites, such as a moiety of the profits of the *Gazette* and profits arising from the Scotch Signet. The *Gazette* averaged approximately £200 and the Scotch Signet about £250 per annum. However, from the profits of the office the 'outgoings' had to be subtracted, and these included a tax on the duke's salary and various fees which the office had to pay to other departments and persons, clerks' salaries, and funding for office supplies and costs. The *net* produce for Newcastle in his new position, for example, was £5,333 for 1725; in 1727, £5,393; and the highest amount, in 1728, £10,542, but this latter figure was unique.[3]

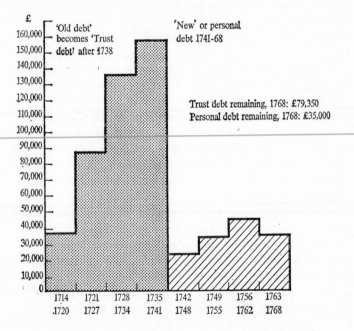

FIGURE I *Newcastle indebtedness, 1714-68, at six-year intervals*

If we add the net landed income of £17,453 from the test year November 1, 1735, to November 1, 1736, to his net office income for the year 1736 of £6,158, we find that the duke had the handsome total of £23,611. We know that he had no additional revenue from dividends

73

from governmental securities or from stock in commercial ventures. Our reconstruction of his income is very close to being correct, for we have corroboration from the duke himself in a memorandum he wrote for his own use in 1736, 'received from the Stewards as well as from the office in 1735—£24,248 & in 1736 £21,761.'[4] Having established his landed net income without much doubt, let us see if we can use the figures available to determine his costs of estate management.

Earlier we posited roughly his direct estate costs but noted the great difficulty of ascertaining the annual changeable costs. Now that we have two fixed figures at hand, for income from estates and from office, we should be able to establish his total management or 'overhead' costs. The duke's memo informed us that he had a total income in 1735 of £24,248 and we know that his office produced in the same year £5,753. By subtracting the one from the other, we find that the net estate income for 1735 was £18,495.

The gross produce of the estate in his hands was calculated to be £24,421 when the Newcastle trust was established in 1738. Subtracting from this amount the net yield of the estate, which we have calculated from the duke's own figures to be £18,495 (for 1735), we find that the total fixed and changeable costs come to £5,926. If we may take this time span as representative, and there is no reason why we should not, for the duke was being very careful and attentive during this period, we see that the cost of management was roughly £6,000 for the estate, of which the annual book value was roughly £24,000. In other words, one fourth of the estate income was never seen by the duke.

It was only Newcastle's salary which brought his annual income up to what his estate alone was supposed to produce. Even with the loss of 25 per cent of his landed income in overhead costs, however, he had an enormous income for this period. Nevertheless, he continued to run into added debt at a great pace. Evidence of his growing financial difficulty is found in the category of bonded indebtedness used by his trustees later. Their schedule of debts showed that he had contracted, in the thirteen-year period 1721–34, bonded indebtedness of £15,005.[5] He had other forms of indebtedness also, such as mortgages, short-term notes and pledges, as well as unpaid household and private debts. The evidence from the trustee accounts makes it certain that the temporary trust of 1721 did not in any way lessen Newcastle's proclivity to spend. It may have given his creditors a temporary sense of security and therefore given him a brief respite, but that would have been all. It must also be kept in mind that most of the debt carried interest, usually at 5 per cent; large amounts of current income were required to cover this interest, which, in fact, was not being paid in full.

By 1728 Newcastle was in desperate need for money to pay off creditors; he had asked Peter Walter to help him find the money but had been rebuffed. Walter had told him that he must put his affairs 'in a Method' before any help could be expected. Walter was already deeply involved personally in Newcastle's financial affairs, for he held a mortgage on the Sussex estate for £7,000. When refused, the duke wrote out in his own hand instructions for the use of Mr Forbes in his talk with Walter. Mr Forbes was to express the duke's concern, 'yt after all that has past Mr. Walter thinks it unpracticable to help me to 10,000£.' Forbes was to tell Walter that the duke must have such a sum, and that he had now taken Walter's advice and put his affairs 'in a Method' (although there is no evidence that he had actually done so in any real way). Now Newcastle suggested a new scheme for Walter's attention, namely, that Walter transfer his mortgage on Sussex to Claremont, its contents and the manor, for the duke felt that it was more than sufficient collateral for the mortgage; and then Sussex would be free to serve as surety for loans Walter might be able to arrange among his friends.[6] This proposal of the duke's did not bear fruit.

In his need, since the money market seemed to be closed to him if Walter would not countenance his plan, Newcastle turned to his father-in-law, Lord Godolphin, and requested that he be permitted to borrow £5,000 on his bond. The noble lord replied that it would not greatly inconvenience him to furnish Newcastle the money he needed, 'yet I can but own it wd in some manner disconcert my affairs were I to be disappointed in my expectation of receiving it again.'[7] Newcastle had indicated that he wanted the money for a short time only, and had promised repayment, but the letter of the earl makes it plain that he knew of his son-in-law's financial history and of his great indebtedness. Much of this sum was no doubt paid by the trustees after 1738, but we find Newcastle himself paying Godolphin £2,000 in October, 1741, a dozen years after it was borrowed.[8]

By early 1730, it appears from Peter Walter's own accounts that part of Newcastle's need was met by borrowing directly from friends and relatives. Walter himself advanced an additional £2,500 with Claremont as security; he lent, along with Colonel Pelham, £5,000 more (we do not know the collateral but perhaps Colonel Pelham guaranteed repayment); and Walter lent an added £1,600 in the name of a Mr Tilson. He was also paying interest to Mr James Pelham, who had lent £5,200. Thus, by 1734, Walter was paying out, from the money he collected for Newcastle, interest on over £20,000 at a rate of 5 per cent, much of it borrowed from himself or from members of the Pelham family.[9]

In the 1730s Newcastle and his advisers made strenuous efforts to establish some control over the duke's financial affairs, especially in regard to costs in the family. Peter Walter had insisted upon the need for this in 1728. The first need was to determine what the annual expenses were for the duke's whole establishment. With five homes to

TABLE 2

Distribution of expenses, 1731

	£	s.	d.
Mr. Burnett [Housekeeping]	12,427	1	8
Mr. Creswell [Stables]	2,966	2	1
His Grace [Pocket Money] & the Journey to Spa	3,173	5	6
Pin Money [to Duchess]	800	0	0
Claremont	2,768	15	3
Sussex—besides the Rents and lands in hand	500	0	0

account for, as well as the various departments within each, it is perhaps not surprising that the busy Newcastle did not really know what his total annual obligations were for his 'family.' He ordered the various accounts to be studied and an abstract of the 'Expenses in General' prepared for the year 1731, and for an estimate to be made as to the ways by which they could be reduced in 1732. The total expenses for the year 1731 were found to be £22,635.4s.6d. Table 2 shows the distribution. For the next year, 1732, it was proposed to reduce the expenses in general to £20,400, certainly not enough to help the duke materially in his perilous situation.

The inadequacy of this plan was undoubtedly made clear to him, for he was soon busy at Claremont, himself, formulating a scheme to reduce his expenses radically. He drew up a budget of £12,000 per annum 'for the Expenses of ye Family, London, Sussex & Claremont,' to be initiated on Lady Day, 1733. He proposed dividing the amount as shown in Table 3. Creswell and Burnett were ordered to prepare schemes for their respective departments which were to be approved and signed by the duke.[10]

TABLE 3
The budget for 1733

	£
Claremont wood, kitchen Garden, House & Farm	1,000
Sussex	500
Pin Money	500
Pocket Expenses, Elections, etc.	1,000
Creswell for all Expenses	2,000
Remains for Burnett & servants wages & everything	7,000

TABLE 4
Categories of household expenses

	£	s.		£	s.
Butcher	600		Apothecary	120	
Fishmonger	360		Milkman	30	
Poulterer	360		Pastry cook	18	
Baker	180		Herbman and fruiterer	144	
Butterman	120		Oylman & Grocer	180	
Brewer	60		Wax lights	120	
Malt & Hopps at Claremont	240		Tallow candles	200	
Tea, coffee, chocolate	120		Wood & coals	500	
Servants Boardwages	200	4	Wine of all sorts	800	
Soap	84		Livery and servant wages	1,000	
Lamp oyl	48		Extraordinaries, contingencies of all sorts & Sussex journey	1,247	16
Charcoal	120				
			Total: £6,900		

Mr Burnett carried out his master's order at once and prepared a detailed budget consisting of twenty-four categories of household expenses which he kept within the £7,000 for the year. These categories present a clear picture of the needs of the great household (see Table 4).

Mr Creswell's scheme or budget for the reduction of expenses in his department was a bit simpler to prepare and shows clearly the areas of his responsibility (see Table 5).

The great house, Claremont, had been assigned £1,000 by Newcastle for its maintenance. The breakdown of expenses which the housekeeper

TABLE 5

Expenses for the stables

	£ s.		£ s.
Oats & Beans	300	Stable rent	100
Hay & Straw	270 8	Servants Wages	112
Servant and Board wages	200 4	Hounds	235
		Hunting Stables	250
Smith & Farriers	120		
		Pointers	50
Coachmaker's contract	90	Tradesmen, Extra-ordinaries, contingencies	272 8
		Total: £2,000	

submitted is shown in Table 6. It was to be understood that the produce of the farm was to defray the total charge for disbursements at Claremont.[11]

The wages for servants for Newcastle House and Claremont and for those employed in the stables was a great item in annual costs. Full-time servants numbered forty-nine in the houses and stables, and eighteen men were employed part-time about the woods and farm at Claremont, making in all sixty-nine servants in 1734. Their annual wages totaled £1,248.17s.4d., while liveries and board wages for those working in the stables added an additional £412.6s.0d., making in all £1,661.3s.4d. p.a.[12] In this scheme, the total annual cost for the whole family was £8,000, which was a reduction of £4,000 from the budget of two years earlier.

The budgets prepared for the Newcastle establishment demonstrates the extent and complexity of the whole operation and show the absolute necessity for careful supervision of staff, and for personal attention and management on the part of the duke and duchess. The duke had

TABLE 6

The housekeeper's expenses at Claremont

Servants Wages & Boardwages in the House

	£	s.
Housekeeper and wife	50	
Porter and assistant	38	
Two housemaids	30	
Two watchmen	36	10
Brewer	48	04
Helper—Brewery & Laundry	20	

Keeping of the Wood & Plantation

	£	s.
Wages & Boardwages. Charge of the Pheasantry & Aviary	300	
Keeping of Fruit & Kitchen Garden	160	
Keeping of the Flower Garden	30	
Tradesmen, artificers, repairs about the House, plants, trees, flowers	287	6
Total: £1,000		

promised Bishop Bowers for years to provide such personal management, and now in the 1730s he actually attempted to do so. He went over his own accounts quite regularly and issued directions to his various agents to pay workers, tradesmen and others. The duke correctly felt that he was paying more for household materials than he ought. Merchants increased unit-costs for items because the duke was so slow in paying bills. By this means the tradesmen hoped to receive some interest on their capital investment, along with their normal profits. In 1734 Newcastle directed payment of various bills and the discharging of the tallow chandler, adding: 'I shall expect ready Money Prices for everything.'[13]

For once in his life Newcastle was actually trying to make his budget work, at least on the expenses of his family. He ordered his servants to supply him with weekly accounts of expenses so that he would know when and where excesses were arising. He seemed to be obsessed with the idea that much of his trouble came from tradesmen who were constantly taking advantage of him in their charges, and he checked their bills personally. 'I would have an account of prices, that several Trades People charge for everything; and also an account from Burnett and Northcote of every Tradesman that refuses to deliver provisions or Goods at the Market price, because there are Bills owing to them on the former Account.'[14] The duke evidently felt that the fact that he was on a new tack should make the merchants ready to co-operate fully and to ignore long-standing debts. He was to find the tradesmen perfectly capable of considering their own interests first, regardless of past patronage.

The day-to-day supervision of affairs was still in the hands of the faithful Peter Forbes, who must have often been put upon to meet the demands of local creditors. The merchants, tradesmen and others who were holders of claims upon the duke had good reason for concern. Upon review of his condition, it is also evident why Newcastle himself took such a detailed interest in his own affairs. The duke had proposed that the new scheme, budget or establishment begin in 1733, but it actually began on May 12, 1734. Newcastle was soon eager to know how it was working.

As usual in such cases, he turned to an expert, Peter Walter, and asked him to analyse the working of the budget for the six lunar months, May 12, 1734, to October 26, 1734. Actually Walter did much more than this, for he undertook a full study of the debt of the estate and only then did he turn to the matter of Newcastle's latest retrenchment effort.

First Walter recapitulated the debt situation of the Newcastle estate as it existed at the beginning of the trust of 1721. The figures he calculated from schedules affixed to that deed are shown in Table 7. Next he calculated, from accounts given him by Mr Forbes, what the debt was when the 'new Establishment' or scheme was begun on

May 12, 1734 (see Table 8). Thus the debt in the 'interspace of time,' i.e. 1721–34, had increased by £57,415, including £9,000 for unpaid interest on the debt.[15] Here we see the full burden of the great estate, £135,998, and the exact reason for Newcastle's deep concern for the

TABLE 7

Debts of the Newcastle estate calculated for 1721

	£	
Debt at interest	60,880	
Debt without interest	17,692	
Debt not mentioned (Ld. Lincoln)	10,000	
	88,572	Debt 1721

working of the new scheme. His debt during that thirteen-year period had been increasing at an annual average rate of over £4,000. These figures demonstrate forcibly the failure of the trust of 1721 and the effort made at that time to retrench.

Only at this point did Walter turn to the working of the budget itself. He reviewed the accounts which had been kept by the chief

TABLE 8

Debts of the Newcastle estate calculated for 1734

	£	
Debt at interest	88,423	
Debt without interest	47,575	
	135,998	Debt 1734

household officers in order to determine if they were maintaining their budgets. Alas, in spite of the greatest attention for the past six months to domestic expenses, the net 'exceeding' was £396.1s.7d. Walter warned Newcastle very plainly:[16]

> If the Scheme be not exactly pursued, and no Exceedings made in it, the end of all past and present endeavours will be frustrated, and the great Debt, which lies heavy upon the Estate (great as the Estate is) will never be paid.

The six-months' excess over the budget was not large and was perhaps
as close as Newcastle would ever come to actually living upon a plan.
He continued to seek advice on how to economize, but there was no
easy way to retrench since each reduction affected some area of his
interest. The duke was liberal with his friends and generous to dependents and relations; he so greatly enjoyed maintaining a style of life
which was wholly out of date, even in his own day, that it was difficult
for him to accept even patently commonsense advice.

A case in point was Newcastle's vast expenditures in his home county
of Sussex, where, although he normally visited them only once or twice
a year, he maintained his ancestral home, Halland, and his hunting
lodge on the coast, Bishopstone Place. The lands attached to these
seats were calculated to be worth about £1,000 per annum in rent, but
it cost an additional £2,000 to operate them. The lost rent was not the
real cause of the uneconomic situation; a custom of open hospitality
was the culprit. Newcastle was informed of what he undoubtedly
already knew:

> It appears . . . that there has been a most Expensive Usage
> practiced at both those Houses by giving small Beer and Doles of
> Wheat to all People of the Country, about them, without stint or
> limitation and of entertaining all comers and goers with their
> Servants and Horses, another boundless Expense.

As Newcastle's adviser pointed out, these practices had been carried on
for so many years that they 'are almost become a Custom,' and their
abolition might 'affect the Popular Interest of the County.' However,
the writer felt that in spite of such a danger it ought to be done, and
proposed a method: 'To do it effectually the two Houses should be
shut up and all the lands tenanted.'[17]

The park at Halland had nearly eleven hundred acres in it and handled
four or five hundred head of deer. The adviser calculated that if it
were to be leased at 10s. an acre, it would produce £550. The writer
also pointed out that the Park or Farm at Claremont cost £80 per
annum more than it produced, yet the officials of the estate felt they
could not do with fewer servants. Hard as it must have been, Newcastle
appears to have taken at least part of the advice regarding Sussex, for
the housekeeping accounts there show a drastic change for a short time.
In 1733, they had been £1,643; in 1734, an election year, it should be
noted, they rose to £2,962; in 1735, they totaled only £477, but they
tripled the following year to £1,340.[18]

One of the most interesting accounts which has survived is one which Mr Waller called Newcastle's Private Account, for the years 1737–54, which demonstrates the ducal areas of interest, concern or responsibility better than nearly any other source. It is difficult at times to see what criteria were used by Newcastle to determine what expenses should be in his private account, and what in others. It is not surprising that one with the duke's public position should spend a great deal for newspapers, nearly £10 a quarter, and for books. Newcastle liked music, and opera boxes were a large expense, £105 in 1737. Annual pensions to various individuals; subscriptions to hospitals and schools; and gifts to individuals, such as the Doorkeeper of the House of Lords, are all noted in these accounts. It is somewhat surprising to find Newcastle paying Mr Waller's salary and the duchess's pin money from his private account at this time. A special instance is that of Newcastle's famous French chef, Peter Clouet (commonly called 'Chloe' by the English but spelled 'Cloiet' by the accountant), who received £105 per annum and whose visit home to France, paid for by the duke, cost £25.5s.0d. One would have assumed that the chef's salary would have been paid from the household account. Such unusual items as nursing charges for two servants of £12.1s.6d.; apothecary charges for Mrs Elliot, the Newcastles' beloved housekeeper, of £66.5s.6d.; and finally the entry, 'John Downs for Mrs. Elliot's Funeral, £24.6.6,' are also found here. More personal and expected entries such as charges for hosiery, shoes, mercer's goods, and tailor costs are included, along with abundant charges for M. August Friard, Perukemaker, usually at or near £20, as well as charges for 'garter ribbon, £15.4.0' and 'Hungary water,' £2.12s.0d. More prosaic items for household necessities abound, together with church offerings, pew rents, water rents, lamplighter costs, the poor rate and even 'beer for bonfire.'[19] With all aspects of life taken into account and with dependents of every description, it would have been difficult for even the best-intentioned of men to retrench.

Thus, it proved to be impossible for the duke and his duchess to live upon a budget, even for their usual family expenses. It was also impossible to stop extraordinary expenses; despite good intentions, the demands of status and politics had to be met. However it was not these annual expenses, both ordinary and extraordinary, which brought Newcastle's financial structure to the brink of total collapse, but the great load of debt which had been building for nearly a quarter of a century, and the interest payments which it entailed. The final element making drastic action essential was the exhaustion of Newcastle's credit resources. As long as he could continue to borrow, all was apparently well; when the great estate became too burdened, individual or corporate credit ceased to be available. Interest on bonds and notes outstanding was falling dangerously in arrears.

At about this time of financial crisis a young man destined to become one of the duke's most trusted advisers and confidants entered his employment. Andrew Stone became the duke's private secretary, and Newcastle made him Undersecretary of State as well, from 1734 to 1739. Stone's work was both in the capacity of a general high-level adviser in the family, and in that of a faithful colleague in the office. Newcastle brought him into the Commons in 1741 for Hastings, which he continued to represent until 1761. It appears that as Peter Forbes became more burdened with work and also with illness, Stone took over some of his work of a supervisory nature, as a transmitter of the duke's wishes to his stewards and other lower servants.

It was the faithful Peter Forbes who had to bear the odium for the duke's slowness in paying his bills, meeting with irate creditors at the office in Newcastle House or replying to their letters demanding payment. A fine example of what he faced can be seen in a letter to one of the stewards, where he asked, 'what shall we do with Master Glen, who has our note for £500 which was payable a fortnight ago. He dunnes my hearts blood out, & has even this morning, plagued me so hard for the payment of the money, that I could no ways help to promise he should have it by the end of next week.' Now the problem was to find the money, and Forbes's suggestion was that each collector 'club' £125 apiece and take repayment out of the first £500 the duke should pay into his account at Hoare's Bank.[20]

Newcastle continued to keep a constant watch on his affairs, conferred with Forbes, and wrote memoranda for himself on his affairs. In June, 1736, he wrote that the whole debt appeared at Midsummer, 1734, to be £137,500, which is slightly higher than Walter had computed it in May. Then he recounted his income from stewards and from the office for 1735–6 at £46,000. 'Out of that Summ £33,094 paid towards Old Debt, plus £5170 from Walter's collection towards sinking the Old Debt.'[21] If Newcastle's figures are correct, it means that he was living on the £13,000 difference, that is, on his £12,000 annual budget. This may be correct, for he was very short on cash and had anticipated his income by borrowing £3,000 of his stewards by drafts, pro-rated and dated, presumably to coincide with the time of their collections.[22]

But the duke's efforts to retrench in his household expenses and to pay his most pressing debts were not enough. He had also ordered a stop to new buildings and repairs in Sussex. He ordered Forbes to inform Mr Burnett to bring all building and other costly activities in Sussex to a halt. New buildings were simply to be covered up and the new stone staircase being added at Bishopstone Place was to be closed off for at least the remainder of the year.[23]

There can be little doubt that Newcastle was making progress in his efforts to retrench and to pay his debts. However, the progress was too slow, and the pressures upon his credit were so great that even Peter Walter refused further money to Newcastle without the additional security of Henry Pelham's name to the note. He had reached the end of the road.

This final emergency forced Newcastle to turn to his brother, whom he loved so well, for his support. The duke's missive must have made light of his situation, for he received in return a letter as plain-spoken as those written years before by Bishop Bowers, although one filled with love and affection:[24]

> Horse Guards
> 14 January 1736–37

I was not the least surprised att the receipt of your letter, but heartily and greviously concerned att it. Not for the trifling contingent security Mr. Walters [sic] desires from me, for when you are undone it little Avails me to what condition I am personally in, and if it did, I am already so involved, that this will make but a very small addition. What goes to my heart is to me, that you continue to deceive yourself in the manner you do, and that you can think it possible others can be deceived also. You say this arises from your having drawn bills on Mr. Hoare beyond what the estate has brought in, why not plainly say, for this is what you must know, that you have spent more than your income, this you say is occasioned by purchases and repairs att Lewes, I know Dear Brother that that has been a great expense to you, but what ruins you, is that att the same time near five thousand pounds laid out at Newcastle House, continued expenses from additions at Claremont, hounds and other vast ones at Bishopstone. and now new buildings and alterations going on there. Forgive the freedom I write to you with, I promise you itt shall be the

last time, but my love for you, your honour and future peace
obliges me to do it, the just concern nature obliges me to have for
my own family calls upon me to do it, when one sees the
honestest and the best natured man that was ever born running
headlong to his own distruction [sic], and that only because he
won't allow himself time to think and see the consequences which
everyone about him does, I know the receipts of your estate both
in Nottinghamshire and Lincolnshire are anticipated, Peter
Walters [sic] receipt is sufficiently so too, if this were known to
your creditors, or if by any accident, there should be removals att
Court, think, Dear Brother, what a condition you would be in,
and if you do think, it is impossible but you will immediately put
your affairs and expenses in such a way, as may satisfy your honest
creditors, and in a few years, make you in reality, what every man
desires to be, a great a sure and considerable support to your
friends and country; forgive I beg once more, and I promise you,
I will never vex you again, it goes to my heart to do it now, but
I can't avoid it, whilst I am Dear Brother your affectionate,
faithful and loving Brother.

H. Pelham

In this excellent letter, full of sincerity and concern, Pelham covered
the major causes of Newcastle's financial plight: his grand style of
life; his political expenses; his unwillingness to face reality; his continual hustle and bustle and refusal to think, coupled with his precarious
position with his creditors; and the fact that his resources were all
engaged in his credit structure. Pelham was as good as his word, for
there is not another letter in which he touched in this vein on Newcastle's continuing difficulties.

The constant labor and the difficulties of Newcastle's affairs seem
to have undermined the health of Mr Forbes, for by July, 1737, he
was seriously ill. Newcastle was much concerned and ordered Mr
Burnett to see that the doctor's orders were not departed from 'ever so
little,' for Forbes's health was of the utmost importance to him.[25] We
have seen that James Waller began his association with Newcastle at
about this time as an accountant and probably took over some of the
work previously performed by Forbes, or he may have been employed
at this time owing to the approaching crisis in the duke's affairs. Waller
wrote to Newcastle in October, 1737, to inform him that the balance
at Hoare's was very low and that when the bills drawn in September

came in for payment, all would be gone. His hope was that the land stewards' receipts might enable him to cover bills drawn upon Mr Forbes.[26] The duke was also indebted to his own agents, especially to Mr Burnett, for over £3,500, and the agent charged interest on the balance. Burnett insisted upon a bond for the amount and desired 5 per cent, but Waller would pay him only 4 per cent, for he thought it would be a bad precedent to give the higher figure.[27] It appears that Mr Forbes desired to leave Newcastle's employ after all his years of service. He indicated that he was making up all of his accounts in December, 1737, so that they could be audited by Mr Waller, and when that was finished he hoped 'His Grace will be so gracious as to give me my Quietus for good.'[28] Although Forbes's responsibilities were greatly reduced, he did not leave the duke's service completely.

Newcastle was living on the razor's edge and was kept from impending collapse only by timely payments from his stewards. Waller warned the duke that he had only £283 at Hoare's, 'and I have promised clamorous People on Wednesday Se'night money for drafts on Mr. Forbes, and some bills on Mr. Hoare not yet come in, so that unless Mr. Bedwell [Clare Market steward] makes his payment, . . . there will not be £300 for clearing Hampton Court, etc., this week.'[29] Thus Newcastle's condition was so desperate that even his court expenses could not be met for certain. In his toilsome search for ready money, he turned to Robert Burnett and asked him about the availability in Sussex of money which might be borrowed, but the quaintly spelled reply held out no hope at all:[30]

I fear it Imposable for me to meet with any person that has near ye sum of a thousand pounds to spare. What I have heitherto Borrow'd has bin a hundred pound or pirhaps some places two or three hundred of some pirtickerlor people but Larg sums are not to be mett with hear. the easeyst way that I can thinke of att presant for your Grace, is if Mr. Waller will please to except of Draughts one him att ye distance of three four five & six munths thay will serve to pay to trading people & such as can give credett to one another. but what is Imediatly wanted is for small sums & Jobs which your grace is very sensible must be wanted att this Juncture to carry things in the manner your Grace should like to have it at ye approaching election.

Thus, there was no money to be had in Sussex; moreover, the agent went on to tell the duke that he needed £800 himself to carry out work in Lewes and at Bishopstone, no doubt in part to put local voters in a proper mood. The duke borrowed £1,000 from Hoare on February 1, 1738, which was repaid by the trustees on July 26, 1738.[31]

The period 1734–8, that dating from his attempt to retrench to the beginning of the trust in 1738, saw an effort by the duke to live within the means available as far as the expenses of the family and household were concerned, although Pelham's letter made clear that capital expenditures continued at his seats. Newcastle always had difficulty in understanding that capital employed in building was as much a drain on his resources as were current operating costs. What he needed to do was to stop incurring new debt and to continue to economize in order to make sizeable reductions in his enormous indebtedness. Yet the duke could not cease participating in the life and events of his time; in spite of his efforts to save money, we find in his personal account at Hoare's such intriguing payments as '1735—to Fred. Handell £121.16.0,' a tidy sum, when we consider his difficulty in meeting the demands of his tradesmen.[32] The expenditures continued; and when Newcastle's account at the bank was balanced on July 5, 1738, he was overdrawn £1,150. This was the final balancing before the new trust came into effect, at which time the overdraft was paid.[33]

The establishment of a trust appeared to be the only way in which the estate could be kept intact and the great debt paid at the same time since it was always possible, if this expedient were not used, that creditors could force the estate into bankruptcy. Negotiations for the trust must have taken a great deal of time and effort; but since the Newcastle papers contain very little direct information about the origin of the great affair, one must assume that much of the effort was made in face-to-face negotiations between the duke's agents and the principal creditors. The deed of trust for the Newcastle estates was signed on June 2, 1738; its basic purpose was to pay the debts owed by the duke, 'who in justice to his creditors,' had resolved to set aside part of the rents and profits of his estates to create a fund for paying them.

The deed was made and signed by the duke and by Henry Pelham on the first part, and by the trustees on the second part. The trustees were John, Lord Monson; Charles Monson of Gray's Inn, a brother of Lord Monson; and Hutton Perkins of Lincoln's Inn, secretary to Lord Chancellor Hardwicke. Newcastle had at first wanted Hardwicke himself as a trustee, but the Chancellor felt such a role inconsistent with his public position and recommended Perkins in his place. The duke thanked his friend, 'I most readily and thankfully agree to the kind proposal of Mr. Perkins, depending upon your kind advice, and Direction in the Whole.'[34] Thus Hardwicke would not be an uninterested spectator in the operation of the trust.

The trustees were resolved to reduce the rate of interest on the vast debt to a uniform 4 per cent. Since the creditors could not know how long Newcastle might live, and since Henry Pelham was heir in law to the estates, it was necessary for Pelham to agree to the trust for his lifetime—that is, to add his contingent estate for life in the premises and join Newcastle in the covenants, declarations and agreements made in the indenture—before creditors could feel that they had sufficient security to reduce the interest on the debt so that the whole might be more readily paid off.[35]

The deed of trust envisaged that the debt could be paid off by reserving most of the rents and incidents from the estate for that purpose, and did not contemplate sales of land. The indenture named the estates to be put in trust, the steward of each and the annual gross rental, as we have noted. Although specific farms and property in Hastings were included, the Sussex estate was excluded from the terms of the trust. The gross annual rental of these lands and properties was computed at £24,421. The annual 'outgoings', that is, taxes, tithes, poor rates, etc., were calculated at £1,308—certainly far too low—leaving a net rental of £23,112. All of these lands were placed in trust for ninety-nine years.

The trustees had two basic obligations. First, they were required to pay the duke, for his support and maintenance, £7,000 'clear and net money' annually in equal quarterly payments, and, in case of his death, the sum was to be paid to Henry Pelham. Second, all money, the 'Surplus and Residue of the Rents, Issues and Profits' of the estates, was to be used towards paying and discharging all debts and sums of interest owed by the duke. The entire debt was to be included in a 'Schedule of Principal Money or Interest' from which, with the approbation of Newcastle or Pelham, the trustees were to make payments until all should be cleared. The trustees were also empowered by the deed to borrow money at 4 per cent upon their trust; all money, current income or sums borrowed, were to be kept by Messrs Hoare and Arnold, goldsmiths, the traditional Pelham bankers.

The Schedule of Debts, written in a book marked with the letter 'A' according to the trust, provides unimpeachable evidence for the deplorable and dangerous state of indebtedness Newcastle had got himself into by early 1738. The debt was categorized in several ways:

first, the type of debt, that is, mortgages, pledges, bonds and notes; second, geographical location of the account, that is, debts on the London Account [Newcastle House], debts on the Claremont Account, debts on the Sussex Account [Halland and Bishopstone Place]; third, Debts in his Grace's Private Account; and, fourth, an account to cover money owed to stewards and others, called 'Balances on Sundry Accounts.'

Interestingly enough, the category of bonded indebtedness—that is, promises given under the duke's hand—was divided into three chronological periods. The first period ended in 1721 and was entitled, 'Bonds before Mid-Summer, 1721,' which is the date of the first trust. One can assume that the bonds covered were from the date of the duke's coming of age in 1714, to 1721, a seven-year period. The second period was 1721–34, that is, 'Bonds since Mid-Summer, 1721 but before Mid-Summer 1734,' a thirteen-year period, which ended with the duke's great effort to retrench and live by his 'Scheme.' The third period was termed, 'Bonds since Mid-Summer, 1734,' that is, the four-year period from the budget to the beginning of the trust, 1734–8.

Simple addition gave the sad and serious picture. By Lady Day, 1738, Newcastle had a principal indebtedness of £143,839.15s.2d. Unpaid interest charges on mortgages, bonds and notes added £14,353.8s.4d., making the total indebtedness the fantastic sum of £158,193.3s.6d.[36] The duke was forty-five years old. (See Figure 1, p. 73.)

The deed of trust was signed and sealed that June day in 1738 in the presence of James Waller and Andrew Stone. A quarter of a century before, it would have been witnessed by Thomas Bowers and Peter Forbes; but now Bowers was dead and Forbes had been partially superceded by Waller. Although Newcastle signed the indenture for the trust, he evidently had not signed over certain deeds for specific properties, for he wrote to his friend the Lord Chancellor on June 10 asking for advice before he signed them. The duke told Hardwicke that he was to have £7,000 per annum under the trust, but what worried him was the fear that he might actually have to live on that income in the future. In case of a change at court and he 'should be out of all Employment,' he would lose his salary and would be faced with relative poverty. He wanted the trustees to agree to increase his trust income in that eventuality, but both they and Mr Hoare, 'who is to advance a considerable sum of Money to pay off the most pressing debts,' refused his request. The debt-ridden duke confessed to his friend, 'it would be a very great alteration to be reduced to £7,000 p. ann. But as these necessities are

the consequence of my own Follies, I will and must cheerfully submit to them, if there be no Remedy.'[37] Now that his estate income
was permanently reduced, it was essential for Newcastle to retain
his great office of state in order to maintain his accustomed style of
life.

NOTES

1 Horace Walpole (ed.), *The Works of the Right Honourable Sir Charles
 Hanbury-Williams, K.B.* (London, 1822), I, 37 footnote.
2 Hoare, Current Accounts, Ledger N, ff. 80–7.
3 Add. MSS. 33138, ff. 177v–8. A close average for the net income of the
 office, 1725–44, would be approximately £5,500 p.a.
4 Add. MSS. 33137, f. 475, Newcastle House, June 16, 1736.
5 L.A.O., Monson papers, 28B/13/2.
6 Add. MSS. 33137, ff. 325–5v, 'Instructions for Forbes to talk with Mr.
 Walter, 1728.'
7 Add. MSS. 33064, f. 351, Godolphin to Newcastle, September 17, 1729.
8 Hoare, Current Accounts, Ledger Q, f. 277.
9 Add. MSS. 33320, f. 188v, Peter Walter's accounts.
10 Add. MSS. 33137, f. 363, Claremont, March 11, 1732.
11 *Ibid.*, ff. 365–6, 367, 368.
12 *Ibid.*, ff. 397–8, 'A scheme for the family,' Claremont, June 5, 1734. This is
 reproduced in Nulle, pp. 184–6.
13 Add. MSS. 33137, f. 414, Claremont, July 28, 1734.
14 *Ibid.*, f. 427, Newcastle Memorandum to Mr Forbes, Claremont, November
 3, 1734.
15 *Ibid.*, ff. 431–2v, Peter Walter to Newcastle, November 28, 1734.
16 *Ibid.*, f. 432.
17 *Ibid.*, ff. 472–4, Memorandum on Halland and Bishopstone Expenses,
 Claremont, 1735.
18 *Ibid.*, f. 493, Abstract of Sussex Housekeeping Accounts.
19 Add. MSS. 33321, *passim.*
20 Add. MSS. 33065, ff. 25–5v, Peter Forbes to ?, Newcastle House,
 January 22, 1736.
21 Add. MSS. 33137, f. 475, Memorandum—Business done with Forbes,
 Newcastle House, June 16, 1736.
22 *Ibid.*, f. 475v.
23 Add. MSS. 33065, f. 170, March 24, 1736.
24 *Ibid.*, ff. 142–3.
25 *Ibid.*, f. 169, Stone to Burnett, Hampton Court, July 20, 1737.
26 *Ibid.*, f. 209, Waller to Newcastle, October 6, 1737.
27 *Ibid.*, f. 213, Waller to Newcastle, October 23, 1737.
28 *Ibid.*, f. 238, Forbes to ?, December 29, 1737.
29 *Ibid.*, f. 213.

30 Add. MSS. 32690, ff. 466–7, Robert Burnett to Newcastle, Lewes, December 31, 1737.

31 Hoare, Money Ledger, 1718–43, f. 141.

32 Hoare, Current Accounts, Ledger N, f. 79.

33 *Ibid.*, Ledger O, f. 87.

34 Add. MSS. 35046, ff. 33–4v, Newcastle to Hardwicke, Newcastle House, March 10, 1738.

35 L.A.O., Monson papers, 28B/13/1.

36 *Ibid.*, 28B/13/2, Trustee Accounts.

37 Add. MSS. 33065, f. 272, Newcastle to Hardwicke, Claremont, June 10, 1738.

CHAPTER 3

THE FUNCTIONING OF THE NEWCASTLE ESTATE TRUST, 1738–68, AND THE PELHAM FAMILY SETTLEMENT OF 1741

The trustees for the estates of the Duke of Newcastle received their commission on June 2, 1738, when the deed of trust was signed and they began their long and heavy task. They had the income from the estates assigned to them by the trust to meet their obligations. The stated rental value of the estates in their hands was £24,421 per annum, but whether by intention or by oversight the costs of estate management, administration and maintenance were ignored. We should not be surprised, therefore, to learn that in the first ten months of the trust's existence, the trustees received from the land stewards only £13,865.16s.0d.—far from the stated annual value. The trustees were required to pay £7,000 per annum to the duke for his maintenance, and this obligation came first in their calculations. Next they had to pay interest on the prodigious debt; and even if interest on it was reduced, either by agreement or by new borrowing, to a uniform 4 per cent, it required at least £4,000 per annum to service it. In fact, the annual interest charge on the old debt and on new sums borrowed by the trustees would total £4,459.11s.0d. by March, 1739. Precious little remained to reduce the principal indebtedness, for about £11,500 of the current annual income of roughly £18,000 was earmarked, leaving the trustees only about £6,500 p.a. to carry out their final obligation.

Since rental income was obviously insufficient to meet the urgent and immediate need to pay interest due and accumulated, as well as principal indebtedness, the trustees began at once to accumulate capital by borrowing upon their trust. Their initial borrowing was from an individual, Mr Thomas Gibson, who lent them £9,000 on June 5 on mortgage. He also appears from the accounts to have lent an additional £2,000 on the security of the family plate, and an added £1,850 on the family jewels; but whether he lent these sums to the trustees or to the duke is unclear; Waller did not include these sums in his later tabulations.[1] The trustees then borrowed £22,000 at 4 per cent from

Hoare's Bank on July 13, 1738.[2] Finally they borrowed £2,000 from Colonel John Selwyn; and the accountant, Mr Waller, let them have £3,500 at the unusually low rate of 3 per cent.[3]

As required by the deed of trust, an account was opened at Hoare's Bank on July 14, 1738, in the name of the trustees of the Duke of Newcastle. On the same day, they began to pay off debts (no doubt at the direction of the duke) to Robert Burnett, his steward and Sussex agent, totaling £3,519; to Mr Waller £4,188 for his mortgage; to Mr J. Cooke, £3,000; and to Colonel Selwyn, £2,615.[4] These debts were largely mortgages and bonds and were paid immediately and in full.

In their accounting, the trustees assumed that their responsibilities had begun on Lady Day, March 25, 1738, that is, at the beginning of the year as it was then calculated in England. The first accounting period ended on March 14, 1739,N.S., and was thus approximately a full year. During this period the trustees had at their disposal a total of £41,365 from landed income and from borrowing, and they paid something in each category employed to describe the debt. Table 9

TABLE 9

Payments made by the trustees of the Duke of Newcastle towards settling his debts, March 1738 to March 1739

	£
Mortgages	10,800
Bonds	8,800
Notes	2,450
Sussex account	3,600
London account	2,200
Claremont account	1,500
Private account	1,050
Stable account	1,100
Balances of accounts	1,950

shows the amounts in rounded totals. In all, the trustees discharged £39,062.2s.7d. in debts during the period and were left with a hefty £149,131.0s.11d. yet to pay. It must have been discouraging from the beginning.

94

In this first trust action, everyone to whom Newcastle was indebted received something. Some mortgages were paid in full, some in part, and interest was paid on others. Outstanding notes were paid in full, while bondholders in each category received some payment. Debts owed to tradespeople and artificers were a large item; about half of them were paid in full while the other half received approximately half of what was due them. Laborers appear to have been paid in full, but servants in the family received only about half of what was owed. It was safe to make them wait another year for their arrears in salary and board wages, since their condition would not affect the duke's reputation or credit; and in any case, they would continue to be fed at the duke's table. It is interesting to note, however, that the duke's charities were paid in full. They were not a major item, of course, but they were expected of a man of his station and long arrearages would certainly tarnish his name. As would be expected, the trustees paid promptly the duke's quarterly £1,750, for without it life would have been impossible for him.

The accounts of the trustees demonstrate that they continued to work manfully to pay off the indebtedness. During the initial trust— that is, from 1738 until January, 1742—the accounts were balanced four times. During each period, the trustees paid something on each category of indebtedness, as noted above. For the whole period they paid debts, interest charges and costs of the trust totaling £70,564.5s.4d. During the same period the duke received from the trust a total of £24,525, making their total outgoings £95,089.5s.4d. Since the trustees had received only £54,963.17s.10d. from the stewards during the period, this means that the £40,000-odd difference between the foregoing figures came from new borrowing. Thus the duke's personal debt was being transferred to the trust and consolidated.[5]

As we know, the purpose of the trust of 1738 was two-fold: to pay the duke's debts and to provide him with current income upon which to live. It became apparent by 1740 or 1741 that the trust's income from rents and estate profits was unequal to the demands put upon it, and further that borrowing alone could never liquidate the debt. First, the trust could not pay off the vast indebtedness at a pace fast enough to satisfy holders; and second, the duke could not live upon his income from the trust and other sources. Newcastle was building a new debt, as we shall see later, and his remaining credit was being ruined, not only on the money market but even among lowly merchants.

THE PELHAM FAMILY SETTLEMENT

The great estate struggled on for months under increasing pressure while a means was sought to save the situation. In the spring of 1740 it became obvious that rents alone would never be able to unencumber the estate, but that only that expedient dreaded by the aristocracy, the sale of landed estates, could provide the capital to pay the principal and interest on the debt, old and new. However, most of Newcastle's estates were held in fee tail and could not be sold without the agreement of the heirs and remaindermen which would permit the barring of the entail in the common law courts. Securing an agreement would be a long and costly process.

Negotiations were soon undertaken to arrange a family settlement that would have advantages for everyone. Some of the best legal minds in England were engaged in the project at one time or another. Lord Chancellor Hardwicke and Hutton Perkins, his secretary and a Newcastle trustee, were involved in giving opinions and in preparing the proper instruments. The attorney general, Dudley Ryder, was constantly consulted, while William Murray, the future Earl of Mansfield, a brilliant lawyer, evidently did much of the planning.

In the spring of 1741, Newcastle wrote to Hardwicke and asked his advice on reaching a settlement. The problem was to secure consent to barring the entail on the lands which Newcastle had inherited by the will of his late uncle, Duke John. The will had entailed the estates on Pelham-Holles and his heirs male; then to Henry Pelham and his heirs male; then to Gilbert Vane, heir apparent to Christopher, Lord Barnard, and his heirs male; then to Henry Vane and his heirs male; and, failing these lines, to the heirs at law of the late duke. The obvious problem was to remove the Vane interest, a remedy which was necessary on two levels. First, the estates could not be sold with a good title as long as the Vanes had a reversionary interest in them; and, second, Newcastle had no children to inherit the estates, and Pelham's two sons had died of smallpox on the same day, leaving only daughters to inherit his property. Thus, the Vanes would inherit the whole by the entail provided by the will and supported by Act of Parliament. Fortunately for Newcastle, the Vanes were in financial need and Lord Vane was willing to join in barring the entail in return for proper remuneration. The duke first understood that Lord Vane wanted a fourth or a fifth of the estate, but Lord Vane later indicated that he would be willing to take money instead of land.

Newcastle wished to control the whole estate for two reasons: first and most pressing, of course, so that land could be sold to relieve him of the pressure of debt; and second, so that he could entail what remained in such a manner as to keep it in his own family. Yet the duke had no desire to take advantage of Lord Vane. 'That, however desirous I may be to get rid of that great load of Debt; (which, however, imprudently, and wrongly contracted I cannot think of doing by any dishonourable means;). . ., no consideration should engage me, to do anything that may have the appearance of imposing upon a necessitous, and weak young Man, without Friends, and without advice' or of barring the remainder now in Henry Vane.[6] Thus it would be necessary, in a sense, to buy out the Vanes.

Since Henry Pelham was the actual heir of Newcastle directly involved, it would be necessary for him to agree to the settlement as well. Because of their personal and political involvement, it would have been difficult for Pelham to have refused to aid his brother in his distress, but Newcastle felt it was his brother, 'whose Goodness to me is the chief, if not the only reason for his consent,' that made it all possible.[7] However, since the money to pay the Vanes, as well as that to pay the duke's debts, could come only by selling part of that estate, the future interest of Pelham or of his daughters would be materially reduced.

Newcastle's current financial condition continued to worsen and his debt to increase. He asked Mr Waller to report to him; and on July 14, 1741, Waller sent the account which told him that his affairs were indeed in a dreadful condition and recited such a list of moneys owing that it must have brought the duke to tears. Even the duchess's pin money could not be paid; over £900 was due Charlton, the coal man; there were over £7,000 arrears of interest; and Messrs Hoare were owed £2,260 due Lady Day last 'but at present there is not £800, & no prospect of any coming in to make up the sum til after Michaelmas.' The absolute necessity of raising new capital to save the duke from the maelstrom was evident in the details of Waller's report: a trust indebtedness (that is, money borrowed by the trustees) of over £40,000 and a 'new Debt' (that is, built by Newcastle since establishment of the trust) of over £21,000. Waller acknowledged the gravity of the situation when he told Newcastle, 'when the affair of Lord Vane [family settlement] is finished, I hope all matters will be made easy, but I don't see it possible to borrow money 'till it is compleated and unless it is compleated we are all undone.'[8]

Newcastle saw as a result of these long and difficult negotiations for a new family settlement the final salvation from his perdition of debts. 'If this thing can be done justly and honourably, It will make me easy for my own life; and give me the Satisfaction of Settling My Estates upon the only Representative of my Own Family; and who must be in every Respect, the dearest to me.'[9] Thus the duke himself explained the foundation for the family settlement and displayed its rationale. It appears that the major item holding up final agreement was the amount of money demanded by the Vanes for their concurrence in barring the entails. The duke's advisers had evidently suggested the sum of £40,000 as sufficient to induce their acquiescence. Newcastle had a very poor opinion of his cousin Lord Vane and of his stability, apparently with good reason; and in the final settlement, the duke would see to it that Vane's sons were protected financially. The duke also suggested, as an additional inducement, that whatever the final agreement should be, the lands be settled in fee tail so that Vane's sons alone could inherit them and not the heirs at law of Duke John.[10] The extended negotiations over the size of the Vanes' portion from the estates to be freed from entail continued until late fall 1741, when Newcastle and Pelham agreed to their demand for £60,000.

The Pelham Family Settlement was signed and sealed on November 17, 1741. It was long and complex; and in its enrollment in the court of Chancery, it covered nineteen skins.[11] The indenture consisted of seven parts or agreements among the principals or those persons necessary for its implementation. The principals were the Duke and Duchess of Newcastle; Henry Pelham; William, Lord Vane; and Henry Vane. The individuals necessary to carry the agreements into execution were: James Waller, who could carry the common recoveries in the Court of Common Pleas; Charles Monson and Hutton Perkins, trustees; and the Duke of Leeds and Henry Furnese, who would supply the money needed to buy out the Vanes' interest in the estates.

The indenture conveyed freehold estates in the counties of Lincoln, Derby, Dorset, Wiltshire, Hertford and Kent to trustees Monson and Perkins, so that Waller could carry out the common recoveries on those lands in order that they might be sold to pay the duke's debts. The lands and farms were enumerated, and the trustees were to 'sell, dispose of the inheritance in fee simple of the said Manors, either entirely or in parcels unto any person willing to purchase them for the most money and the best prices that reasonably can be gotten.'[12] The lands recovered in Lincolnshire were to be conveyed to Thomas,

Duke of Leeds, and to Henry Furnese as security for the £60,000 they were to provide. The money arising from the sale of lands was to be used to pay the expenses of the recoveries; for the charges and expenses of the trust; to pay all debts and encumbrances as contained and specified 'in a Book marked with the Letter Z,' which was to be signed by both Newcastle and Pelham; and to pay interest on the debt. In case any principal should remain after all of the debts were paid, that money was to be used by the trustees to buy land in the duke's name. The trustees were to receive rents from all lands not sold and to use the money for debt retirement or interest payments.

Further provision was made that the trustees could mortgage estates in Nottinghamshire and in the town of Nottingham to raise funds if sales were not sufficient. In addition, with the permission of the duke and Henry Pelham they could borrow a sum not to exceed £20,000 on the Nottingham, Yorkshire and Middlesex estates,[13] but were limited to a maximum interest of 4 per cent. As usual, all money arising from the actions of the trustees was to be deposited in the trust account with Benjamin and Henry Hoare.

The provisions of the family settlement concerning Lord Vane and Henry Vane were most singular. As we have seen, the Vanes demanded £60,000 for their consent, but of this sum the needy Lord Vane was to receive only £14,000 in cash. The remaining £46,000 was to be laid out in land which was to be in the hands of trustees and settled so that the contingent remainder could not be destroyed—that is, the rents and profits of the lands purchased were to go to Lord Vane during his lifetime, but the lands were in law entailed upon his sons and then to Henry Vane and his heirs male.

In a sense, all of the principals had profited from the settlement: the duke had been relieved of his new debt and 'made easy' for the rest of his life; Henry Pelham had strengthened his interest and that of his daughters in the estate and had in fact secured partial control of it; the Vanes present and future had been provided for and protected.

The long and difficult procedures to secure the family settlement had been finished by the end of October, 1741. They had demanded the expert legal and financial advice of many persons, but particularly of the Lord Chancellor and of William Murray, as we have noted. Newcastle gratefully acknowledged his indebtedness to all:[14]

As I have the prospect of having my private affairs settled greatly to my satisfaction, I cannot but remember with the utmost gratitude those to whose favour and goodness, I entirely owe it. My first obligation is to the kindest Brother, that ever man had, of which I begg you would assure him, that I have the sense. The next, to that affectionate advice, with which you have honoured me & directed this whole proceeding & in the third and last place, to those who under you have carried this great affair into execution. And in this, I cannot but think myself greatly indebted to Mr. Murray, who took the great pains he has taken in the way of his profession [and] has singly secured the consent of all parties, without which I should not have been thoroughly easy.

The legal procedures for the settlement were complex, and the work of securing agreement from the parties was arduous; but much needed to be done to secure the funds necessary to carry it into effect. In May, 1743, Hutton Perkins presented his bill to Newcastle for all of his labor of five or six months in carrying out the settlement, in securing money on the Nottinghamshire estate, and in selling land. The bill totaled £780.6s.4d.; yet Perkins reminded the duke of his constant attendance during the negotiations, which was not covered in his bill, and which might be compensated 'as the Duke pleases'—in other words, by an added gratuity.[15] The attorney general, Dudley Ryder, had been offered one hundred guineas for his advice and refused to take it; but Mr Murray evidently accepted the three hundred guineas offered to him for his great labor.[16]

Newcastle's trustees had, as a result of the settlement or the second trust as they sometimes termed it, more adequate means of meeting their responsibilities. They were empowered to sell a vast acreage to raise principal sums; they collected rents on lands assigned to them; and they had the power to borrow upon the security of certain lands. The second trust also relieved them of the obligation to pay the Duke of Newcastle £7,000 annually, since certain freehold and leasehold lands in Middlesex, Lincolnshire, Nottinghamshire, Yorkshire, Suffolk and Dorset, not in trust, provided him with a net income of over £8,600 p.a., which made him better off than he had been. Half of this sum came from the Clare Market estate, which had been released from trust in the new agreements.[17]

OPERATION OF THE NEWCASTLE
TRUST, 1741–68

The trustees began to labor at once under the terms of the new settle-ment. Their actions can be fairly accurately reconstructed, because the trust accounts have survived, and the day-to-day receipts and payments can be followed in the ledgers at Hoare's Bank.[18]

One of the first actions of the trustees was to borrow £14,000 from Hoare on a deed of assignment on November 19, with which to pay Lord Vane the cash sum due to him.[19] Next, the trustees began to search out sources of available money for borrowing and to seek per-sons who were interested in buying landed estates. It was during this tense period that Newcastle's plight was spoken of freely by his brother-in-law Sir John Shelley when talking with the Earl of Egmont. Shelley made the interesting observation that 'most of the money went in vanity, which had run him so into debt,' that it made it necessary for the duke to sell land worth £12,000 per annum. 'In the mean time, 'tis a shame to see how his duns pester him.'[20]

The trustees' work was evidently arduous, as Perkins indicated; it was not until August 27, 1742, that they were able either to borrow additional money or to sell land, a time lapse of nine months after the settlement had been signed. On that date they deposited £30,000, which they had borrowed from the Earl of Mountrath and others, on the security of the Nottinghamshire estate. At the same time they deposited £21,000, which was the purchase price of two parts of the Dorsetshire estate bought by Mrs Lora Pitt and John Brown, Esq., respectively.[21]

The functioning of the trust under the new arrangements can be studied most conveniently by using the accounting periods as they stand in the accounts, for there we see all of the trustees' financial actions and the balances of the various accounts. The first full account-ing period under the new trust ran from January 11, 1742, until January 17, 1743, just over a full year. The resources available to the trustees in this period are shown in Table 10. With this great sum they undertook to pay creditors of every description, as listed in the schedule of debts. They paid off bonds and notes totaling £12,000; London debts of over £11,000; Sussex debts of over £8,500; Claremont debts of over £3,000; and a host of smaller ones—totaling in all £61,749, which left them with the lowly balance of £1,695. Although we cannot say exactly how much the preparation of the family settlement cost the estate, a sum of £3,000 was set aside to cover it; but an item which was termed 'Miscellanys' by the accountant and included 'Settlement, wages, gratuities, etc.,' totaled £4,726.19s.6d., which may be the exact cost.[22] Certainly these vast payments lessened the pressure upon the estate; but great debts, both old and new, remained. The new trust indebtedness was carrying interest at the rate of 4 per cent to Hoare and to Lord Mountrath; and to Lord Vane, for the unpaid or uninvested principal due him of £46,000.[23]

TABLE 10

Resources of the trustees, 1742–3

	£	s.	d.
Rents from stewards	11,270	19	$11\frac{1}{2}$
Money borrowed	30,000		
Purchase money (i.e. sales)	21,000		
Balance of last account	1,174	6	3
	63,445	6	$2\frac{1}{2}$

In the second accounting period under the new trust, January 17, 1743, to August 11, 1743, the triple means of raising capital continued: rents, land sales and borrowing. The stewards returned £5,030; the trustees borrowed £22,000 from Thomas Gibson and an additional £11,000 from the Earl of Mountrath and others—both sums on the security of the Nottinghamshire estate; and they sold the Derbyshire estate to the Duke of Devonshire for £33,375, and a part of the Wiltshire estate for £1,700, plus a few other small parcels. In the eight-month period the trustees had in all £73,456 in new money for their use.[24] Major payments during this period went for mortgages, bonds and notes; but lesser amounts went for debts listed under the various Newcastle seats, for the trustees had by now cleared the small debts and consolidated them in the new borrowing. In this short period they had discharged an additional £71,000 of debts.

The trustees were now paying three types of debts, according to their own terminology: the so-called 'old debt,' that contracted by Newcastle before the trust of 1738 had been established; the debt accumulated by the duke between 1738 and the Pelham family settlement of 1741; and the 'New Debt,' that is, the sums borrowed by the trustees themselves on the security of the trust estates, which they also occasionally termed 'the new Securities.'

The accountant for the trust, Mr James Waller, from time to time drew up abstracts from the various accounts so that the total trust situation and the progress made to date might be more readily seen. In July, 1744, he provided figures to show the working of the trust since

TABLE 11

Trust income, 1738–44

		£	s.	d.
Rents		76,696	12	11
Borrowed:				
First Trust	£41,300			
Second ,,	63,000			
		104,300		
Purchases [i.e. sales]		81,970		
Total trust income		262,966	12	11

its initiation on Lady Day, 1738, to July 17, 1744. First Mr Waller gave the income of the trust and the sources (see Table 11). Next he indicated the original state of the debt or the full burden of the trust (see Table 12). Finally the accountant totaled the trust debt remaining and gave the annual interest charge which it carried (see Table 13). This remaining debt carried an annual interest charge of £7,037.[25] Thus

TABLE 12

The original state of the debt

	£
Total debt on first trust was	162,996
second trust was	63,000
Lord Vane	60,000
Original state of debt:	285,996

by simple subtraction we see that the trustees had paid off during the period from 1738 to July, 1744, encumbrances of £105,896.8*s*.10*d*.

TABLE 13

Trust debt remaining

	£	s.
First trust [1738]	71,809	12
Second trust [1741]	11,290	
Lord Vane	34,000	
Borrowed—Notts Estate	63,000	
	180,099	12

In this period, 1738–44, the trustees had in new money—that is, in resources which did not constitute an additional burden upon the estate—a total of £158,000 from rents and sales. We have seen that they paid off £105,000 of trust encumbrances during the same period, and we must immediately ask, what happened to the £53,000 difference between the two figures? The bulk of the difference is accounted for by the required payments to the duke of £7,000 p.a. from 1738 to 1741, which totaled £24,500. The remainder was probably accounted for by interest charges on the debt; the costs of the new settlement, which were at least £3,000; and the accountant's salary, which was extremely high at £500 per year. For the future, Mr Waller informed the trustees that they had still in hand estates valued at £138,600 which could be sold to pay the remaining indebtedness.

In the following accounting period, August 11, 1743, to May 3, 1745, the trustees received in rents £11,474, which was not large considering that the period covered twenty-one months. However, sizeable sales of land in Lincolnshire totaled £29,120, while many small parcels in Hertfordshire realized £4,239. Their total income, including balances, was £46,500.[26] Nearly £38,000 of this went to pay principal or interest on the new securities, and the remainder went for bonded indebtedness contracted before 1738. It should be noted that the sale of land in Lincolnshire to Charles Pelham and Charles Reynolds produced £26,000; and the trustees borrowed an additional £20,000 of Hoare on June 13, 1744, to pay to the Duke of Leeds and Henry Furnese the remaining £46,000 of the original loan of £60,000 which was used to buy out the Vanes's interest in the estates.[27]

As the trustees were able to sell more and more of their lands, obviously the income from rents continued to diminish. During the accounting period from May 3, 1745, to August 6, 1746, a fifteen-month period, the trustees received only slightly more than £6,000 in rents. The sales of land were small also; the Kent estate was sold for £3,500, only £100 less than its valuation, and a £2,500 portion of the remaining Lincolnshire estate went also, in all only £6,000. Once again old bonds were paid in part, but more of the income went to pay interest on the consolidated debt and the charges of the trust.[28]

The trust's landed income continued to average about £6,000 p.a.; but this was hardly sufficient to pay the interest alone and it was essential that sales of land should continue. In the accounting period covering twenty-three months, August 6, 1746, to July 16, 1748, the trust had a landed income of slightly over £12,000; but finally a buyer was found for another large portion of the Lincolnshire estate. In June, 1748, Mr Abraham Hume purchased the South Kyme estate for £30,000, which made in all over £43,000 for the trustees' use. Once again nearly all of this great sum was expended to reduce the new securities debt; £22,000 went to Henry Pelham, who was assignee of the debt originally owed by the trust to Thomas Gibson; and over £5,000 went to Hoare's Bank in part payment of a total of £34,000 still owed to them.[29]

It was nearly three years before the trust accounts were balanced again, on August 7, 1751. Because of large land sales, the rents now totaled only slightly over £11,000 for the period, which was a very great reduction. Yet once again, sales of land made possible the operation of the trust, for the Earl of Clinton purchased the Tattershall and Sempringham estates in Lincolnshire for £34,340, while Mr George Crowle bought the Hatcliffe and Irby estates in the same county for £19,700; these, plus other small sales, made in all £54,750. Then the trustees borrowed £10,400 of John Temple, James Pelham and James Waller in order to pay off the bonds. Thus, the trustees had a grand total of £76,000 to use, all of which except for £266 they expended in bond and new security payments. Some of the 'old debt' bonds dated back before 1721 and had been drawing, or accumulating, interest all of these years. The trustees liquidated their loans from Hoare in March, 1750, for they paid off the £10,000 remaining on their original loan of £22,000 made at the beginning of the trust in 1738, and also paid the remaining £29,000 of the original debt of £34,000 contracted in 1741.[30] The £11,000 borrowed of the Earl of Mountrath in April, 1743, on the Nottinghamshire estate, was assigned to Horatio Walpole on June 1, 1749.[31]

Although the trust accounts in the British Museum end in 1751, for some unknown reason, a full run of the accounts exists among the Monson papers, as has been noted; and from these and the trust's accounts at Hoare's Bank the activities of the trust can be observed. However, the major work of the trust ends in the decade of the fifties, even though the trust continued to function until the duke's death, and a couple of years beyond.

It is interesting to note that the firm of Hoare—or at this time Hoare and Arnold—lent to the trust, or to Newcastle himself, nearly £100,000 in the period 1738–54, either as an original loan or in order to refinance earlier loans. However, by 1755 only £13,000 remained to be paid to the bank; this sum, plus interest and a small bond, was fully paid by October 3, 1759, and neither trust nor Newcastle borrowed more from Messrs Hoare.[32] The Duke of Newcastle and his trustees must have been among the prime clients of the bank, and only once did Hoare's confidence in the ability of the great estate to pay its obligations appear to have weakened. On November 30, 1749, the bank increased the interest charges one per cent on the remaining £29,000 due on the loan of 1741. This was an astute move on the bankers' part, for the estate was at that time becoming deeply indebted once again. Eighteenth-century bankers had sensitive antennae for picking up information or rumor regarding the financial life of their major creditors, or perhaps they employed an informal intelligence system arising from the talk at clubs and coffee-houses.

The current income of the trustees remained very small, consisting of only £3,102 in the calendar year 1752–3.[33] The trustees had unsold estates in Dorset, Wiltshire and Hertfordshire valued at £36,500, which they hoped to sell, but there appears to have been some question regarding clear title to some parcels. The Nottinghamshire estate served as the security for £51,400 of the trust debt held by the Earl of Bradford's Committee (the young earl was mentally incompetent), by Horatio Walpole and by the Earl of Abergavenny, respectively.[34] Thus we see that much of the trust debt was held by individuals and would continue to be until the end. The trust regularly paid to Lady Lincoln interest on £10,000, which was the marriage portion provided in part by the duke and held by him as an unsecured debt before the trust. In 1758, Andrew Stone was paid interest on a mortgage of £11,000 but whether this was his money or that of another cannot be determined. The trustees paid the Duke of Newcastle himself interest at 3 per cent on £2,950 which he had in the trust; this sum no doubt represents trust 'excesses' which might have been paid into his private account but which were retained for trust uses. Little new borrowing by the trust took place, except in order to refinance the £45,000 when the executors of Lady Mountrath were paid off in 1767, at which time a like sum was borrowed from Lord John Cavendish and Charles Yorke.[35]

The great reduction in the annual rental income of the trust because of sales caused the trustees to attempt to increase rents where they held large acreage. The Nottinghamshire estate provided the best opportunity for improvement, so they had a survey and valuation made by Mr George Mason (the new steward or collector who had replaced Mr Bristowe), which indicated that the estate there could produce at 'improved rents' £5,335 p.a., an increase of £1,184. Mr Mason was directed by the trustees to let the estate to tenants-at-will at the new rents, and Newcastle's approval was sought, as required by the terms of the trust.[36] The duke gave his general approval to the plans of his trustees and to his steward for the management and improvement of this estate, yet he could not ignore the danger to his fixed political interests and influence which he had cultivated for so many years. In his memorandum to his estate managers he added a firm direction: 'As to the Estates lying in or possessed by Tenants living in Retford, Newark and Nottingham, an account to be sent of the Improvement that may be made, but those Improvements, not to be carried into Execution, without my further Direction.'[37] Obviously, fear of offending tenant voters was of greater moment to the duke than was the need of the trust to increase its annual income.

We saw earlier that significant changes were made at this time in the management of the duke's affairs. Mr Waller was dismissed as accountant and replaced by the able Mr James Postlethwayt. Mr John Sharpe, a barrister who had had some connection with the duke's affairs for years, was put in overall direction of both trust and non-trust matters. In March, 1755, both Sharpe and Postlethwayt were added as trustees, but unfortunately Sharpe died in 1756 and Postlethwayt in 1761.[38]

It appears certain that from about 1754 the trustees saw that they would not be able to pay off completely the principal indebtedness. They continued to pay the interest due regularly and punctually, but reduced the principal only slightly. On July 31, 1754, the trust debt stood at £93,450 with interest and at £3,609 without interest, in all £97,059.[39]

In the last fourteen years of Newcastle's life, the trust debt was reduced by only a little more than £18,000, for in 1768 the debt stood at £79,350 and was held by relatives, friends or dependents (see Table 14).[40]

TABLE 14

The debt in 1768

	£
Lord Lincoln	10,000
Lord Abergavenny	10,400
Lord John Cavendish	35,000
Charles Yorke	10,000
Andrew Stone	11,000
Newcastle	2,950
Total trust debt, 1768	79,350

All so-called 'excesses' over interest, trust charges and some small debt payments were transferred to Newcastle's private account at Hoare's. In the period 1756–68, they paid into his account over £24,000, that is, roughly £2,000 per annum. In the year of the duke's death, the landed income of the trust was £4,590; interest payments on the trust debt totaled £2,880, and the duke received approximately £2,000.[41]

Let us calculate the total debt paid off since the beginning of the trust in 1738. First, Mr Waller's accounting rendered on July 17, 1744, showed that the inclusive debt of the trust—that is, of the 'first trust' of 1738, the total costs of the family settlement, and that of the 'second trust' of 1741— had been £285,996. Next, he indicated that the 'trust debt remaining' as of 1744 was £180,999, which means that in the six-year period, the trustees had liquidated £105,000 of the debt. By subtracting the total remaining debt in 1744 from that remaining in 1768 as noted above, we see that in the twenty-four-year period the trustees paid off an additional £101,649, a very slow rate indeed compared to that of 1738–44. By simple addition we see that in the thirty-year period, 1738–68, the Newcastle trust paid off encumbrances of £207,546. Compared with this great figure, the £79,000 trust debt remaining at the duke's death was quite manageable.

The total operation of the Newcastle trust over the thirty-year period provides insights into the complexities of the financial world of the eighteenth century as it related to the landed classes. One important question concerns the source of capital for borrowing; we have seen that Hoare's Bank played a central role in the affairs of the Pelham family. This bank had from its earliest times been closely allied to the nobility and gentry, and in fact specialized in service to the aristocracy, as did a few others.[42] Although the bank was one major source of capital, we have noted the great importance of individual lenders and the virtual necessity for employing a scrivener, or person such as Peter Walter, who had intimate knowledge of probable sources of ready capital.

A survey of the persons named in the trust accounts who served either as sources of capital or as purchasers of parts of the estate will give us some indication of the locus of capital. It appears that the trustees borrowed from fourteen individuals, and of this number five were noblemen in their own right: Abergavenny, Bradford, Leeds, Mountrath and Walpole; three were closely related to noble families: Pelham, Temple and Selwyn; two had much liquid wealth, for they were financiers in the City: Henry Furnese and Thomas Gibson; two, Stone and Waller, were professional men who were also men of substance; and the remaining two we know nothing of. Thus, more than half of the individuals who lent money to the trust came from the nobility or from persons closely related to a noble family.

The purchasers of parts of the Newcastle estate, in so far as they can be identified, form an interesting lot. There were sixteen individuals; one, a woman, Mrs Lora Pitt; and one, a clergyman, the Reverend Frederick Williams. Of the remaining fourteen, two were noblemen, the Duke of Devonshire and the Earl of Clinton, and three who made large purchases were termed 'Esq.' by the accountant, and were probably substantial gentry: Abraham Hume, John Browne and Robert Hucks. George Crowle and Charles Reynolds, who invested heavily in land, were probably also of the gentry. The remaining seven purchasers took only small parcels and cannot be identified.

It is obvious from the information we have that the landed class itself provided the greatest source of both capital and purchasers of portions of the Newcastle estates. There is no doubt at all that the noble families provided the greatest source of liquid capital. The largest purchases were also made by noblemen, the Earl of Clinton and the Duke of Devonshire; while the next largest was made by a member of the substantial gentry, Abraham Hume. It is regrettable that the correspondence of the trustees has not survived, except for a few items in the Newcastle papers. Its loss makes it impossible to trace the trustees' search for lenders or purchasers; we do not know if that work was done by the trustees themselves, by Mr Waller, or by another. We have only one letter of Hutton Perkins, in which he indicated his labor in finding money and purchasers during the early days of the trust. Perhaps the persons seeking such looked first to the landed families known to be affluent and largely ignored those in the financial or mercantile community, for we have here only Furnese and Gibson who lent directly to the trust. There can be no doubt that since so much capital was needed, the trustees would prefer large unit sales to many small ones. The value of the three largest purchases noted above was about half of the value of all other sales combined up to 1751, the period of major trust activity. If one were seeking to demonstrate social mobility in early Georgian England by noting transfers of land, one would find scant support in this data.

The interest rate charged on mortgage loans in the early eighteenth century seems very low when compared to rates in effect in the late twentieth century. The deed of trust of 1738 noted that much of Newcastle's debt carried an interest rate of 5 per cent and implied that that was too high. Most of the duke's debt was secured on his landed estate, but some of it was on his signature only. One of the motivations for consolidating the debt in the hands of the trustees was to reduce the interest rate to a uniform 4 per cent. The fact that Henry Pelham joined in the deed of trust gave the security to lenders, which made them willing to take the low rate. Since it was better to have interest paid at a rate of 4 per cent than to have it unpaid or heavily in arrears at the rate of 5 per cent, it appears that some individual creditors voluntarily reduced the rate to 4 per cent. We noted earlier that the trustees were limited to a rate of 4 per cent for any money they should borrow on the security of the Nottinghamshire estate. Only in one instance did the rate fall to 3 per cent, and that was for a loan of £3,500 in 1738 from Mr Waller, the accountant.[43]

What did the trust of the Newcastle estates accomplish? First, it saved the duke from certain financial ruin in 1738, when his credit was gone; and it saved him once again, with great help from the Pelham family settlement, by taking over his new indebtedness in 1741. Second, through income from land rents and from sales of land it paid off all of the encumbrances listed in the Schedule of Debts, some of which dated from Newcastle's youth. Third, it consolidated the remaining debt and faithfully paid interest on it. Fourth, it provided what was essentially a board of directors for nearly all of Newcastle's financial past; we have seen the great income of the trust and can sense the financial knowledge necessary to manage it. We know that the trustees did not have absolute control; Newcastle held the power to lease lands, and therefore they could not improve rents without his co-operation. We also know that most of the trust lands were let at beneficial rents rather than at economic ones.

The trust of the Newcastle estates was largely a success in that it paid off a mountain of debt; at the same time it was destructive in that, by its very nature, it radically reduced the economic foundation required to support a ducal title. This is what Horace Walpole knew, or sensed, when he termed Newcastle 'a duke without money,' or at least without enough.[44]

Meanwhile, be the care and devotion of the trustees ever so great in carrying out their obligations, the duke still remained a free agent and could continue to spend, as his income and his restored credit would allow him. If Newcastle had not now learned from the financial mistakes of his youth and early manhood, he could yet effectively undo all of the trustees' good work and endanger his financial well-being once again.

NOTES

1 Add. MSS. 33320, ff. 20 and 30, Trust Accounts.
2 Hoare, Money Ledger, 1718–43, f. 141.
3 Add. MSS. 33322, f. 13.
4 Hoare, Current Accounts, Ledger O, f. 89.
5 Add. MSS. 33322, ff. 13, 20, 26.
6 Add. MSS. 33065, ff. 401–3, Newcastle to Hardwicke, March 25, 1741.
7 *Ibid.*
8 *Ibid.*, f. 420, Waller to Newcastle, July 14, 1741.
9 *Ibid.*, f. 403, Newcastle to Hardwicke, March 25, 1741.
10 *Ibid.*, f. 448, William Murray to Newcastle, n.d. [1741].
11 Public Record Office, Close Rolls, C 54–5668.
12 *Ibid.*
13 Add. MSS. 33138, ff. 61v–2.
14 Add. MSS. 35407, ff. 121–1v, Newcastle to Hardwicke, Newcastle House, October 31, 1741.
15 Add. MSS. 33066, ff. 7–9, Perkins to Newcastle, May 6, 1741.
16 Add. MSS. 33222, f. 51, February 24, 1741.

17 Add. MSS. 33138, ff. 159–60.
18 Trustee accounts from 1738 to 1751 are in the British Museum, Add. MSS. 33322, 84 ff; they are also found in the Monson papers in the Lincolnshire Archives Office for the whole period 1738–70; Hoare's Bank, 37 Fleet Street, has its ledgers complete from its founding in 1672.
19 Hoare, Money Ledger, 1718–43, f. 141.
20 H.M.C.R., *Manuscripts of the Earl of Egmont (Viscount Percival)*, III, 244, January 18, 1742.
21 Add. MSS. 33322, f. 37; Hoare, Current Accounts, Ledger P, f. 337.
22 Add. MSS. 33066, f. 8.
23 Add. MSS. 33322, f. 52.
24 *Ibid.*, f. 59.
25 Add. MSS. 33138, ff. 162–3v.
26 Add. MSS. 33322, ff. 60–6.
27 Hoare, Current Accounts, Ledger R, f. 177, Trustee Accounts.
28 Add. MSS. 33322, f. 71.
29 *Ibid.*, f. 66; Hoare, Money Ledger, 1743–73, f. 16.
30 Hoare, Money Ledger, 1743–73, f. 16.
31 Add. MSS. 33322, f. 81.
32 Hoare, Money Ledger, 1743–73, f. 16.
33 Hoare, Current Accounts, Ledger W, f. 20, Trustee Accounts.
34 Nottingham University Library, Newcastle papers, Ne D 132, f. 19.
35 L.A.O., Monson papers, Trustee Accounts, March 24, 1767.
36 Add. MSS. 32337, f. 428, Sharpe to Newcastle, December 11, 1754.
37 *Ibid.*, f. 452, Claremont, December 15, 1754.
38 Add. MSS. 33066, f. 431, Newcastle to Trustees, March 3, 1755.
39 Add. MSS. 33138, f. 429.
40 L.A.O., Monson papers, Trustee Accounts, July 31, 1767; Hoare, Current Accounts, vol. 70, f. 43.
41 *Ibid.*
42 D. M. Joslin, 'London private bankers, 1720–1785,' *Economic History Review*, 2nd series, VII, No. 2 (1954), p. 176; H. P. R. Hoare, *Hoare's Bank: A Record 1672–1955. The Story of a Private Bank* (London, 1955), pp. 28–40.
43 Add. MSS. 33322, f. 13.
44 Horace Walpole, *Memoirs of the Reign of King George the Second* (London, 1847), I, 166.

CHAPTER 4

LIVING ON A BUDGET AND BEYOND, 1738–52; OR HOW TO BUILD A NEW DEBT

Happily the Newcastle trustees had taken over the great responsibility of paying off the debt of youth and early manhood of £158,000 and the duke was free again. He had promised himself and everyone connected with him that he would retrench and actually live within his means. It was necessary for him to attempt to control disbursements since he was attempting to live on a scheme or budget. However, the public life which went with his great cabinet office called for constant expenditure from his own pocket, for the office carried no expense account. It is impossible to determine the costs of what was essentially state entertaining in the growth of Newcastle's debt but it must have been a considerable factor in the housekeeping and extraordinary accounts. These costs, added to those required of one of his rank and station, would make the task of limiting his expenditures to his income a difficult one.

We can say with certainty what Newcastle's spendable income was for this period. First, we know that the trust of 1738 allowed him £7,000 per annum for his expenses. Second, we can determine from the office account his net income as Secretary of State. In the year 1738–9 the office produced £5,534.[1] Therefore his total usable income during the first year under the trust was £12,534. Although the Sussex estate was not in trust we can safely ignore it as a source of additional income, for annual costs in the county exceeded the produce of the estate.

The budget drawn up for Newcastle was extremely close to his actual income; in fact, it was almost exactly that, for it totaled £12,500. This sum was divided into allowances for each area: Household, £5,000; Stables, £2,500; Claremont, £1,200; Sussex, £1,200; Duke's Private Account, £800; Duchess's Pin Money, £600; Extraordinaries, £1,200. Current expenses were watched very carefully, for Mr Waller informed the duke of 'exceedings' as the year progressed. He noted that these were mainly in his Private account, in the Claremont account

113

and in the Stable account, which included hunting dogs, under Mr Coates. Newcastle was in Sussex at Bishopstone Place, when Waller wrote, 'I hope your Grace will remember now you are on the Spot to reduce the Hounds, which is a heavy article in the allotment for Mr. Coates.'[2]

It is doubtful if Newcastle followed this advice to retrench in current expenses, for in December he issued directions to his agents there, Mr Bristowe and Mr Morrice, to undertake immediately new painting, new wainscoting, and new floors at Bishopstone Place.[3] The duke was unable to separate in his mind the current charges for his own personal expenses and those of his family from the costs of capital improvements, which appeared to him to have no bearing on his current financial state. Capital improvements could be paid for in the future with future income. However, with most of his current income in the hands of the trustees, Newcastle appears not to have comprehended the fact that his real income could not be significantly increased and that the new encumbrances could not be paid.

Because of the eighteenth-century custom of abstracting various accounts so that the whole could be seen more readily, we have certain evidence of how Newcastle's budget of 1738 worked. The abstract for the first year survives and it shows clearly where the money went and just how well the duke was able to manage (see Table 15).[4]

Alas, Newcastle actually spent £17,664, or more than £5,000 above his budget. Yet this does not give the full story, for only £10,012 of the amount spent had actually been paid, which left him with a new debt of £7,652 during the first year under the new arrangements provided by the trust. The largest of his unpaid accounts were for Sussex, £2,520, and for Claremont, £2,307. The duke would continue to exceed his budget at approximately the same rate for the next two years, for when the 'new trust' was established his additional debt was approximately £21,000.

It is obvious that the existence of a budget made no difference in the rate of expenditures. It should be noted that in categories directly related to the duke's public and political life, i.e. Claremont and Sussex, the overages were vast and largely unpaid. On the other hand, only in the area of housekeeping was a saving made, and this may mean that the duchess closely supervised this area. Indeed, the duke told her in a letter that he had been 'applauding [you] for being the best Steward I ever had.'[5] Perhaps Henrietta had inherited some of the financial acumen of her grandmother Sarah, Duchess of Marlborough, and it is perhaps unfortunate that she did not have full authority in her husband's financial affairs, for we have noted her care in accounting for the expenditures from her pin money.

Newcastle approved his wife's action in dismissing a servant, but when it came to economizing in an area of his own interests, evidently at her suggestion, his attitude abruptly changed: 'I can never think of parting with my pine-apples after I have been att £500 expense to build houses, etc. The expense of keeping them now will be very inconsiderable, if rightly managed.' He hoped that such things as garden expenses could be reduced and was 'sorry and surprised' that expenses in several categories exceeded the budget; but, as always, he was hopeful. 'But this

TABLE 15

Abstract of accounts

Lady Day 1738–Lady Day 1739 Budget of £12,000 per annum

	Allowed	Spent	Difference	
	£	£	£	
Housekeeping	5,000	4,568	432	saved
Stables [Coates]	2,500	2,878	378	exceeded
Claremont	1,200	3,791	2,591	exceeded
Sussex	1,200	4,100	2,900	exceeded
Private Account	800	1,727	927	exceeded
Pin Money	600	600	—	
Extraordinaries	1,200	[blank]	[blank]	

is the first year, we must be better managers the next.' He blamed the excess at Claremont on new building going on there and felt that, even with his pineapples, it could be run on its allotted £1,200 p.a. when the building was completed.[6]

Newcastle loved to visit Sussex, where he could be with old family and personal friends, where he could be away from his London duties and tensions, and where he could relax, enjoy himself and at the same time maintain his political interest. His descriptions of his life in Sussex show him as a human being, enjoying simple country activities among friends, and not as the caricature of the eighteenth-century courtier as pictured by the malicious Lord Hervey, or the scurrilous Charles Hanbury-Williams.

The information on Newcastle's life in Sussex comes largely from his letters to his wife. He had the custom of writing to her frequently, when he was away, to tell her of his activities or of the state of his health. The duchess rarely visited Sussex with her husband, for she disliked the life she had to live there, and, besides, hunting and politics were largely men's affairs. The duke particularly liked to be in the county for the Lewes races in August and often stayed longer. During his visit in the fall of 1738 he reported to the duchess on his safe arrival at Halland, of his having spent the evening there in company, and that he had gone to his favorite hunting seat, Bishopstone Place, in fine weather. 'Jogged out this morning and killed a brace of hares' and went out later to shoot, 'shot once and killed a patridge [*sic*].' The duchess was frequently concerned about Newcastle's consumption of alcohol, especially when he was with his old political friends, so the duke assured her that the evening entertainment for his party of friends was quiet, for 'we are mighty sober, drink nothing att all, & play at whisck att night.'[7]

The duke would be entertained in turn by his friends in Sussex and he told his wife of the group's activities at the home of Lord Wilmington. The men ate, drank and engaged in various sports. They spoke of going fishing for whitings and also played games of skill. 'There is a cricket match between Lord John Sackville & Sr. Wm Gage on Monday, Sr. Wm. is so taken off, yt he is always beat.'[8] Thus in the informal and rustic pastimes Newcastle could forget his problems, financial and otherwise.

However pleasant and relaxing the jaunts to Sussex might have been, they also meant an expense, not only for ordinary costs of travel and living, but in giving entertainments to all and sundry. The races in August brought many persons to the town of Lewes and it was incumbent upon Newcastle to participate in the general festivities. For example, in this August of 1738 Newcastle paid for two balls given in the town, including the cost for dinners, wine and music, all of which came to £120.10s.10d. The lavishness of the duke's entertainment is shown by the types of wine 'expended': 'clarett, Burgundy, Champagne, Calquallia, white French, Greeke, Renish, Turkey, Hermitage, arrack, Red port.'[9] This liquid refreshment cost him eighteen guineas.

As we know, Mr James Waller was the accountant and paymaster for the trustees, as well as for Newcastle himself. He had great responsibilities but was unusually well paid for undertaking them. For Newcastle he had the burden of trying to pay current expenses, as well as for paying on certain unscheduled or non-trust debts. He also carried on a wide correspondence with agents, creditors and others, and often stood between the duke, his creditors and his own agents. In replying to the request of John Collier of Hastings, an attorney and Newcastle's political representative, for payment of sizeable legal costs of the corporation of Hastings, which the duke had promised to take care of, Waller demonstrated the duke's practice in meeting current expenses. Collier had requested payment often and had been put off, so Waller attempted to explain why he could not be paid from the current quarter's income:[10]

> when my Lord Duke before he went into Sussex was distributing
> the money to come in, I mentioned this Debt to you, but so
> much was wanted for the Journey, & my Lady Duchesses'
> [sic] Journey into Derbyshire, & for Lewes, & other extraordinary
> occasions, that the whole is quite exhausted, & nothing left hardly
> for Housekeeping necessarys, which are greatly in arrears & at
> this rate it is impossible to fix times for any Payments
> whatsoever.

This quotation clearly demonstrates the Newcastle priorities in money matters, for first came the immediate personal claims of himself and the duchess, then the extraordinary expenses, no doubt political for Lewes and other places, next came ordinary housekeeping needs, and, finally, payment of debtors. It is obvious that current quarterly income, or anticipated income in this case, could not meet all demands.

In many ways Mr Waller had a most unpleasant task, and it is not surprising that he would from time to time find himself in conflict both with creditors, who felt that the rich Duke of Newcastle certainly should be able to pay them, and also with the duke himself. Newcastle complained of Waller's lack of communication with him, saying that he had given him no account of the moneys he had received and paid out for over six months, but added with his usual candor that it was probably his own fault for not giving him an opportunity to do so. Yet what angered the duke and what he found inexcusable was 'the answers he gives to people and the small debts he leaves unpaid.'[11] Some small creditors, when thwarted in their requests for payment by Waller, would write to the duke personally, asking for payment, and through such letters Newcastle saw something of his condition and of Waller's method of operation. Newcastle's pride was hurt and his anger stirred by a letter received from Mr Cole, his hay merchant, who told him that Waller had informed him, when he had requested payment, 'that he must never expect the money & must look upon it as lost.' This led the duke to one of his rare outbursts of anger against the harassed Mr Waller: 'how is it possible for a man in his senses to say so, sure there must be some mistake, but he is so proud, so hasty, & so ill bred, yt I can almost believe anything of him.'[12]

Newcastle's financial condition was becoming ever more precarious; and it appears that it was the small merchants who first reacted to his worsening credit situation. Their capital reserves were quite limited, so they had to be insistent upon payment. It would be surprising if the merchants' disquiet did not provide the ripples of information upon which the great creditors, such as the bankers, formed their opinions, at least partially, upon the health of the estate. Here, in 1740, Newcastle's current credit situation was so bad that even the Kingston butcher would no longer sell to him, and the common laborers at Claremont had received no payments for over three months.

In this situation Newcastle told his wife, 'as my Business will really not allow me to look into these things, I must begg you would do it for me, & keep Mr. Waller constantly to his Business, & make him come to you every week.'[13] He asked her to have Waller prepare accounts covering all of his income, disbursements, debts, trust, etc., and to have them ready for a conference, in which the duchess would be included, the following week. The pressure of his official business was used fairly often by the duke as an excuse for not knowing about his personal affairs, and there is probably a good bit of truth in his rationale. However, it is doubtful if it would have made an appreciable difference even if he had attended to his accounts each week with Mr Waller and the duchess, for we have seen repeatedly that he spent money with little attention to his disposable income.

Late in 1740 Mr Waller gave the duke an interim accounting of the status of his private account, which covered part of the second year following the institution of the trust. He had handled a total of £8,040 from quarterly payments from the trust, salary, etc., but had paid out £8,299.5s.0d. Much more important than this small imbalance was Waller's report that he had, as of November 13, 1740, a total of £7,168.1s.0d. in unpaid bills, while he had only a little over £450 cash in hand. In fact, the amount of overage was increasing at a faster rate than in the initial budget year, although Newcastle had hoped to better his circumstances. Thus, one can see why Waller had so often to disappoint impatient creditors. Waller begged assistance from Newcastle for Mr Burnett, his steward and Sussex agent, who had written to him saying that very large sums were needed there, 'and if I cannot help him out, begs your Grace will give him leave to leave the Country for he shall not be able to stay in it.'[14] Newcastle, then, was paying only about half of his way in 1740, according to his accountant's figures: £8,000 of expenditures paid and £7,000 of expenditures remaining unpaid.

This interim financial accounting should have made it fully apparent that the situation could not continue; for, as we know, the trustees controlled most of his estate and he could not increase his income in order to pay off the new debt. Newcastle struggled on but it soon became obvious that only drastic changes could alter his situation. The trustees could not pay off their debt rapidly enough to make the creditors happy, while Newcastle had no way of paying off his newly created indebtedness. These are the prime reasons why the negotiations for a new family settlement were undertaken, the details of which we have already noted.

While those negotiations were under way, Newcastle was in serious need of capital. He turned to Mr Waller for help, evidently wanting to borrow from him or from him and others. In spite of the general artificiality of manners and the extreme formalism in human relations in the eighteenth century, the accountant was one person who could speak the naked truth to the employer. We know that Newcastle received much economic advice from Bishop Bowers; now again he received it from a purely professional person and a man to whom he was indebted, as well. With some very plain speaking, sweetened by a compliment, Waller told the duke:[15]

> If I could supply the whole of what your Grace says is at present
> wanting, it would be a great pleasure to me, and much greater if
> your Grace would in earnest resolve to extricate yourself out of
> these difficulties in your affairs, as it depends intirely [sic] upon
> a little Self Denyal, which without flattery I really think is the
> only Virtue your Grace does not abound in, I am in hopes it will
> be no such hard matter to put it in practice.

Mr Waller submitted to the duke at this time a full and complete account which covered his income and expenditures for the preceding fourteen-month period, that is, from May 1, 1740, to July 13, 1741. The accountant had handled for the duke £18,007.5s.11½d. from all sources: salary £6,589.6s.5½d.; from the trust £10,500; from Secret

Service money £711.6s.0d.; plus a few smaller amounts from fines, and such items as 'Prize in Lottery, £8.10.0.' The duke must have been pleased to read that only £17,810.5s.0d. had been expended during this period: housekeeping £4,000, his private account £2,500, and Claremont £3,800, while Sussex in this election year took the enormous sum of £5,700. The duke thus had a balance in his favor of £197.[16] Yet we must remember that Newcastle was trying to live on a budget of £12,000 p.a.

If Newcastle had not had to turn to the next page of Waller's accounting, he would have had a better day. The next page gave him the extremely sad news in its title: 'Unpaid Debts.' These debts were those contracted from the date of the creation of the trust, Lady Day 1738, until July 14, 1741, a period of three years and four months. At the bottom of the column Newcastle saw the great sum: £21,846.1s.6d. Included were housekeeping debts of nearly £6,900, Claremont at £3,500, a vast new debt for Sussex of over £5,560, Stables £3,200, plus many smaller ones.[17]

The evidence is clearly before us of the plight which necessitated a new financial foundation for Newcastle and which led to the Pelham Family Settlement. During this period Newcastle was spending at a £39,000 rate, while his income was at an £18,000 rate. He was spending about £546 per month *more* than he was receiving from all sources. Thus he was amassing a new debt at a furious rate. While his trustees at this time were paying off £54,000 of old indebtedness from their landed income, Newcastle was creating a new debt of £21,000.

We have seen how, after a vast amount of effort and at immense cost, the new family settlement and the new trust arrangements were signed and sealed on November 17, 1741. The trustees had had a great responsibility in attempting to bring order out of the chaos which the duke had created in his affairs up to that year; this marked the limit of their task. In the years following, Newcastle was his own financial master once again. Actually the period after 1741 would mark the fourth opportunity for the duke to set his feet on the straight path of financial solvency, if we consider his first rescue from bankruptcy to be the trust of 1721, the second the trust of 1738, and, the third to be the Pelham Family Settlement of 1741. As we know, the duke felt that the settlement would make him 'easy for the rest of [his] life.' It is now our task to see if this hope was fulfilled: that is, now that Newcastle had a new financial start in life after 1741, how well would he manage his affairs? Had he learned anything from the experiences of the painful burden of debt which he had repeatedly contracted in his earlier life?

We know that the Pelham Family Settlement and the new trust arrangements relieved the trustees of the obligation of paying New-castle £7,000 annually. We also know that the duke could not come close to living on trust and salary resources, so how could he live with-out the trust payment? The answer to this query lies in his income from non-trust estates and from estates which were released from the trust as a part of the new settlement. We have an account of the estates *not* in trust as of 1743, the first full year of the new arrangements, and

TABLE 16

Income from estates outside the trust, 1743

Location	Collector	Net	
		£	s.
Middlesex	Mr. Bedwell	4,000	
Lincolnshire	Mr. Dobbs	679	10
Nottinghamshire	Mr. Bristowe	1,058	10
Nottinghamshire	Mr. Twells	775	
Yorkshire	Mr. Williamson	656	
Suffolk, Dorset, etc.	Mr. P. Walter	468	10
		£8,637	10

this gives us his *net* landed income. (Only Sussex is excluded, for the income there was small; in fact, because of the duke's political expendi-tures, the estate cost more to maintain than it brought in.) Table 16 shows these estates, their collector or receiver of rents and their net produce.[18]

It is apparent that the new arrangements gave him a larger landed income than he had received from the original trust. During this year of 1743 he received as net income from his office as Secretary of State £5,544.[19] Thus in the first full year of his new lease on life, Newcastle had a net income from all sources of £14,181.10s.0d. However, since the duke had not been able to live previously on a budget of £12,000, which had been approximately his income, the likelihood of his living within his improved income did not seem great. A new debt would certainly be amassed. (See Figure 2, p. 133.)

It would be expecting too much for a man nearly fifty years of age to change his pattern or style of life. In fact, considering Newcastle's territorial, political and social position and the concomitant responsibilities, it would have been very difficult to have changed markedly even if he had desired to do so, for as head of the family and as co-chief of the Pelham interest, his role was clearly fixed.

As head of the Pelham family, Newcastle's relations with his brother Henry were at times difficult. Family problems may have been exacerbated by political competition and jealousy, but the duke's affection for his brother was sincere and he needed his support in every way. As we have seen in the arrangements of the family settlement, Newcastle's estates were to descend to Henry's children. It was a family tragedy when Henry's two small sons died of smallpox on the same day in 1739, leaving only daughters to inherit both their father's and their uncle's estates.

Henry's eldest daughter was named Catherine, after her mother, and her choice of a husband was a major family concern. It is doubtful whether she had a free choice, since her marriage had every mark of having been arranged by the family. Catherine's husband was to be her first cousin Henry, the ninth Earl of Lincoln, son of Newcastle's and Henry's sister Lucy. If Catherine were to marry Lord Lincoln, it would mean that their children would be doubly descended through the Pelham name.

The negotiations for the marriage treaty between the two branches of the family were carried on by Hutton Perkins. It appears that the Lincoln side of the family asked, as a condition of the marriage, that the right of the duke and Henry Pelham to revoke the settlement of the Newcastle estates be given up. Pelham was quite willing to do so, but the duke was very hurt because the demand was sprung on him without prior consultation. He wondered why he should give up all power over his estate for a marriage the whole family wanted and felt that his brother distrusted his affection for him.[20] Newcastle suggested that their good friend, the Lord Chancellor, arbitrate the dispute. He was evidently successful, for the marriage took place on October 3, 1744. Thus the duke's hands were tied; regardless of events or actions the estates would go eventually to their late sister's grandchildren. It may appear that Henry Pelham was pressing every advantage; but considering the duke's financial past, perhaps it was only good sense to ensure that the estates could not be alienated in case Pelham should pre-decease the duke.

We have seen that Newcastle's income was restricted to rents from lands not in trust, to his salary and office perquisites, and to any 'overages' paid him by the trustees. However, in case of immediate need he could borrow or take advances from his land stewards, since most of them had both trust and non-trust lands in their collections. Such action had a bad effect on the ability of the stewards to pay moneys into the trust account at Hoare's and led to complaints from the trustees. In April, 1746, the trustees met in Great Queen Street, London, to pay the interest on the debt, 'but upon examining Mr. Hoare's accounts we find they have not in their hands money enough even to pay themselves their own Interest. This puts us intirely [sic] to a stand.' They also informed the duke that Mr Bristowe, the Nottinghamshire steward, owed the trust nearly £2,600 and that Newcastle in turn owed him £1,700; they entreated the duke to pay him what he had taken in advance. They also reminded Newcastle that the interest must be paid regularly, for it was very low at 4 per cent.[21] As we have seen, Newcastle retained full administrative control of his estates, and this can only be considered a weakness, although perhaps a necessary one, in the arrangements.

The trustees kept a close eye on estate management even though the major responsibility was the duke's. They informed him that estate expenses were too high in Nottinghamshire under Mr Bristowe and also that Mr Waller's salary of £500 per annum was excessive now that the debt had been consolidated and the exacting work of paying off hundreds of small creditors had been finished. The 1745–6 period was one of tight money, according to the trustees, and they did not receive enough money in rents to pay the interest on the great debt. They added a final explanation of their problem: 'we have not been able to sell any of your Grace's Estates for two years last past, so we are under a necessity of having all the Rents punctually applied for the purpose of our Trust, and that we are greatly pressed for Interest.'[22] If the trust rents were slow to come in, so were the duke's and he was hemmed in from every side by his new creditors.

The costs of maintaining the Pelham political interests were constant and were in part carried by credit with local political agents. We found Newcastle owing money in 1740 to John Collier of Hastings, who no doubt owed his position in the customs there to Newcastle. Again in 1746 Collier complained to Sam Burt, the duke's faithful servant, that he had not been paid his costs for celebrating two birth-days, i.e. the king's, and for newspapers which he had sent. He had an added expense in 1746, 'this year was my Lord Duke of Newcastle's turn being once in four years to fill the silver Bowle with arrack punch on the Coronation Day. These amounted to £38.17.9.' The corpora-tion of Hastings' silver bowl must have been refilled many times and the coronation fittingly remembered in loyal toasts. Collier was sober enough to remind the duke that he owed him now a total of £111.0s.6d. and to request payment.[23] Regardless, Burt replied to the agent that the duke 'says he has not yett money to help him.'[24] Slowly but surely a new debt was being built up.

We have seen that the duke and duchess had in their various homes a large number of family servants and that their wages were frequently in arrears. Few of them, however, appear to have left Newcastle's service willingly, and there is little evidence to show that many were sent away. The duke disliked change and evidently put up with much inefficiency and with many bad practices, as Murray would indicate later. The servants with whom the duke was most intimate seem to have been those regularly serving at his beloved Claremont. It also appears in some cases that the children of servants took service with the duke. The Greenings had been with him for years, and their son, called by the duke 'young Greening,' became a valued servant as steward of the grounds, gardens and trees at Claremont. This John Greening must have begun his service with the duke at a very early age, for he indicated that he had been with him for sixteen years in 1747. In that year he was engaged to be married and asked the duke to deliver on his repeated promises to 'do something for him.' Greening was not a bit subtle with his employer but simply informed him that he had instructed his foreman on the management of affairs and that he would be departing if Newcastle could not do as requested.[25] The duke could hardly envision life without his melons, pineapples, etc., which he loved to eat and to send to friends, and he valued Greening's ability and loyalty. He evidently responded to the appeal, for Greening continued in his service for many years and, in fact, was given much added authority.

By the late 1740s Newcastle's personal financial condition was becoming very difficult again. During this period he had had great responsibilities as Secretary of State, and no doubt the fact that the War of Austrian Succession dragged on so long made the internal money situation difficult. One of the most poignant evidences of arrears in payment of the costs of 'the family' and of the expense of maintaining a large establishment is seen in the letters written by a merchant who had long supplied Newcastle with tea and coffee. It also gives a fair hint of small business practices in the eighteenth century:[26]

> My Lord,
>   I take the Liberty of acquainting your Grace I have delivered to Mr. Greening Two Years Bills for Tea & Coffee due at Michaelmas 1747 for £164.9.4 since that time there is £102.13.6 more due. I assure your Grace I charge the same price in your Bill as I do all my ready money customers and therefore hope your Grace will be so good as to order the Payment.
>   I am my Lord wth the greatest Respect,
>
> Collet Mawhood

In the summer of 1747 Newcastle had been busy masterminding the general election in the Whig interest so that the government would be secure in the peace negotiation aimed at ending the War of Austrian Succession. Newcastle accompanied the king to Hanover as Secretary of State in 1748 and carried on the negotiations. While he was away, the burden of looking after affairs continued to be in the hands of Mr Waller and the various officials of the household. Greening wrote quite regularly to the duke about conditions at Claremont, the state of the gardens and the trees, and other matters. Since he was a much less sophisticated man than Waller, his reports of financial problems provide a detailed catalogue of the attitudes of merchants and artificers.

In the summer of 1748 a Mr Packer, who had done much work for Newcastle, sued him for non-payment of his charges. Both Mr Waller and Greening had faced the irate Mr Packer, and the duke was given a fine picture of the event. 'Mr Waller talked to him a considerable time in a very obliging manner, but Packer was rediculously [*sic*] surly and obstinate, and would not withdraw his Suit,' even though Waller promised him £100 immediately, another one hundred in a fortnight, and to pay the bill in full by the next Christmas. The accountant even promised Packer additional work on repairs at Newcastle House, but the aggrieved Packer 'said he did not want to do any more work for your Grace,' and he would proceed as the law directed unless he was paid £500. Packer's full bill was £630 but he was willing to withdraw his suit and pay his lawyer himself, if he were paid the £500 immediately. Packer did not receive the sum demanded and therefore refused to stop his suit; but Waller was able to have the hearing of the case before the court stopped until the following October.[27] Such suits, or even the threats of suits at law, were a very serious matter, because they were public witness to a weakening of the duke's credit and of his ability to pay.

Ever hopeful, Newcastle expected the trust to be able to pitch in and help him in his new difficulties, for the trustees were to pay excesses into his personal account, as we know. Waller informed the duke that the trust debt was greatly reduced but that the trust was so confined 'that your Grace must not flatter yourself with any assistance from it, otherwise than that, as Sales are made, your Grace will thereby be eased the extra Interest money paid to Mr. Hoare, and by making the Nottinghamshire Estate a proper security for money.'[28] The duke could look forward to more borrowing only when the great estate had unburdened itself of its debt; but this was no comfort in the face of immediate need.

In spite of warnings, given by his accountant, that his credit structure was weakening, he continued to live in his accustomed manner. In the summer of 1749 George II dined at Claremont, as his father before him had in 1717. Upon this occasion the duke's faithful house steward, Sam Burt, recorded in his 'Extraordinary Account' the costs of the great dinner, as well as the costs of entertainment—music, bell-ringers and gunners for the royal salutes.[29]

In many ways the year 1749 was a most memorable one for the Duke of Newcastle. His genius as a political manager was recognized and evidenced by the House of Commons, elected in 1747; the peace of Aix-la-Chapelle of 1748, of which he was very proud, had brought at least a temporary end to hostilities; finally, 1749 saw his election as Chancellor of Cambridge University. Newcastle always had a kind feeling for his college, Clare Hall, and for the university. His election was made possible by the support he had from George II, who insisted that his own son should not be elected to the position. The honor and prestige gained by his election as Chancellor brought the duke great personal joy; and he set out to make the ceremony of his installation a memorable one. He must have spent as much time and careful attention upon this event as he did when planning campaigns in counties and boroughs for a general election. For once in his life he alone would be the center of attention. He would make the ceremony a symbol of his own status in the country, as well as a display of his interest and concern for his university, before his family, his personal and political friends and his dependents. The expense of this grand affair would not weigh in the balance.

The day chosen for the actual installation ceremony was July 1. As we know, July was always a special month for Newcastle, for it was the month in which he had been born. It is doubtful if the time chosen for his great day was accidental—it could be two celebrations in one. Newcastle arrived in Cambridge and was lodged in his old college, Clare Hall, next to Trinity College. He had planned to stay not just one day—that was not enough to show the new Chancellor's encouragement to learning—but for nearly five days. Thomas Gray wrote to a friend to give him 'an account of our magnificences here ... that adorned that Week of Wonders.'[30] The gala week consisted of the installation ceremony, feasting, formal visits to colleges and religious services.

About noon on July 1 the Vice-Chancellor, heads of houses and other officers of the university, noblemen, doctors and students assembled in the Senate House for the great ceremony of installation. A deputation was sent to Clare Hall to bring the Chancellor-elect to the steps of the Senate House, where he was met by Dr Chapman, the Vice-Chancellor. Dr Chapman brought Newcastle into the Senate House and accompanied him up the aisle to the chair of state, while an *Ode* written by Mason and set to music by Mr Boyce, composer to his Majesty, was performed.

Mr Mason, a fellow of Pembroke Hall, called his work an *Ode for Music*. It consisted of nine airs and a recitative, and appears to be one of the most graceless of the many odes composed in that century. The recitative set the stage:

> Here all thy active fires diffuse,
> Thou genuin [*sic*] *British* Muse:
> Hither descend from yonder orient sky,
> Cloth'd in thy heav'n-wove robe of harmony.

The airs are too tedious to be repeated in full but two of them do give some insights into the realities or the hopes of the occasion:

VIII

> O Granta! on thy happy plain
> Still may these Attic glories reign:
> In unaffected grandeur great;
> Great as at this illustrious hour,
> When He, whom George's well-weigh'd choice
> And *Albion's* gen'ral voice

Have lifted to the fairest heights of pow'r,
    when He appears, and deigns to shine
    the leader of thy learned line;
And bids the verdure of the olive bough
    mid all his civic chaplets twine,
And add glories to his honor'd brow.

Recitative:

IX

Haste then, and amply o'er his head
    The graceful foliage spread;
Meanwhile the Muse shall snatch the trump of Fame,
    and lift her swelling accents high,
To tell the World that Pelham's name
Is dear to Learning as to Liberty.

The full chorus ended the performance by picking up the final air and repeating it from 'The Muse shall snatch the trump of Fame.'[31] Mr Mason's *Ode* was printed in 500 copies, which were sold both in Cambridge and in London, but he does not appear in the records to have received any reward from Newcastle. This may account for his unkind references later to the duke as 'Old Fobus' and 'the Owl.'

When the performance was finished, the Vice-Chancellor made, in English, an elegant address of about twenty minutes on the honor done the university by the duke's acceptance of election. The speech was very well received by the great audience. Thomas Gray told his friend 'that our Friend Chappey's [Dr Chapman] Zeal and Eloquence surpassed all Power of Description ... all people join'd to applaud him: everything was quite right; & I dare swear, not three people here but think him a Model of Oratory.'[32] Newcastle was then presented with his patent of office and with a book of the statutes of the university; following this, the Senior Proctor administered the oath of office. Only then did the Vice-Chancellor seat the new Chancellor in the chair of state, thereby installing him. Next the University Orator read a Latin oration of about twenty minutes.

Now the time had arrived for the new Chancellor to deliver his address to the university. Newcastle arose from his chair of state and 'in a very handsome speech returned his thanks to the University for the honour conferred on him, enlarged on the benefits arising from an academical education in general, shewed how much religion, literature and loyaly were advanced by the principles cultivated in this University.'[33] The correspondent added that the words and the music were well suited to the occasion.

A clever satirist looked upon the memorable events and wrote *Cam, an Elegy*, in which he touched upon the devout donnish interest in the duke's great day:[34]

> Each Fellow, quick as glancing thought,
> Quick as the glass, the circling ardour caught;
> From heart to heart, from lip to lip it ran —
> But did they hail the *patriot, scholar, man?*
> No 'twas the enchanting ministerial charm
> That struck each bosom with a wild alarm;
> Each in idea grasped preferment's prize,
> While scarfs, stalls, mitres, danced before their eyes.

After the formal installation ceremonies had ended, the new Chancellor, the Vice-Chancellor and members of the Senate, together with noble, ecclesiastical and other guests, walked in procession according to rank to Trinity College for a great banquet which was provided by the new Chancellor for the university. The assembled notables made 'a most numerous and polite company. Not less than 800 gentlemen dined in the Hall and Master's Lodge. Great plenty of Champaign, Burgundy and Claret flow'd, in which loyal healths were drank [*sic*], and prosperity to literature in all its branches.'[35] Gray reported that 'the duke's little court came with a Resolution to be pleased. ... Everyone, while it lasted, was very gay, & very owlish & very tipsy at night. I make no exceptions from the Chancellour to Blew-Coat [the University Marshal].'[36]

Newcastle's 'little court,' which came to do him honor, to feast and to join in the rites of Bacchus, had been invited to be present. Horace Walpole, who always put the unkindest interpretation on all matters pertaining to the duke, informed his friend Mann in a rather witty way, 'the whole world goes to it: he has invited, summoned, pressed the entire body of nobility and gentry from all parts of England. His cooks have been there these ten days distilling essences of every living creature, and massacring and confounding all the species that Noah and Moses took such pains to preserve and distinguish.'[37] Walpole was not far from correct that the guests came from all over England. Present for the duke's great day were the dukes of Richmond and Marlborough, the earls of Lincoln, Radnor, Dalkeith, Halifax, Tankerville, Waldegrave, Ashburnham and Godolphin; Viscount Galway, and Lords Burghley, Onslow, Monson, Montfort, Cornwallis, Dupplin and others. The ecclesiastical peers were represented by the bishops of Ely, Lincoln, Chichester, Peterborough and Londonderry. Sir William Calvert, the Lord Mayor of London, was also present. Close personal or political friends, such as the Yorke brothers, sons of Lord Chancellor Hardwicke, Sir William Yonge, Sir Thomas Robinson and Andrew Stone, as well as several members of the Saville and Townshend families, were also in attendance. Newcastle's own family was represented, of course, by his brother Henry Pelham, who stayed at Peterhouse, by James Pelham, William Conally and Henry Vane, Jr. Most of these invited guests received honorary degrees of one kind or another from the hand of their host, the new Chancellor.

On July 2 Newcastle attended both morning and afternoon services and heard sermons in Great St Mary's Church, although after the festivities following his installation he must have been in poor condition for spiritual reflection. Yet he found time that day to stop long enough to write his wife a description of his triumph. His exaltation is quickly seen:[38]

> I have this moment received my dearest's most kind letter, I am just come from King's Col. chappel. Nothing ever went so well, & so magnificently, as our ceremony yesterday. Near two thousand people, & all the Joy, and Satisfaction, that could be seen in all faces. The University appeared in the highest splendour. The Nobility, & persons of Quality were very numerous. The Chancellor I dare say nothing of, let others speak for him. Those who envy him, should not have been here. I am just going to visit, & sup tonight at St. John's.

Although very busy, the duke savored each moment of his glory. It was on the next day, July 3, that he awarded honorary degrees to his close friends, making them Doctor of Physic, Doctor of Laws or Master of Arts for *honoris causa*. Following this ceremony he was busy again, visiting colleges, and did not get to his quarters in Clare Hall until 11 p.m.

On July 4 he attended a meeting of the Congregation and reported to the duchess that he had 'not one moment unemployed.' He informed her Grace that he was to visit three colleges before dinner and six in the evening. The duke was earning his high honor, but was extremely pleased. 'Everybody, & everything is as I could wish, & I really believe the Chancellor is as well liked, as he has reason to like. ... I really think I am not the worse for the hot weather, tho now it is grown cooler. I sweat, & shift four or five times a day.'[39] The festivities and visitations were finished on the fifth and Newcastle could head back toward London via Newmarket. On the way he hoped that he 'might make free wth a Bed at pappa's,' that is, that he might stay with his father-in-law, Lord Godolphin. He actually had little time for rest, for he was called back to court on the 8th. In leaving Cambridge, Newcastle departed from a scene which gave him one of the unfeigned pleasures of his life. He must have felt that any expense he was put to for it had been money well spent.

Perhaps the item of expense may have entered the minds of some of the participants in this 'Week of Wonders,' especially that of the new Lord Monson, who no doubt knew much of the duke's financial problems from his late father, and that of Andrew Stone, who was becoming increasingly important in Newcastle's affairs, official and otherwise. Henry Pelham, of course, was particularly and most intimately acquainted with his noble brother's habits of expenditure.

We know the costs for these great events, both to the new Chancellor and to the university itself. Newcastle's Steward of the Household, Sam Burt, kept a careful account of 'Bills Paid at the Installation at Cambridge'; and the university's costs were preserved by Dr Richardson, '1748–1749—Expenses at the Chancellor's Election and Installation.'[40] Sam Burt actually paid out £1,554.9s.2d.; only one person, namely Mr Boyce, the composer, was paid 'on Acc't.' Thus Newcastle's costs, as here recorded, are very close to being exact. On its part, the university paid out £229.19s.11d. apparently in full. Thus at least £1,784.9s.1d. was expended for the grand affair. Both Newcastle and the university received, or were to receive, full return on their respective investments.

Mr Burt's accounts help us to reconstruct this memorable installation. The duke himself was properly attired for his great day, for he paid William Jordens £47.10s.0d. for his robes of office and £101.7s.6d. for the gold chain which he wore about his shoulders. It seems strange that Mr Boyce should receive £200 for composing the music to accompany Mason's *Ode*, with more to come evidently, but that Mr Mason himself should go unmentioned in the accounts. It is possible that payments to him could have been included in the largest single item in Burt's accounts, 'To several, gratuities £454.7.0.' This was a vast sum of money, which probably included tips to the servants and others in each of the colleges visited by the duke.

Payments were made by Burt to butchers, poulterers, cutlers, bakers, grocers, fishmongers, carpenters, innkeepers, carriers, pewterers, brewers, and wine sellers, to say nothing of cooks in the various colleges. It is difficult to categorize all of the payments, but it appears that food cost over £200, wine and spirits over £200, labor over £180, supplies over £30, lodging twelve guineas, and coach hire another nineteen guineas. It appears that great amounts of venison were consumed or perhaps presented to the colleges, for Burt paid out £31.10s.0d. in fees, alone, to keepers. No doubt the animals came from Newcastle's own parks; their actual cost does not appear in these accounts. The main courses for the great feast were fish, over £30; meat, over £75; and poultry, over £45. As Horace Walpole noted, Newcastle brought his own cooks from London and hired others as well; their salaries and those of their helpers cost the duke over £80, plus their lodging, transport and food. After meat and drink, one of the larger items was a payment of £40 to 'Messrs. Thornton & Harrison, Gardiners.' This may mean that the dinner also included fresh vegetables and salad; and, since four guineas were for Morello cherries, it may be safe to assume a fresh fruit dessert or many cherry tarts.

The university's expenses were a bit simpler and were directly related to the ceremonies themselves. Costs incurred by the election and notification of the duke came to over £10. However, a major expense was the official patent itself, its embellishment, and a cover and silver-gilt box for it, all of which came to over £40. We have seen that, as a part of the ceremony, the new Chancellor was given a copy of the statutes of the university; this copy, properly illuminated, cost nearly £10. The large expenses were connected with preparing the Senate House for the traditional ceremony, which came to nearly £70, and the charges for making Great St Mary's, the university church, ready for the services there. Seventeen pounds was spent in cleaning the church and nearly £15 in repairing the organ. Some items in the university's accounts are not as clear as they could be. For example, the entry, 'Mr. Mason—500 copies of his Ode £12.4.6,' does not indicate if this sum was paid to Mason or to the printer for the copies of the work. There is no doubt that the university was careful in its preparations, for pavements were repaired with new broad stones, walks newly gravelled, and new paint applied where necessary. Perhaps the university did not forget Newcastle's hard-working Sam Burt and others, for included in its accounts is the item, 'Chancellor's Servants at installation—£21.'

Newcastle's expenditure for his installation was extravagant, but it showed the academics both the splendor of the ducal way of life and the type of Chancellor they had elected. More importantly, no doubt, it demonstrated the Pelham power and influence in the nation. What it most certainly did not demonstrate was the dangerous personal financial condition of the new Chancellor. However, even while in the midst of his great crisis in October, 1751, he signified his intention of establishing two annual Chancellor's Medals to the value of ten guineas each, to encourage classical literature. The reverse of each medal included the ducal arms on a shield with the inscription: *Exergue Liberalilas Tho. Holles Duc: Novocastr: Acad. Cancell.* Two medals were awarded annually from 1752 to the time of the duke's death.[41]

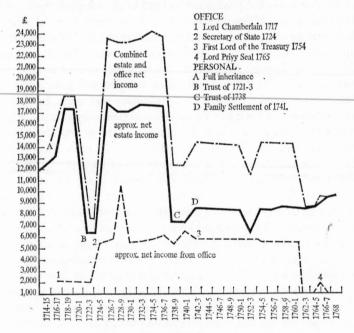

FIGURE 2 *Newcastle's income, 1714–68*

The pressure of debt and the importunity of creditors continued to increase throughout 1749 and 1750, until only renewed borrowing could save the situation. To meet immediate pressures Newcastle was able to borrow by mortgage from Hoare £13,000 on April 10, 1750, probably upon the Sussex estate, but this appears to have exhausted the credit resources which he could use without his brother's consent.[42] The settlement of 1741 permitted £20,000 to be raised on the security of the Nottinghamshire, Yorkshire and Middlesex estates, but this right was vested in Newcastle and his brother jointly. Only Nottinghamshire lands appear to have been used as security for mortgages, however. The duke had now to secure Pelham's consent to burden that estate; this effort would lead to a major conflict between the brothers.

As we have noted, the relationship between the two brothers was complex. Henry Pelham was the younger, and of a very different temperament from the duke. The former was calm, almost phlegmatic; the latter excitable and nearly always agitated. Newcastle recognized his brother's political precedence as head of the administration but at times had policy differences with him. In personal financial matters they were un-alike also; after a fast-spending youth, Pelham changed and became conservative in his money usage, accumulating a respectable fortune through investment. Interestingly, neither brother was ever accused of using political office for personal gain, not even Pelham as Paymaster, where the opportunity was great. In spite of their differences a basic affection and interdependency existed. Whenever a situation arose which was likely to lead to trouble between them, Newcastle usually turned to a third party to act as intermediary. Earlier this unpleasant and troublesome job of go-between had been performed by Lord Hardwicke; in this instance, it was Andrew Stone.

Andrew Stone had been Newcastle's private secretary for many years, was Undersecretary of State, and M.P. for Hastings. He was a man of great ability, possessed loyalty to the two brothers, and knew well the foibles of each. At the duke's request, Stone approached Pelham for his reaction to the idea of further borrowing on the Nottinghamshire estate. The message he brought back to Newcastle was far from reassuring. Pelham felt that his brother needed to have a 'clean State' of his financial condition laid before him. He needed to know how the trustees were progressing with their task, that is, the amount of trust debt remaining and what the unsold estates held by the trustees would bring in which could be applied to debt reduction. In that way Pelham would know if it would be wise to agree to further borrowing on the estate for non-trust uses. Pelham was not unfeeling about his brother's difficulties, Stone was to assure him, but felt that some of his problems came either from lack of knowledge of his affairs or from not having the proper agent to manage the whole of his affairs. Here Pelham was demonstrating his lack of confidence in Mr James Waller, whom he also felt to be highly overpaid for his labor. So Pelham laid down conditions to his agreement for additional borrowing, namely that Newcastle have a full account of his situation prepared; that he have it examined by Hardwicke, by William Murray, the Solicitor General, by Hutton Perkins or by another; and that if the inspection demonstrated that borrowing would help Newcastle's situation, then he (Pelham) would agree to it.[43]

The duke proceeded immediately to order the full accounting of the trust estates. He instructed Mr Waller, in a long memorandum, to give him specific information: (1) an account of the whole debt charged on the trust estate, (2) the particular estates sold and the sums sold for, (3) yearly produce of the trust estates, (4) application of the money, (5) debts discharged by sales or income, (6) yearly and incidental charges of stewards and agents, (7) net money received from the trust estate, (8) the debt discharged, (9) the debt remaining, (10) the trust estate remaining unsold, (11) trust estate sold, (12) yearly income of the trust estate remaining, (13) the computed value for which the remainder of the trust estate could be sold, (14) a short abstract of the uses of the trust, and (15) an account of the power of the duke and his brother to raise £20,000 more upon the trust estate. In his haste Newcastle asked for some of the information twice over. He also wanted to know the yearly income of his non-trust estates, including Sussex, an account of the debts omitted from the trust of 1741, and finally an account of the 'whole debt now standing out by Mortgage, Bond or Book Debt since the Trust was created, to this Christmas Day.'[44]

The duke's order was peremptory, for his need was urgent. It probably was not difficult for Waller to extract the information requested, for the duke soon had the data. If it was unpleasant, he at least knew where he stood. First, Waller gave the duke the picture of his *total* non-trust debt as of Christmas, 1751 (see Table 17).[45] He then presented what he termed 'new debts' from Michaelmas, 1741, to Christmas, 1751. This was the debt accumulated by Newcastle since the family settlement and the new trust of 1741; its total was included in the general abstract given in Table 17. However, the list is somewhat less specific (see Table 18).

TABLE 17

Abstract of debt, Christmas 1751 [1738–51]

	£	s.
Mortgage, Bonds, Interest	21,820	
Book Debts:		
London	17,457	07
Servants	2,386	
Claremont	7,842	2
Personal Account	2,865	11
Small Debts:		
London–Claremont	369	7
Sussex Rents	2,297	
Lewes Bills	4,657	18
Halland	2,286	9
Bishopstone & Seaford	3,100	16
Small debts [Sussex]	317	1
	12,659	4
	65,399	11

TABLE 18

New debts, Michaelmas 1741–Christmas 1751

	£
Messrs. Hoare on Mortgage	13,000
Bonds to Sundry & Interest	9,038
Mr. Burt's List for Tradespeople & Servants in London, & Rents & Some debts in Sussex	21,508
Mr. Nesbitt, Mr. Crew, & others not in other lists	1,200
	44,746

This disparity between the two totals for debt and new debt can be explained by Newcastle's request that Waller inform him of the debt *not* included in the total of trust indebtedness in 1741. We see that this totaled over £20,000; and why this great sum was not included in the book of debts prepared at this time is nowhere explained. Regardless of whether the debt was old or new, the duke had a huge obligation of over £65,000 for which the trustees were not responsible. Obviously Newcastle's budget efforts were fruitless, since he was apparently spending about £4,000 per annum more than he could cover from his income. (See Figure 1, p. 73.)

All of the figures presented by Mr Waller were evidently studied by one or more of the persons named by Pelham and a recommendation made. They certainly would convince anyone that Newcastle needed money to save himself once again. Newcastle evidently had expected to be able to secure needed money at once but obstructions were soon put in his way. He needed to have his affairs in some order, for he and the duchess were about to depart for Hanover with the king. In an almost defeated vein he wrote to his wife from Claremont:[46]

> I am afraid My Dearest we will not be able to get the Money we want before we go, tho' my Brother should consent, I therefore beg you would send for Mr. Waller, & talk the whole over with him, & know of him, & Sam Burt, what debts are most pressing, that if possible they may be discharged. It will also be necessary to settle the Family that is to go with us, & to give every Servant his particular Business, & also to settle the two families, that are to be left behind, in London and here.

The multitude of problems of statecraft, diplomacy, politics; his anxiety about sea travel; and his longing for sympathetic understanding and support, led Newcastle first to anger and then to suspicion of his brother, as Henry took longer and longer to signify his willingness to aid him. When the duke learned of his brother's price for consent to raising £20,000 on the Nottinghamshire estate, he was deeply hurt, humiliated and angered. This led to one of the greatest altercations between them and touched all of their friends and even the king himself.

Henry Pelham's demand, simply stated, was that Newcastle settle the remainder of his Sussex estate, valued at about £1,500 per annum, upon his children as an equivalent for the money to be raised. This demand was conveyed to Newcastle by the faithful Stone. In return

Stone received, as background for his future negotiations with Pelham, a torrent of explanation, feeling and justification in a very long memorandum.[47] It was the 'bargain' aspect of it which hurt and infuriated the duke. 'The D. of N. could not but be extreamly affected with such a condition,' for it showed Pelham's reluctance to ease the duke in 'his great Distress, without making a Bargain for it' and because it meant that Pelham felt that the duke was to be bought, to consent to a reasonable settlement in favor of his family.

Newcastle believed that he had good grounds for considering his brother's treatment of him as ungenerous. He wrote furiously of his kindnesses to his brother, of which Stone was to remind him. The duke recalled all of his financial help to Pelham: he gave him £1,000 p.a. even before he came of age; at Henry's marriage he gave him £800 more in Sussex from the Newcastle and Pelham estates. 'The D. of N., tho then far from abounding in Money, & encumbered with Debts . . . all of which Mr. P has enjoyed (the free gift of the D. of N.) ever since 1726. The amount far exceeds the value of the £20,000, now proposed to be laid . . . on the Nottinghamshire Estate.' Since Newcastle had helped his brother when he was in need, that kindness now ought to be reciprocated. The duke could simply not resist the temptation to have Stone remind Pelham that he had been a spendthrift earlier. 'The D. of N. thinks it unnecessary to observe that Mr. P. had very soon spent the whole Fortune left him by his Father. This is no otherway material, than as it may be some Excuse, or alleviation with Mr. P. of the D. of N.'s Indiscretion in the Debts he has contracted' —and demonstrates that Newcastle had helped him when he was in need.

The duke went back to the Pelham family settlement of 1741, which, although it had given advantages to him, had conferred even greater ones upon Pelham, since by the re-settlement and the barring of the entails, Pelham's daughters, rather than the Vanes, could inherit the estates. Newcastle felt that Pelham had been a close and demanding person in those arrangements and that he, himself, had received less consideration since the family settlement than he deserved, for 'from that Time Mr. P. bargain'd with him, like a Purchaser, & did not treat him like a Brother.' This may well have been a figment of Newcastle's imagination; Pelham's letters show a continuing concern and affection for his brother in spite of many provocations.

Although Newcastle could dredge up from his memory all favors to his brother and the family, as well as real or imagined slights and failures of affection, he was not so able to face his own weaknesses and actions. 'It is unnecessary to enter into the Causes of the D. of N.'s present Distress. His own Indiscretion to be sure, is the Principal one. ... He has however this comfort, that there is nothing Vicious in it & Folly is all that it can be imputed to.' If the duke had been as specific regarding his own financial life as he was about his brother's, the job of the economic historian would have been easier in this case. 'Indiscretion' and 'Folly' are not adequate causal explanations. The assumption here is that both Stone and Pelham knew well the real causes of Newcastle's plight.

In spite of the duke's emotional catharsis over his brother's demand, he had little choice but to agree to it. He asked Stone to inform Pelham that he was willing to settle the Sussex estate on Lord and Lady Lincoln or, if Pelham intended to marry his second daughter to Mr Thomas Pelham of Stanmer, he was willing to settle it on him. It had always been Newcastle's desire to keep his estates, especially the Sussex lands, in the family; his anger over Pelham's demand was justly due to the manner in which it was made.

Finally, seeing his brother with no financial problems and at the head of the administration, Newcastle in a petulant mood indicated that he might have been aided by Pelham in another way. 'The D. of N. might have expected that in Mr. P's present Situation, His great good Fortune arising singly from his Employments, Equal to that of any of His Predecessors, Mr. P. might have thought of other Means, of making the D. of N. in some degree share that good fortune.' Pelham knew of his brother's refusal to take financial aid from the king, and of his abhorrence of pensioners, but in his anger the duke used this possibility as a weapon against him. He did not wish to remain on bad terms with him, however, and told Stone, 'It is vain to look back and if Mr. P. will henceforward act as a Brother, & really take the D. of N.'s situation into consideration, the D. of N. will endeavor to forget what is past.'[48] Thus ended the long memorandum to Stone; he was placed firmly in the middle of this acrimonious family quarrel. It would be interesting to know what material he used from this memorandum in his conferences with the prime minister. Be that as it may, Newcastle and his duchess had to go off to Hanover with the affair unsettled and the money not in hand.

Newcastle must have found some relief from his hurt and anger in writing the memorandum for Stone's use in his talks with Pelham. On the next day, February 27, 1752, he wrote quite calmly and soberly to

his wife telling her of the 'strong' letter to Stone and of his brother's
expected agreement on the borrowing of the money as a result. But
the immediate need was to quiet things at present and to see that the
crisis situation did not repeat itself in the future:[49]

> and on both these, I must depend upon My Dearest, Mr. Stone,
> & Mr. Murray. . . . Our Hanover journey should be as cheap as
> possible, the expenses of the houses & Repairs settled, & as low
> as can be & in ye course of the summer, the Family, & all
> expenses put upon a low foot, within the Income. . . . In these
> things my whole dependence is upon My Dearest.

The 'crisis of 1752' brought the duke once again to the resolution to
live within his means; but for the doing of it, he placed the responsibility upon others. After all of these years, it would seem obvious that
only the duke himself could prevent over-spending, but this is the one
thing he either could not, or would not, do. He often suggested that
others had to watch his personal financial affairs for him because his
own time was fully taken up in state service. In all fairness, however, he
never blamed another for his 'exceedings' when time after time his
dangerous financial plight became known to him.

We do not know when Stone had a conference with Pelham about
the matter of a new mortgage on the Nottinghamshire estate, but we
do know that Pelham agreed to it and that the needed £20,000 was
borrowed on April 2, 1752. The mortgage was negotiated by Murray;
the money was apparently provided by Sarah Manvillain, spinster,
of St Martin's parish, together with Andrew Stone. Miss Manvillain was
probably a relative of Stone's wife, who was born Hannah Manvillain
and who was also a party to the mortgage, which may possibly suggest
that she was her relative's heir.[50]

While Newcastle was in Hanover with the king, his financial affairs
at home were in the hands of Mr Stone and Mr Waller. With the
mortgage money available, Waller and John Greening, temporarily
acting as Steward of the Household, studied the various accounts and
prepared lists of creditors, both tradesmen and servants, and established
priorities for payment. When this process had been completed Greening went to Mr Stone, who signed a draft on Hoare and Arnold for
£4,228.9s.0d., so that Greening could begin the next day to pay
merchants, whose bills had been examined and approved, the money
due them and the servants their back wages.[51] Of course, the sum
drawn from the bank represented only a very small part of the moneys

owed by the duke, in fact, not a quarter of the London book debt alone.[52]

While his agents at home were attempting to meet the financial emergency, Newcastle's current expenses in Hanover were taken care of by the faithful and able Sam Burt, who accompanied the duke and duchess. He was Steward of the Household and kept careful account of every expense, at least from March 21 to July 9, 1752. During that period he drew £1,258.13s.4d. but spent £1,307.8s.0d., leaving the duke owing him over £48. The major item of expense was the ten 'weekly bills' ending July 9. These totaled £1,013.16s.9d., which shows clearly enough that it cost the duke over £100 per week to live in Hanover, while on official business, yet sizeable expenses continued at home. He and the duchess no doubt entertained members of the Hanoverian court, as well as diplomatic representatives from various German and other courts. Sam Burt did not miss an item which was to his master's advantage, noting in his account even such a small item as: 'By gain in the Exchange at Hanover 0.13.0.'[53]

Newcastle appreciated Burt's long and able service and was deeply grieved when he died suddenly while in Hanover. In a letter to his nephew, Lord Lincoln, Newcastle demonstrated his feelings 'about poor Sam Burt. It goes to my Heart to write about him. I shall never get such an one again; and I don't conceive, what I shall be able to do. He was the best, the Honestest, and most agreeable, and affectionate Servant, that ever was.'[54] Burt had been in a position of responsibility in Newcastle's family for many years, had served as a buffer for creditors, a secretary and family paymaster and was an intimate in many of the duke's affairs. When his accounts were audited following his death they showed that in the period 1742–52 he had received and paid away over £39,000.

The accounts kept by Sam Burt ought to give some idea of where the duke's income was going during this very period, that following the resettlement of the estates in 1741 to the new financial crisis of 1752. These do shed some light but obviously the accounts show what was actually paid, not what was left unpaid. By using Burt's figures, however, plus those given for 'new debts 1741–1751,' we can demonstrate the areas of Newcastle's greatest expenditure during the decade.

Since housekeeping costs were the major item which caused Newcastle constant problems, let us attempt to determine their total for London and Claremont for the years 1742–52, while remembering that other such costs existed for Sussex, although on a much smaller scale, for the duke was not regularly in residence there. Housekeeping costs included food and other groceries, wine, fuel, light and general household supplies, but excluded wages, liveries, repairs, and stable expenses. One cannot be exact in such computations for the various officials of the household and the accountants themselves were not always consistent. This is especially true when we consider the category they so often used, 'Extraordinary Bills,' for this heading makes it impossible to know exactly where money was going. The term referred to the purpose for which the expenditure was made, not for the materials, objects or services which were paid for. Expenditures which were not encountered in normal and daily routines were thus categorized; they included costs for special dinners or entertainments, for major repairs or even for new building. Although the costs of the installation at Cambridge were certainly extraordinary, Mr Burt listed them separately. Bearing all of the difficulties of interpretation in mind, let us attempt to determine housekeeping costs for the decade.

First, we know from Sam Burt's accounts that he actually paid housekeeping costs of £10,558.5s.2d. If we add to this the total of book debts for London and Claremont for approximately the same period, which are found in Mr Waller's abstract of debts, and which total £25,299.9s.0d., we find that housekeeping costs were £35,857.14s.2d. We know that this cannot be the true housekeeping costs for the decade, for Burt had in his accounts extraordinary bills for £11,697. By dividing the total of paid and unpaid costs of £35,000, we see that the household costs would be only a little more than £3,500 annually for the decade; yet even the proposed budget of 1738–9 allotted housekeeping £5,000. Therefore many housekeeping costs must be hidden in the extraordinary category.

There can be little doubt that during the ten-year period, housekeeping and closely related costs, such as stables, liveries, servants' wages and boardwages, were the largest sources of ducal expenditure and the major cause of growing indebtedness. In Burt's accounts direct election costs were a minor item indeed. He listed for the years 1743–50 only £1,102 as 'Paid, and Gave [sic] away, on acct of Elections.'[55]

Burt's death while with the duke and duchess in Hanover and our look into his audited accounts have taken us away from Newcastle's immediate financial problems, as well as from his quarrel with Pelham. The two brothers evidently remained estranged during the whole spring and summer of 1752. We have seen that the additional borrowing was made in April, 1752, apparently with Pelham's consent, but it appears from the correspondence that it was not until September that they were fully reconciled. Newcastle, who had accompanied the king to his hunting lodge, wrote to tell the duchess that he had had a fine letter from his brother, telling him that he approved and asking him how he could have thought he would not do it. Newcastle was extremely pleased and he reported, 'The King afterwards said, I *think you* two agree better at a distance, than *together*, to which I answered, when we *agree in great points, the rest follows.*'[56] Peace was restored between the brothers; this was the last major conflict between them. However, the £20,000 which had been borrowed was but a stop-gap and the duke's affairs continued to worsen while he was in Hanover.

Perhaps it was at Henry Pelham's suggestion that Newcastle requested their good and able friend, the Solicitor General, William

TABLE 19

Net annual income, 1741–51

	£
From Office	5,000
From your estate	6,500
	11,500

Murray, who also sat as M.P. for Newcastle's Yorkshire borough of Boroughbridge, to make a detailed study of his affairs and to suggest a remedy. Murray's study of Newcastle's tangled financial situation was the most thorough and business-like ever made, and the duke actually made an effort to live by his recommendations.

Murray had full access to all of the accounts and abstracts made by Mr Waller, and by the officers of the household and stables, for the whole decade from Michaelmas 1741 to Michaelmas 1751. After what must have been an extended period of study, Murray wrote his long report to Newcastle on November 5, 1752. He began by telling Newcastle that what he had to say made such a sad story, that his head and heart were too full for him to compose the usual polite preface.[57]

First, the duke was given his net annual income during the decade (see Table 19). Second, Murray found that during this period Newcastle had contracted debts to the amount of £66,000, so that he had been spending, as Murray calculated it, at a rate of approximately £17,500, or about £6,600 more annually than he was receiving. Third, Murray pointed out that the interest on this unsecured debt totaled £2,560 p.a., which made his spendable income actually only £8,940 p.a. The £20,000 secured on the Nottinghamshire estate was a permanent debt but the duke was responsible for the interest. Thus he had a personal unsecured debt of £44,000 plus accrued interest. Murray indicated that many of the holders of this unsecured debt had not been paid their interest, and, if they were not paid, could not be expected to remain quiet for much longer.

Murray was brutally frank with Newcastle:

> Out of this annual Sum of £8,940 you are to live and discharge £44,000 during your life. There is no other fund sufficient to satisfy it. There are no Jewells, etc. of value, not so much as Plate that can be sold, for that is entailed, the Timber, proper immediately to be cut, is represented to me not to exceed the value of £1,600.

This was a black prospect for a man nearly sixty years of age who had lived in the greatest magnificence for so many years. How was he to manage to maintain his style of life? How could he, who had a high moral sense, be certain his creditors would not be victimized by his past actions?

The immediate concern was not a moral one; it was how to keep his credit structure from collapsing. Murray was ready with advice and warning. 'The greatest care therefore must be taken to keep the creditors quiet and to do them justice. Upon the first alarm they will certainly distress, & run Races for Priority.' If actions were begun at law, Murray felt that it might add a third to the debt. The really dangerous thing was that if a run began there was no means of stopping it, for there were no resources left which would 'prevent their taking possession of the whole Reel [sic] & Personal Estate,' except the destructive means of selling annuities on Newcastle's life. Even that would not cover his total indebtedness. Bankruptcy was a possibility.

It appears that Murray was purposely attempting to frighten Newcastle by showing the utter seriousness of the situation. Even pathos was called forth by Murray. 'When I saw your affairs at Kew [his home] in this State, I do assure your Grace they drew Tears from my Eyes, & lost me several Nights Sleep. There is not a moment to be lost in taking and executing the necessary Resolution.' There is no doubt that Newcastle was convinced he was nearly lost, for he had great and just faith in the ability and acumen of Murray. Yet how could such resolution be taken and not undermine his position in the ordered scheme of things for one of his rank, position and influence?

The Solicitor General was well aware of the requirements of one in the duke's station and he ranged his arguments like heavy artillery to demolish the nervous Newcastle's reservations about resolutions for retrenchment. Murray tried to convince the duke that he was in a lucky period when he could 'execute such a Resolution so safely and so creditably.' The parts of the rationale which Murray provided give some indicators of the areas of the duke's major costs. First, he pointed out that things at present in the country freed Newcastle 'from Election Servitude, Management and Expense.' Second, affairs at present made the support the duke might acquire 'by a Table in Town not worth Courting.' Third, Murray tried to convince Newcastle that his reputation was already solidly built, 'Your *eclat* for acts of Beneficence & Magnificence has been so dearly bought, your contempt for Money is so universally understood, you can risque no Deminution of Character from a rigid scheme of honourable economy.'

Murray tried to convince Newcastle to admit publicly his financial problems, to laugh at his need to retrench, and thereby he would see that the world would applaud him. He wanted the duke to state proudly that he was determined to discharge all his debts so that 'no man shall suffer by your Generosity but yourself.' By this means, carefully done, the duke could rebuild and strengthen his credit, provide time to extricate himself, and 'in the Intrim make you easier & happier in private than you have been for several years & in publick add a Lustre to yr Honour, Justice & firmness of Mind.' Murray provided a truly ringing rationale to strengthen the duke's resolution; but what was more material was the means to accomplish it.

Obviously there were only two means available to Newcastle and he did not need an expert to point them out: lessen his expenses, and, as Murray stated it, 'Enlarge your Fund,' that is, increase the produce of his estates. Murray did not have sufficient information at hand to make suggestions about increasing landed income but he did know that the duke's farms were under-rented. 'I am convinced, that by boldly striking off many unnecessary Deductions, and by letting the Farms at what they will very well bear, great additions may be made to your Revenue.' It is doubtful if Murray had the knowledge or experience necessary in this area, to know how difficult and full of hazards his suggested policy was.

Murray was well equipped, nevertheless, by both knowledge and experience to propose a budget which would help Newcastle to reduce his expenses. He had all of the accounts of the various departments in Newcastle's establishment and so knew current costs. He also knew the duke's spendable income; it was his task to see that the one matched the other. Murray prepared an elaborate and detailed 'Scheme' for Newcastle: in it the noble household was truly dissected and the current and proposed expenses clearly seen.

The most radical of Murray's proposals was the first, which must have taken the duke's breath away. It was that he actually live on £6,000 a year 'hard money.' No more credit buying. Since the duke had been spending at the rate of £17,600 per year, this proposal meant that Murray had to find about £11,000 to cut from the annual expenditures. Such economy obviously could not be accomplished without a great alteration in the duke's style of life. This factor probably accounts for Murray's frightening account of Newcastle's situation and his careful development of the rationale for retrenchment. The Solicitor General probably did not know the duke had already received, more than thirty-five years before, fervent admonitions to retrench from his old friend, Bishop Bowers; that he had attempted to live on one budget in the 1720s and still another in the 1730s. Alas, the duke's ability to change his way of life was practically non-existent.

Nevertheless, Murray was a veritable cost accountant as he looked into expenses. He made proposals on every head. He felt that expenses of the stables could be greatly reduced by having the needed service performed on contract. Fire and candle could be reduced from £1,200 to £800 per annum—twelve wax candles were being burned each day, winter and summer. The cost of managing the woods at Claremont was too high at £700 p.a.; he felt it could be done for half that amount or less. Servants were far too numerous, 'Servants are the great Load because they are Springs of Riot, Waste & Mismanagement.' Buying in bulk for cash would save a great deal. Murray felt that household expenses of every sort ought to cost no more than £50 per week.

Murray also proposed that all accounts be balanced weekly and that proper credit be given at market prices for the produce of both the home farm and the duke's gardens. He proposed that the duke and the duchess each 'should have a little book ... in which should be entered weekly in one Line the week's expense & in another the Saving or Excess upon the £50 a week,' and that they should not invite company or entertain if it would cause an excess. Murray assured the duke that such care would take only a minute a week.

It was also suggested that the household be reduced, at least temporarily. The household could get along without a confectioner, a cook and a maître d'hôtel for a time. Mr Greening, who was an old and able servant, could manage the family if he were armed with full authority, even to discharging servants, for there were many bad customs to break. Both Murray and Stone had talked with Greening about it. Although he was reluctant, he had agreed to do so for one year, 'from duty and affection' to the duke.

Above all, the accounts must be properly kept and must cover all items, except for the duke's clothes, and for his pocket money, which included expenditures for charities, pensions, and donations, all of which, Murray felt, needed regulation. Again Murray emphasized, the duke must use cash, and not credit, in his purchases, for it 'is certain £50 ready money will buy as much as £100 credit as before.'

Murray's detailed analysis of the costs of Newcastle's establishments in London and at Claremont makes interesting reading. For the twin items of 'Fewel [sic] and light' for the two seats, that is for sea coals, 'Scotch coals,' faggots, candles, lamps, etc., the duke was paying £1,372.18s.2d. p.a., but Murray felt that the same could be reduced to £843 by using ready money.[58] Certain charges could not be reduced, for example, taxes. In London the taxes totaled £119 in all for land tax, wheel tax for his coach, poor rate, window tax, and the like. For Claremont the land, window and poor tax came to £97 p.a. and the tithes to £35. Other fixed costs of the household could easily be overlooked but were essential. For London, lamplighting at Newcastle House in Lincoln's Inn Fields, which was a notorious haunt for unruly characters, was £53.5s.10d. p.a., while Claremont cost only £10 on this head. The water supply, 'new River water,' added £10; scavengers nearly £2; and 'watering the streets,' which presumably meant cleaning them about his town house, cost the duke five guineas a year. The costs of supporting the church were duly noted: 'Piew [sic] rent £4.10.0; Evening Lecturer £2.2.0 and Easter Offering, £2.0.0.' These costs, along with the duchess's pin money of £600 p.a., came to nearly £1,000 per year. One in Newcastle's position was expected to support local schools, hospitals, etc., where he had interests; on this head the duke expended in Lewes, Seaford, Brighton and London £377.10s.0d. p.a. Murray noted that these items required review but they could not be eliminated. Thus in all, for essential expenses in London, Claremont, taxes, pin money and charities, the budget had to carry over £1,300.

It was a favorite theme of masters, that their servants were a source of great cost, waste, confusion and petty thievery. Murray was convinced that this was the case in Newcastle's household, so he made a close study of both numbers and costs. Let us consider the servant situation for both Newcastle House and Claremont in 1752: first Newcastle House, its servants and their salaries (see Table 20).

The servants in Newcastle House, twenty-two in number from Greening down to the lowly platemaid, cost the duke £738.10s.0d. a year. Murray did not attempt to cut here, but simply recommended that the apothecary be dismissed, since he held a sinecure worth £300 p.a. from the duke.[59]

Claremont, upon which Newcastle had lavished so much love and expense since the early days of Vanbrugh and Kent, and where he both relaxed and entertained, required a great staff (see Table 21). Claremont's servants, fifteen in number, which was probably close to minimal for the needs of the seat, cost the duke over £200 a year. Murray could only suggest that the gamekeeper might be let go.[60]

Thus, the Duke and Duchess of Newcastle employed thirty-seven servants in their 'family' for Newcastle House and Claremont at an annual cost of £986.12s.0d. Salary was a large item of expense, but only in relation to Newcastle's reduced income. It alone would not account, directly, for much of the drain on his resources. Indirectly, however, through costs of maintenance, through waste, pilferage or perquisites, the cost of the servants might have been several times higher. It should be noted that Murray's study did not include Sussex, where two more seats were maintained with a small permanent staff at all times. The costs of these seats were paid for by the Sussex steward out of his collection, but we know that the profits of that estate were inadequate for the purpose and had to be supplemented by Newcastle from other sources. Because of the constant debt on that estate, we know that he could not actually cover these costs; it would have been wise for the situation there to have come under Murray's eye.

Murray's incisive study covering a decade of Newcastle's private financial affairs was important, for it provided what the duke and others had often claimed he lacked—knowledge of the true state of his finances. The assumption made by the duke's friends was that

TABLE 20

Cost of servants at Newcastle House, 1752

London Position Men	Salary per Annum
	£ s. d.
Groom of the Chambers	25 0 0
Cook	30 0 0
Valet de Chambre	25 0 0
Usher of the Hall & Butler	25 0 0
3 footmen: £8,8,7	23 0 0
Porter	8 0 0
Chairman	30 0 0
Chairman	30 0 0
Drudge	10 0 0
Housewatchman	18 5 0
Street Watchman	18 5 0
Apothecary	100 0 0
Greening [John]	200 0 0
Liveries 'for about 7'	140 0 0
	682 10 0

Women	
	£ s. d.
Housekeeper [Mrs Twells]	20 0 0
Housemaids—4 at £6	24 0 0
Kitchenmaid	6 0 0
Platemaid	6 0 0
	56 0 0

TABLE 21

Cost of servants at Claremont, 1752

Claremont Position Men	Salary per Annum		
	£ s. d.		
Wm. Swaine	30 0 0		
Gamekeeper	14 0 0		
Porter	14 0 0		
Flower Gardener	18 0 0		
Drudge	12 0 0		
Brewer	20 0 0		
Watchman (when the Duke was there)	9 2 0		
		117 2 0	

Women; other staff and expenses

	£ s. d.		
H. Greening—Housekeeper	20 0 0		
Housemaid—3 at £6	18 0 0		
Laundrymaid	6 0 0		
Boardwages	18 5 0		
Milkmaid	5 0 0		
Cowboy	5 0 0		
		96 10 0 [*sic*, 72 5 0]	
Lodge Porter	19 10		
Livery for Gamekeeper	15 00	34 10 0	
		248 2 0 [*sic*, 223 17 0]	

once he knew his true condition, he would establish his expenditures on a rational basis. As had been indicated many times, however, there was little ground for this easy assumption. The only way in which his vast expenditure could be effectively curtailed would be from insufficient credit or lack of additional estates or property which could be mortgaged. We have seen that in this period he added a mortgage debt of £20,000 to his remaining estates, which represented almost the end of his uncommitted resources.

Murray, however, was a rational man in both his personal affairs and his career; and he assumed that his benefactor and friend was, as well. He appealed to Newcastle to change his ways, not only upon the basis of knowledge of his affairs, but upon his public reputation and status and his personal happiness. Murray's analysis of Newcastle's household costs was masterful and indicates their centrality as a source of the duke's problems; his suggestion of a drastic reduction of such costs to £6,000 p.a. was very bold. By such means he convinced the duke that great care was essential in money matters for the future, if Newcastle were to save himself. As we shall see, the duke seriously attempted to follow his guidelines by practicing some economy.

In this chapter we have looked at Newcastle's financial life covering fourteen years; it began with one budget and ended with another. In 1738 he proposed to live on £12,500 p.a., and in 1752 was expected to live on £6,000. The establishment of the trust in 1738 lifted from Newcastle's shoulders a great burden of debt, and the family settlement enabled it to be paid, so he had indeed a new financial beginning in 1738, and was saved again by the 1741 arrangements. Our problem has been to see how he managed his financial affairs following his near escape from catastrophe, to see if the settlement of 1741 actually made him easy for the rest of his life, as he confidently expected.

The decade had seen the consolidation of the political power of the Pelhams and had brought Newcastle himself much success in politics and diplomacy, to say nothing of his personal satisfaction in the Chancellorship of Cambridge University. However, his various successes had cost much money, as we have demonstrated. Simply stated, he was either unable, or unwilling, to curtail his expenses to fit his reduced income; at the end of the decade he found himself at the brink once again. At this time he could save himself from going over the precipice only by using his own meager resources. This fact necessitated both the Murray analysis of his financial situation and the duke's resolution to abide by the new scheme. It was an attempt to reduce

his expenses, so that he might have funds to diminish the personal
debt he had created during that decade.

NOTES

1 Add. MSS. 33138, ff. 177v–8.
2 Add. MSS. 33691, f. 347, Waller to Newcastle, London, September 10,
   1738.
3 Add. MSS. 33137, f. 530.
4 Add. MSS. 33138, f. 1.
5 Add. MSS. 33073, f. 129, Newcastle to duchess, Bishopstone, September 11,
   1738.
6 *Ibid.*
7 *Ibid.*, f. 128, Newcastle to duchess, Bishopstone, September 2, 1738.
8 *Ibid.*, f. 128v.
9 *Ibid.*, f. 524.
10 East Sussex Record Office, Sayer MSS. unfolioed, J. A. Waller to John
   Collier, London, January 15, 1740.
11 Add. MSS. 33073, ff. 137–8, Newcastle to duchess, Claremont, April 27,
   1740.
12 *Ibid.*
13 *Ibid.*, f. 138v.
14 Add. MSS. 33138, f. 33v.
15 Add. MSS. 33065, f. 420, James Waller to Newcastle, July 14, 1741.
16 *Ibid.*, f. 425.
17 *Ibid.*, f. 426.
18 Add. MSS. 33138, ff. 159–60.
19 *Ibid.*, f. 178.
20 Add. MSS. 33066, ff. 16–19, October 13, 1744.
21 *Ibid.*, f. 29, trustees to Newcastle, April 23, 1746.
22 *Ibid.*, f. 30, trustees to Newcastle, July 10, 1746.
23 Sayer MSS., unfolioed, John Collier to Sam Burt, November 1, 1746.
24 *Ibid.*, Sam Burt to John Collier, November 18, 1746.
25 Add. MSS. 33066, f. 46, John Greening to Newcastle, Claremont, August
   10, 1747.
26 *Ibid.*, f. 107, Mawhood to Newcastle, January 5, 1748.
27 *Ibid.*, f. 56, John Greening to Newcastle, Newcastle House, June 17, 1748.
28 *Ibid.*, f. 87, Waller to Newcastle, September 1, 1748.
29 Add. MSS. 33158, Burt's Account, 1742–52.
30 Paget Toynbee and Leonard Whibley (eds), *The Correspondence of Thomas
   Gray* (Oxford, 1935), I, 322–4, Thomas Gray to Thomas Wharton,
   Cambridge, August 8, 1749.
31 The Ode is found bound in a volume *Poems, London, etc., 1747–1752*, in
   the British Museum.
32 *Gray Correspondence*, I, 322–4.
33 *Gentleman's Magazine*, July, 1749, p. 328.

34 Arthur Gray, *Cambridge University: An Episodal History* (London, 1927), p. 229.
35 Add. MSS. 5832, ff. 231v–2. Copied from the *Cambridge Chronicle*, July, 1749.
36 *Gray Correspondence*, I, 322–4.
37 Walpole/Mann Corr. IV, 71, to Mann, Sunday, June 25, 1749, O.S.
38 Add. MSS. 33074, f. 4, Newcastle to duchess, Clare Hall, July 2, 1749.
39 Add. MSS. 33074, f. 5, Newcastle to duchess, Clare Hall, July 4, 1749, one o'clock.
40 Add. MSS. 33158, ff. 68–9, Sam Burt's Accounts; Add. MSS. 5852, f. 197v, Dr Richardson's Collections Relating to the University.
41 Add. MSS. 5832, f. 144. As reported in the *Cambridge Chronicle*, Saturday, March 12, 1763. The winners of the Chancellor's Medals from 1752 to 1765 are also listed.
42 Hoare, Money Ledger, 1743–73, f. 16.
43 Add. MSS. 33066, f. 255, Andrew Stone to Newcastle, n.d. [1751].
44 Add. MSS. 33138, ff. 341–1v, Newcastle Memorandum to James Waller, Newcastle House, December 20, 1751.
45 *Ibid.*, f. 343.
46 Add. MSS. 33074, f. 137, Newcastle to duchess, February 9, 1752.
47 Add. MSS. 33066, ff. 258–67, February 26, 1752.
48 *Ibid.*, ff. 265–5v.
49 Add. MSS. 33074, ff. 138–8v, Newcastle to duchess, Newcastle House, February 27, 1752.
50 Sussex Archaeological Society, XXVII (1890), No. 438 Indenture, April 2, 1752.
51 Add. MSS. 33066, f. 268, John Greening to Newcastle, Newcastle House, April 10, 1752.
52 Add. MSS. 33138, f. 343.
53 Add. MSS. 33158, Sam Burt's Accounts, March 21–July 9, 1752.
54 Add. MSS. 33066, f. 307, Newcastle to Lord Lincoln, Hanover, July 29, 1752 O.S.
55 Add. MSS. 33158, f. 84.
56 Add. MSS. 33074, ff. 139–40, Newcastle to duchess, Gohide, September 16, 1752.
57 Add. MSS. 33066, f. 339 *et seq.*
58 *Ibid.*, f. 358.
59 *Ibid.*, f. 350.
60 *Ibid.*, f. 351 *et seq.*

CHAPTER 5

THE LAST DECADE OF POWER AND THE LAST BUDGETS, 1752–62

The final decade in Newcastle's active political life brought both tragedy and joy. The death of his younger brother, Henry Pelham, upon whom he had depended and with whom he had yet been in rivalry, was a tragedy for him. That loss surely lessened the joy of reaching the pinnacle of political power in the kingdom. The exercise of power would have to be shared all too soon with one of the most gifted and most difficult of eighteenth-century Englishmen, William Pitt. If the king exclaimed when he learned of Pelham's death, 'Now I shall have no more peace,' Newcastle might well have made a similar statement. Behind the turmoil of public life the ageing duke was burdened with continuing concern for his personal finances.

The masterful study and analysis of Newcastle's situation made by William Murray gave him not only knowledge of his real situation but also a program to follow. What the duke needed now was the resolution to put into operation the new plan; but this was slow to take place. In January, 1753, Murray wrote to the duke from Lincoln's Inn Fields that a lie was being put around by his enemies that his creditors had foreclosed on him. As an example of the rumors being spread, Murray told the duke, 'Among people of Fashion it was said, that his chariot was seiz'd, and prov'd by his being seen going to Court in a chair.' The duke was always concerned about his enemies, real or imagined, and Murray warned him that the same sort of rumor might be started by his opponents, 'and if ever an alarm can be sounded among the creditors, so as to make the least appearance of Uneasiness, the authors of the last lye may buy up Debts in borrowed names, and begin the run.'[1] He also informed the duke that small debts left unpaid, often to small merchants, caused real hardship, as well as magnified damage to his financial reputation; 'the less the Sum the worse the non-payment is.' The able Scotsman did not fear to tell the duke that some did not believe him capable of following a budget:[2]

> Another thing his Grace will not wonder, if there should be in some persons some little Diffidence at first setting out, whether he will obstinately pursue a Plan of this kind. Whereas, if there was the Experience, but of a year, that he is absolutely determined to do it, and after that, any suddain unforseen emergency, or Distress would happen, Persons might be induced to lend any Moderate sum, for which there may be immediate occasion, in Confidence of his Perseverance in it.

In other words, the duke was told that his reputation was well known by persons of means and that only by actually living on a budget could he refurbish his image.

Murray again urged the necessity for having and following an 'entire Plan' so that each expense could be seen in relation to the whole. It is obvious from his questions that Newcastle had not yet begun to retrench. Murray asked if a plan was settled about the number of servants to be retained. Was a resolution taken about pensions and annuities? About expenses relating to elections? Finally he indicated that he had seen no materials which indicated that the duke had taken any measures to increase the revenues from his estates.[3]

While Newcastle was in Hanover with the king, Murray had, upon his own initiative and without informing the trustees or Mr Waller, sought to reduce the interest on the trust and personal debt. Miss Manvillain and Stone, who were creditors for £20,000, readily agreed; but the first to join the plan was Mr Hoare, who held over £15,000 of the duke's debt. The interest on at least the major portion of the duke's personal debt was reduced from 4 to $3\frac{1}{2}$ per cent and the saving made thereby was to go into the duke's pocket.[4]

Once committed to the budget, Newcastle was eager to know how well he had been able to abide by it and had been informally told that he was close to it. However, at the end of six months it appeared that he was exceeding it somewhat and this gave him very great concern. He reported to the duchess, 'I have flattered myself much upon what first appeared, but I agree with my Dearest, we must & we *will* reduce our Expenses.'[5] The duke understood well Murray's intention, that they live on £6,000 per year and that £5,000 be used to pay debts and interest. He had been informed that he was exceeding the scheme by between £400 and £600 for the half year, but the ever-sanguine duke was sure that much more than £2,500 of debts and interest had been paid off in the same period. He was unable to believe the computations of the experts he had hired, for he felt that his estate was worth, 'moderately speaking,' £2,000 more than had been stated. Unfortunately for him, it was not.

Murray's continual harping at Newcastle, and his frequent questions, finally had some effect, for in August, 1753, the duke made an effort to study his own financial condition. In a fashion typical of his method of business in affairs of state, he wrote a double-columned memorandum for his own use. He introduced his study: 'I have looked over the abstracts of the several accounts, and I find the following sums have been paid, since my return from Hanover in the end of November last.' The duke was reviewing his finances for a nine-month period and he was concerned to learn several things. First, he wanted to know how well he was living within the budget. Second, he was projecting ahead to what the condition might be at the end of a full year. Third, he was noting how much old debt had been paid off during his absence and what would most likely be paid off by the end of the year. It is difficult to understand these notations of Newcastle's, for he jumbled together past and future, paid and unpaid obligations.[6]

While in Hanover attending George II, the duke and duchess had attempted to minimize their expenses at home. The duke was surprised that these expenses in London, at Claremont and in Sussex made 'a very considerable article' of between £2,000 and £3,000. This sum apparently had not been paid. He noted, as well, that he had overdrawn an account with a Mr Nester by £1,300 while he was abroad. The duke wrote with seeming pride and determination when he came to current expenses for both London and Claremont, 'This [item] is, and has been constantly, & regularly paid . . . even provisions laid in for Claremont, such as live stock, feeds, etc.' Yet even with such unusual cash payments, he still exceeded Mr Murray's scheme in the household area by over £800. Nevertheless he felt that, all in all, the 'exceedings' of the scheme would be only about £1,000.[7]

The duke was forever hopeful when he thought of the payment of debts. He noted that £2,500 of old debt had been paid off while he was away. He was certain that by Christmas another £4,000 could be paid off by sales of timber in Sussex. He added a mysterious allegation, 'at a moderate computation the old debt will be further discharged by Christmas next £2,000.' Thus he computed that £8,500 of debt would be paid off and that he had received from a source he did not specify, perhaps the trust, a sum of £5,000 towards the discharging of other debt, making in all a total debt reduction of £13,500 for the year ending Christmas, 1753.

It is difficult to be exact in indicating where Newcastle stood at this time, for he himself was inexact. However, we can take him at his word and see without any doubt that he was living beyond Murray's budget. He guessed that he would be over it in the housekeeping area by about £1,000; he noted that his expenses while in Hanover had been nearly £3,000; and he overdrew one account by £1,300. Thus he admitted to bills which were no doubt unpaid of approximately £5,300; Murray had planned for the duke to live on a budget of £11,500, with £5,000 of that sum earmarked for debt payment, but Newcastle was far from being able to do so in 1753.

Throughout the remainder of 1753 the duke was conscious of his difficult condition and carefully noted income from the trust and from his land stewards which would be available for debt reduction. He did not overlook household expenses, for he described a newly employed chef as 'a new *Hervé*, good looking, young, dependable but no appearance of a coxcomb or of one who thinks highly of himself. . . . I have preached *economy*, as absolutely necessary, and I think he is prepared for it.'[8] He instructed the young man that he must govern his area of the household and requested that he prepare a bill of fare for each day. The new chef was a Frenchman who had come over with Lord Stormont, who recommended him.

There is some evidence that Newcastle actually considered raising rents in Nottinghamshire in return for money he had laid out there. In 1753 Job Staunton Charlton, his chief election agent there and his manager for Newark,[9] who also acted as receiver of trust rents, instructed the tenants at Stockwich, through Mr Bristowe, the actual steward, to be prepared to pay more. The method proposed was unique and indicates clearly that Mr Charlton knew little of the give-and-take which was habitually engaged in by tenants and stewards in negotiations for rent increases. The tenants were to be told that the duke expected either a fine or an advanced rent for a lease of twenty years. Each tenant was to make his proposal for the new rent, which would be examined, and 'if reasonable they will have first choice, if not they will be discharged' and the farm let to the best bidder. Each tenant was to be asked when the proposal was made, 'Is this your best?' Then if the tenants at Stockwich were discharged when their terms were refused, they were not to plead that they had not had the customary notice six months before.[10] Mr Bristowe must have known that this was not the country way of doing things and there is no extant evidence that rents there were, in fact, raised.

Late 1753 was one of the most active periods for Newcastle in his concern for his personal affairs. He kept account of each hundred pounds which came in both from the office and from the stewards and noted his balances at Hoare's. He even superintended the payment of current creditors, for he told the duchess that he intended to give Mr Greening a large sum, to assign more for his Private Account and '£200 for Farmer, the Plumber . . . £400 for Symond's executors, & £400 for Morse, the Malster [sic, Maltster].' As usual he asked his wife to have the year's accounts made up and divided properly into categories. The duke even noted that he had lost small sums by gambling with the ladies at court but that the sums were of no importance.[11]

Perhaps the reason for Newcastle's unusual attention to the detail of his affairs was that he had learned that his chief accountant, Mr Waller, had been performing his duties irresponsibly. Both the duke and Mr Murray had become discontented with him and rightly so, for his accounts were done only perfunctorily and incompletely after 1750 or 1752. He had an unusually high salary, which apparently ended in 1752 after his receipt of a lucrative sinecure, for Murray noted this fact and said that he ought to obey orders even though he was receiving no allowance from Newcastle. Waller evidently continued to perform inadequately and was dismissed in September or early October, 1753. In his place the duke hired James Postlethwayt as an accountant for both trust and non-trust estates and later had him added as a trustee for his estates.[12] Mr Postlethwayt's salary was £200 per annum.

It was essential for the new accountant to know the status of Newcastle's affairs, which estates were in trust and which were not, as well as the names of the collectors or receivers of rents. The duke himself wrote to Postlethwayt on October 12, 1753, to give him the information. The collection of the Nottinghamshire estates, both in and out of trust, was in the hands of Mr Bristowe in one area and of Mr Spraggins in another. Still more lands, all in trust at or near 'Notts. town,' were collected by Mr Clay. In Lincolnshire, where Mr Dobbs collected, all lands were sold for the use of the trust except for some leasehold estate. In Yorkshire the moneys were collected by Mr Wilkinson, and none of the estates was in trust. In Middlesex the Clare Market estate was collected by Mr Hammond and was not a part of the trust. Other estates were largely sold.[13]

Postlethwayt was also informed by the duke of the method used to pay the great amounts of interest due on his personal debt each year. He was told by Newcastle that the interest on Mr Stone's £20,000 was now at 3½ per cent p.a., although it had previously been at 4 per cent, and that the payment of it came from Mr Wilkinson's collection in Yorkshire and from Mr Spraggins's in Nottinghamshire. The interest on the debt held by Hoare, which then stood at £13,000 according to the duke, was paid by Mr Bristowe from his Nottinghamshire collection.[14]

Newcastle explained the situation in Sussex to his new accountant by telling him that he had no accounts of the lands there from Mr Waller but that Mr William Mitchell of Lewes had been appointed sole steward and agent and that he was to make up his accounts with Postlethwayt. Then the duke explained to him, 'The greatest part of this estate was my Father's. I settled £1500 p.a. on my brother at his marriage. I added £300 p.a. out of the Pelham estate and settled £500 of the Newcastle estate in this county on my brother and later sold £300 p.a. to him.'[15] The duke did not indicate the annual income of the lands he retained but it was small, as we shall soon see. Thus Mr Postlethwayt had from the duke himself an explanation of his total situation. In addition, the new accountant proved to be a careful and a studious man.

Newcastle had in all of his concerns, public and private, advisers in plenty. Andrew Stone served as a confidant in both areas of Newcastle's life at this time; and as we have seen, William Murray was also coming more and more into the same role. Newcastle attended an opera rehearsal at Lord Holderness's one evening and liked it. He informed his wife, 'My Dearest would have laughed to see me Coquetting with Visconti, Frazey, and a little Muscovite singer.' However, after all of his fun he faced a long conference with Stone, 'who seemed graver than usual.' He was probably dealing with his financial problems, in which they were both active at this time.[16]

The duke continued his personal interest in his financial affairs as 1753 moved on. The relative tranquility in political life probably made more time available to him, but the seriousness of his situation as outlined by Murray was perhaps a greater motivation. Even with all of his help he had trouble understanding the estate accounts. John Dobbs, who collected rents in Lincolnshire, had sent his accounts to the duke but

Newcastle replied, 'I own, I don't very well understand them—what money you have in your hands, and what you propose to receive, the next collection, and whether the £1000 ... you intend to remit ... is old arrear, or Part of, or all the Rents, due last year, which are now to be received.' He ordered Dobbs to send all money and all accounts to him, 'and I should be glad, that your Son would come to Town, in order to explain any Matters, that may not appear, upon the Face of the Accounts.'[17] The duke was tightening up on his stewards and was demanding prompt remission of moneys due to him. One can sympathize with the duke in his inability to make sense out of some of the accounts. They always balance, but this does not mean that they tell the viewer all he needs to know, as the duke noticed.

Newcastle's life seemed to be in a condition where his affairs could be managed intelligently by late 1753. He knew his situation and was actually attempting to manage his finances with the help of the duchess and others. In public life the Pelham brothers held firm control and the king was satisfied. Newcastle's relations with his brother had remained harmonious following the settlement of their differences over the duke's financial plight and the family settlement. Probably for one of the few times in his life, he had approached by early 1754 a condition of security and general well-being.

This equilibrium was to be short-lived: on the 6th of March, 1754, Henry Pelham died unexpectedly. Newcastle's love for his only brother was deep and his dependency real. His death was a terrible blow; Newcastle retired to his home for days to give full vent to his grief. While the duke grieved, Lord Hardwicke made efforts to guide public affairs and to see to the necessary reshuffling of public offices. It was obvious that Newcastle would be first minister, but leadership in the Commons presented great problems. The duke wished to lead and to control in both policy and personnel, but there were few able men who would accept these conditions and work under him.

Our major concern is not with the duke's political problems with Fox or Pitt, or with his leadership of the country as it approached the crisis of the Seven Years' War, but with his personal financial condition. How did the death of his brother and the change of office from Secretary of State for the Northern Department to First Commissioner of the Treasury affect his income? Newcastle was officially replaced by the Earl of Holderness as Secretary of State on March 23, 1754; thus the political negotiations had taken nearly three weeks to complete, following Pelham's death on the 6th. The duke had reached the pinnacle of political power, but it meant a lessening of his salary.

As First Lord of the Treasury the duke's official salary was only £1,480 per annum, while that of his former office was £5,780 p.a.—a vast reduction and one which the duke could in no way afford to contemplate. It was usual, however, for the king to add to the traditional salary, and this George II did for him. However, it was not until July 2 that the king authorized the increase, no doubt retroactive to the date of the duke's appointment to the new office. Newcastle proudly wrote to the duchess, 'Things went so well this morning in the closet that the king ordered me in the best manner imaginable to put down 1000 guineas every quarter for myself, which with the profits of the Treasury, makes clear 5680 pds. pr. ann., 100 only short of the Secretary's office.'[18] These comments make perfectly clear his careful attention to his official income, for without an adequate salary he would have been in immediate peril of financial collapse.

Part of the trouble in which the duke found himself can be blamed on his former chief accountant, Mr James Waller. Waller's accounts made it nearly impossible to tell the actual state of his affairs, whether all moneys due had been paid, and whether or not dishonesty had been practiced by stewards, receivers or other agents. In 1754 Newcastle began to employ an able solicitor, Mr John Sharpe of Lincoln's Inn, to assist and to advise him in his personal affairs. The duke was so pleased with Sharpe that he decided that he and Postlethwayt should be added as joint trustees for his estates. The Court of Chancery decreed their inclusion on December 21, 1754.[19] Sharpe was very grateful to the duke and promised to work hard and to 'supervise the whole' of the duke's affairs. Under the duke and Sharpe, Mr Postlethwayt would serve as chief accountant or auditor. Sharpe was complimentary about Postlethwayt's abilities but felt that at times he was too busy to do full justice to the duke's affairs. It appears from the correspondence that Sharpe kept a tight rein on the men responsible for the duke's local affairs, whom he termed 'country stewards,' and saw to it that their accounts were rendered when due. It also appears that following a survey and valuation of part of the Nottingham estate by the steward, Mr Mason, the estate was let at an advanced rent. The possibly advanced rent totaled £1,184.13s.8d. above the old one but we do not know if the steward actually was able to negotiate all of the advances with the tenants.[20] Mr Sharpe also set out to reduce the cost of management for the Nottinghamshire estate, for it appears that the former collector, Mr John Bristowe, had been wasteful and perhaps dishonest.[21] Slackness in the management of the estates was at least lessened after 1754; it is apparent that Sharpe, Postlethwayt and Job Staunton Charlton were co-operating in the endeavor.

There can be little doubt about the improved management of the various estates; but the perilous condition of Newcastle's finances could not be cured overnight. In fact it appears that his financial condition worsened after he became prime minister. His new eminence undoubtedly increased his costs, for he did even more entertaining than usual and received no special financial support for it, while his salary was slightly less than formerly. Such expenses made it an absurdity to attempt to live on a budget; no more is heard of 'Mr. Murray's Scheme.' To Newcastle the expectations from one of his rank and station were more important than financial solvency. That the duke enjoyed the necessity of entertaining, there can be no doubt. John Greening, who now acted as steward of the household, reported on an unusual dinner in 1755. 'My Lord Duke had a Grand Company at Dinner here on Monday, there were fifty-two Noblemen, the most I ever saw here at one Dinner and his Grace was pleased to say he never saw a Dinner better Served and everything as well as possible.'[22]

We know that the major part of the indebtedness accumulated by the duke earlier was now the responsibility of the trust but that the 'new Debt' he had amassed was his own responsibility. For example, when in need of cash in 1751 he had mortgaged his beloved Claremont to Messrs Hoare and Arnold for £15,000.[23] The duke was probably paying $3\frac{1}{2}$ per cent p.a. on this sum after 1753, but by 1756 the bankers came to feel that the security for the loan was insufficient. If the duke would add to the security, they would be willing to reduce the interest rate to 3 per cent. John Sharpe could not prevail upon them to be easy regarding the security; they were very firm with him, stating that 'If they couldn't get a better and more effectual security given them for the money, they would take the proper Methods to get it paid in.' They were sorry to have to act this way but they were adamant in rejecting Sharpe's arguments, replying tartly that if such were true, that Claremont was sufficient security, he would 'be under no difficulty in getting it from some other friend.'[24] Thus the agent of the First Lord of the Treasury was effectively rebuffed by the bankers, Newcastle House was added as additional security, and perhaps the rate of interest on the loan was reduced.[25] Mr Sharpe died in 1756 and Newcastle had to rely on the advice of Stone, Postlethwayt, Charlton and others. He eventually employed Mr Edward Woodcock as his solicitor and adviser, while more responsibility at the center of his affairs was given to Mr John Twells.

In September, 1758, Newcastle was once again disturbed by the condition of his affairs and initiated a study of them by Charlton and Mr Postlethwayt. He wrote a long memorandum which he entitled, 'Instructions for Mr. Charlton assisted by Mr. Postlethwaite,' which provides a full picture of the duke's concerns at that time. He began by giving the rationale for the study: 'Finding for some time past, that my affairs in general, but more particularly those of my Family & Houses in Town and Country, were again going into great Disorder for want of proper Care and Inspection,' he needed their help. He wanted Mr Charlton, 'in whose ability and care . . . I have an entire confidence,' to come to Claremont from his home at Staunton Hall, Nottinghamshire, so that Mr Charlton, along with Mr Postlethwayt, could review the duke's affairs in order that abuses could be rectified and the finances so regulated that they would not go into disorder again.[26]

The duke wished to know from the two men the general state of his affairs, that is, the produce of his estate and office, the debt remaining and the debt paid, as well as current debts, under proper headings for London, Claremont and Sussex. He wanted them to receive all outstanding bills for every area in which building had been taking place. Once all of this was finished he wanted them to make new regulations for every area, 'in order to prevent the like Inconviencies [sic] for the future . . . that being under regular and constant Inspection, I may know every Branch of Expenses Weekly, or at farthest Monthly,' so that he would know to whom he was to go for an accounting and who should receive orders from himself or the duchess.

The sad condition of his domestic affairs the duke blamed on Mr Greening, who 'has for some years past wholly undertaken the Management of my affairs' as they related to areas covered in the instructions. We know that Greening reluctantly agreed to serve as Steward of the Household following Sam Burt's death in 1752 with the understanding that it would be temporary, for he retained his former responsibilities at Claremont. Additional responsibilities were heaped upon him, probably following Sharpe's death in 1756, until he became in effect the man of business as Newcastle noted. The duke was conscious of these burdens. 'I am sorry to observe that either from too much business, or some other uneasiness [?] unknown to me; they have been for some time past so totally neglected & unconstrued [?], that I am determined to put them into a new Method.' The Greenings, both father and son, had been in his service for many years and this is the only criticism in the papers. However, the duke did not suggest that he be dismissed, but only that his responsibilities be limited to some specific areas at Claremont, that he continue to have 'a general Inspection of the Whole,' and that he carry all accounts to be audited and passed to Mr Postlethwayt every quarter in the normal manner. In other words, the duke suggested that he continue to be the man of business, if Mr Charlton should agree. The duke's suggestion to Charlton pointedly demonstrates the duke's fairmindedness, as well as his faith in the rectitude of his old servant.

In order to lessen Greening's work Newcastle suggested that Tom Perry be appointed Steward of the Household along with 'a *proper person* to assist him in keeping his accounts.' It seems strange to appoint a person to this important post who did not know how to keep or check accounts, for the duke proceeded to define the man's responsibilities and they deal largely with this very area: he was to receive household accounts from all departments, including those of the housekeepers at Newcastle House and Claremont; check all casual disbursements for the family; keep account of wages of servants and the payment for liveries; and receive quarterly stable bills and disbursements, costs of repairs and accounts of other disbursements. The house steward was also to account each week for the daily consumption of wines and other liquors. As if he did not have enough to do, he was also to 'lay in proper provisions of Coals, & Fuel, at the proper Seasons of the year & to have Money to pay for them at the Cheaper Rate.' We can see that the duke suggested a broadening of the responsibilities of the house steward to include some duties formerly performed by the gentleman of the horse, which may mean that that position was left unfilled. With all of these suggested duties Tom Perry would indeed have needed additional help, even if he had been an expert accountant; we can also understand why Greening, earlier, had fallen behind in his work. Later an official called 'Clerk of the Household' was added, and his accounts were examined by Mr Twells or by the duchess regularly.[27]

Full responsibility for the farm and dairy at Claremont was placed in the hands of John Whiston, who had authority to appoint persons under him to carry out the detailed duties. He was also to see that proper wood fuel was available for the house, although the purchase of coal was evidently the responsibility of the house steward. Whiston remained at Claremont for some years; his accounts show him to have been very careful and indicate that the farm was actually being run at a profit in the duke's later years.[28] In his directions Newcastle also ordered Mr Mitchell of Lewes, his Sussex steward; Mr Coates, his steward and keeper at Halland; and Tom Swain, perhaps in charge at Bishopstone Place, to come to London in order to bring their accounts to be audited and to receive directions for the future.

Newcastle, realizing that he was asking Charlton and Postlethwayt to perform a very great task, gave them full power to require any of his servants or agents in town or country to answer questions and to show their accounts. He anticipated that the study could be completed in one month and made available to Mr Charlton any apartment at Claremont which he might feel would best suit his needs. During the process of this financial review the duke, himself, did not want to be involved unless urgently needed: 'Mr Charlton knows my necessary avocations, & consequently will have the goodness to have recourse to me *only*, when this is absolutely necessary. The Duchess of Newcastle will always be ready to answer his questions and give him what assistance he may want.' However, the inspection of the accounts, the conferences with stewards and household officials, and the preparation of the report and recommendations evidently took about five months instead of one, for it was not until the next April that Newcastle noted the results of the Charlton–Postlethwayt study, when he wrote to his wife, 'My Dearest I am afraid will be sadly vexed to see Mr. Charlton and Mr. Postlethwaite's accounts.'[29] The debts came from continued building, which had been completed by this date, from servants' wages unpaid for half a year and from interest due on bonds. The new debt situation had been called to the duke's attention as early as the previous summer—1758—but nothing had been done about it. The new debt must have been in the neighborhood of £8,000 or £10,000, for the duke had been told that it might be paid off by securing advances on existing mortgages of almost that amount. Newcastle feared, however, that the scarcity of money would make the mortgage holders, Lord Middleton and Mr Honeywood and Co., loath to advance more credit. The financial stringency created by the war was affecting the duke's personal financial situation.

As usual the duke asked his wife to look into the details. 'I beg My Dearest would get an explanation of all these things, & direct Mr. Postlethwaite to put down in writing, all the new Debts; when they should be paid; also the Method, he would propose to pay them.'[30] He asked her once again 'to settle our Several Families, & the Expenses of them,' and then he proposed what might be done, such as discharging some servants, saving on wine, beer, coal, candles, board-wages, and the stables. 'The housekeeping which is generally thought the most material article, is the least of all & the other Extravagancies may be prevented without any Inconvenience, Reproach, or even great appearance of Alteration, especially the articles of coals & candles.' Thus the duke was willing to cut back by keeping the houses cool and dark. As usual the servants were blamed as the chief cause of excesses.[31] Once again the duke appears to look upon current expenses in his various establishments as the real cause of his problems, when it is obvious to one studying his financial condition that it was his extraordinary expenses in building, entertaining, general politically related expenses in the counties, especially Sussex, and in all of the things that both Newcastle and his accountants found convenient to place under the heading 'Extraordinaries.'

Perhaps it was the stringency of the money market which made Henry Hoare call in his mortgages on Claremont and Newcastle House. This was evidently done in the summer of 1759, for during that time Newcastle or his agents turned to Mr Edward Woodcock of Lincoln's Inn for help in finding the money. By the middle of July Woodcock had the promise of the money from Robert Clive, through his agent, and attempted to set a time for the execution of Hoare's assignment of Newcastle's mortgages to Clive and the payment of the money.[32] Evidently the assignment did not take place at the suggested time, for Newcastle reported to his wife a month later, 'My Dearest will be glad to hear that we are now sure of our Money, Judge Clive was with me this morning, & told me that I might depend upon the 15000£ on the 14th of September next.' The duke was much relieved and hopeful that this would ease their situation, for 'now the Expenses in Sussex, & some necessary contributions towards Recruiting the army, will lie hard upon us.'[33]

The assignment could not be made as quickly as anticipated, however, for a question was raised about a clear title to Newcastle House. This problem was overcome by the agreement of Lord and Lady Lincoln, and with the arrangement that Lord Mansfield would validate the deed so there would be no later misunderstanding.[34] Finally, on September 29, the money was deposited to the account of the Duke of Newcastle by Clive's bankers, and Hoare was paid off by October 3.[35] It is interesting to note that the Newcastle mortgage was the largest held by Clive, at least until 1766, for his attorney reported that he had out in mortgages and bonds a total of £29,512.10s.0d. and that his income for 1766 was £9,184.2s.0d.[36]

Perhaps October 3, 1759, came and went unnoticed by the Duke of Newcastle, but it was a signal day in his financial life. On that day his indebtedness to Hoare was paid off and he would borrow no more from that source. The final payment was in all £17,304.11s.3d. and covered the mortgages, a bond for £1,600 and probably accumulated interest or other costs.[37] Newcastle's borrowing began on July 4, 1716, when he was advanced £2,000 on his bond and it continued through personal and trust borrowing for forty-three years. In that long period the bankers had advanced to the duke or to his agents a grand total of £112,600, had lost not a farthing, and had received rates of interest which ranged from a high of 5 to a low of 3 per cent.[38] By 1760 Newcastle's trust and personal debt were under control in that interest could be, and was, promptly paid, owing largely, as we have seen, to the fact that income from specific estates was earmarked for the payment of interest on specific indebtedness.

It was the item of current expenses which was not in control, but this was nothing new in the duke's life. No better example exists of his difficulty in controlling current expenses than the situation in Sussex. We have often noted in this study that the high costs there were a constant drain on the duke's resources, for they required more money than the estate in the county produced. It is easy to conclude that these expenditures were in large part directly political—the town of Lewes was costly in this respect—but upon closer examination the culprit was the never-ending costs of maintaining his major seat, Halland, and, to a lesser degree, Bishopstone Place.

Fortunately the interesting and at times amusing diary of a man who lived in the parish of East Hoathly near Halland and who visited there frequently, gives us many glimpses of the duke's entertainments and demonstrates the great difficulty of limiting his expenses. Thomas Turner was invited to Halland on what he termed 'publick days,' when literally hundreds would be entertained, each according to his degree. It seems that there was always at least one such day when the duke came in August for the Lewes races, but others were held when the duke was not present in order to celebrate public events. It is obvious from the diary that Turner loved the entertainments, but his guilt at over-indulgence or at Sabbath-breaking made him cast a hypocritical eye upon what he observed at Halland. On Sunday, August 7, 1757, he visited the seat three times and noted, 'There was a great company of people, of all denominations, from a duke to a beggar,' naming several of the nobility who were present.[39]

Turner's description of an entertainment at Halland in the afternoon of August 23, 1758, to celebrate the taking of Cape Breton, shows us that guests were well provided for but each according to his status in the community:[40]

> About four P.M., I walked down to Halland with several of my neighbors . . . where there was a bonfire of six hundred faggots, the cannon fired, and two barrells of beer given to the populace, and a very good supper provided for the principal tradesmen of this and the neighboring parishes, as there had been. a dinner for the gentlemen of Lewes and the neighboring parishes After supper we drank a great many loyall healths, and I came home in a manner quite sober. There was I believe, near 100 people entertained at Halland this day, besides the populace, and so far as I can see, everything was carried on with decency and regularity.

Turner was usually invited to Halland by Mr Coates, Newcastle's steward there; although he knew he always drank too much when a guest, he claimed he feared to disoblige Mr Coates by not attending. At the end of the previous June he had been invited to Halland to celebrate the victories of Prince Ferdinand of Brunswick on the lower Rhine and had drunk over a dozen loyal healths but 'About ten I deserted and came home safe; but to my shame do I mention it very much in liquor.'[41]

It is obvious that the Seven Years' War was an additional cause of expense to Newcastle, for he felt that the victories won by his administration should be properly celebrated. In early August, 1759, he was again in Sussex with many of his friends; a great public day was held on Sunday, August 5, and Turner was once again at Halland. He named some of the nobility present, including the Earls of Ashburnham and Northampton, Viscount Gage and Lord Abergavenny, as well as the two judges of the assize, 'and a great number of gentlemen, there being, I think upwards of forty coaches, chariots, etc . . . I came home about seven, not thoroughly sober.' Turner could be very critical of the duke in the security of his diary, and was particularly disapproving that during the great war against France Newcastle should bring French cooks to Halland, remarking upon this occasion, 'there being no less than ten cooks, four of which are French . . . as busy as if it had been a rejoicing day.' Turner always felt that a general thanksgiving should be ordered to celebrate national victories rather than the Newcastle variety, and in a self-righteous tone he wrote, 'Oh, what countenance does such behaviour in a person of his Grace's rank, give to levity, drunkeness and all sorts of immorality.'[42]

Newcastle's continuing political activity was demonstrated by his return to his home county for the general election of 1761, the eighth and last of his political career. Turner reported on the assemblage at Halland which demonstrated Newcastle's political influence: 'In the morn down to Halland, where there was, I believe, near five hundred people to attend his Grace to Lewes—the election being there for the county, today, but no opposition.'[43] No doubt following the election the usual treats and entertainment were provided at the duke's political club in Lewes, all at his Grace's expense.

Turner's diary demonstrates fully that at nearly the end of his career Newcastle was continuing a style of grand 'county entertaining' which he had engaged in for nearly fifty years, at least since his great feast in 1714 to celebrate his coming of age. These affairs were such a part of the fabric of the duke's being in all of its aspects, social, political and psychic, that he could not have considered ending them, regardless of the chaos they helped to maintain in his current expenses for his household year after year. It is little to be wondered at that a budget or scheme never worked.

Every accountant or auditor the duke ever employed had to warn him at one time or another that he was on the brink of serious financial embarrassment. In January, 1760, Mr Postlethwayt made a survey of the still incomplete accounts of the previous year and discovered, 'that the Expenses upon many of the articles exceed what the future ease and quiet of my Lord Duke will admit of' and that since there were no resources left for increasing his income, the duke would have to economize. It is apparent that the Murray scheme or budget had not worked and was in fact abandoned; now the accountant was indicating to Newcastle the necessity for a 'diminuition of the general Annual Expenses' to £10,500, two thousand pounds less than the last budget.[44] The Postlethwayt plan or Scheme of Regulation would have the expenses in each area reduced to a weekly maximum, have each official keep weekly accounts and require that any expense above the budgeted weekly maximum be reported to the duke or duchess. What the accountant failed to realize was that the spending itself was at base controlled or ordered by the very persons who were to check on it. Of course Mr Postlethwayt's actual concern was that their Graces know what the expenses were.

In the annual budget of £10,500 proposed by Mr Postlethwayt, the housekeeping expenses for Newcastle House and Claremont were calculated to be £120 per week or approximately £6,200 annually. The remaining £4,300 was to cover all other expenses and each category received its share, with the exception of the duchess's pin money of £600, which was now paid to her directly by the collector of the Clare Market estate and did not go through the general accounting procedures (see Table 22):[45]

TABLE 22

Budget proposed in 1760

	£
His Grace's apparal [*sic*] and pocket money	600
Coals	600
Equippage and horses	800
Servants wages	700
Liveries	500
Sussex	600
Extraordinaries	500

This budget, like its predecessor, was close to the duke's income from estates, office and trust surpluses. The duke had informed Postlethwayt early in 1758 that his estate income, including Clare Market in London, was approximately £6,200 and that he expected about £1,500 from the trust that year. We know that his salary as First Lord of the Treasury was £5,680 gross; we must characterize his salary as gross for he had the usual office costs to defray, as well as assessed taxes. The tax on his salary was not an inconsiderable item when it was at four shillings in the pound. Among the Newcastle papers is a receipt issued by Mr Henshawe, Collector for the Verge of the Court, for the fourth quarterly payment of £60 on the duke's salary for 1761.[46] This £240 annual tax on his place brought his net salary to £5,440 p.a. We see that his annual income was roughly £13,000, but the trust excesses paid into his personal account varied from year to year. Mr Postlethwayt was being realistic in his budget; knowing the duke's spending habits, he provided a £2,500 cushion for the duke to fall back upon.

Unfortunately, or perhaps fortunately, Mr Postlethwayt did not live to learn whether or not Newcastle would follow his advice and his budget. On September 6, 1761, Postlethwayt died at his home in Hatton Garden. Upon learning of this event Newcastle sent a servant at once to the widow to secure control of all of his papers, accounts and correspondence in her possession. Mrs Postlethwayt replied in a letter to the Duchess of Newcastle, saying she 'had rec'd orders from [her] dying husband to act with greatest Care and Secresy [sic] in every-thing concerned with my Lord Duke,' asserting that she was sole executrix of her husband's estate and that no other eye should see the papers.[47]

Although Mr Postlethwayt was not present to keep a check as he had intended, a more regular method was employed in attempting to keep track of food costs. From at least 1761, weekly abstracts of the daily bills of fare for the whole family were prepared and several volumes of them are among the Newcastle papers.[48] These volumes cover costs at both Newcastle House and Claremont and are carefully divided to show costs of consumption in various categories: Pantry (especially bread), Cellar, Chandry, Kitchen, Poultry, Spicery (tea, coffee, chocolate, etc.), Farm (butter and eggs), Woodyard and Scullery (including vege-tables). These bills of fare show the source of some foods and demon-strate the movement of food from the estates in Sussex and Notting-hamshire to London and Claremont. They include, as well, food given as gifts, especially game, fowl, fish and 'wheatears,' and in turn they list the receipt of such items from others. These accounts show that separate tables were maintained for the Steward of the Household, Thomas Perry; for Mrs Spencer, the housekeeper; and for Mr Hurdis, the chaplain. For particularly large dinners or for special events, extra cooks were hired, extra china rented and certain items, such as desserts and confections, were provided by contract with caterers, as was the charcoal used in cooking. There was no such thing as a normal week, for the weekly costs fluctuated greatly but would average over £50. In a test year, July 1762–July 1763, the lowest weekly cost of the tables was £14.8s.0d. while the highest was £179.13s.4d. This latter figure was occasioned by a special five-course dinner costing £98.1s.10d. given at Claremont for the French ambassador on May 17, 1763, which was after the duke had left office, it will be noted.[49] It appears that Mr Postlethwayt included many items besides food in computing the weekly cost of £120 for the duke's household.

The Duke of Newcastle was famous for entertaining, and as we know he enjoyed it. Now that he was head of the Treasury he had even more social demands upon him. He was also in the habit of giving certain dinners annually, such as the Sussex dinner and the Cambridge University dinner, and perhaps also one for his old friends from Westminster School. The year 1761 was an unusual one, for it was the year of the young king's marriage and coronation and naturally the head of government would be expected to celebrate both joyous events.

The annual Sussex dinner was given in order to entertain his friends and supporters from the county. At Newcastle House on Wednesday,

TABLE 23

Cost of the annual Sussex dinner, in 1761

	£	s.	d.
Cellar	12	11	0
Spicery		2	0
Meat	4	1	0
Fowl	9	16	0
Fish	7	12	4
Disburst [labor?]	6	12	0
Butter—Eggs	1	9	6
Scullery	1	4	9
	45	9	4

The Desart [*sic*] not included.

January 28, 1761, the duke provided twenty tables for his Sussex friends, and we know the costs in detail (see Table 23).[50]

The dessert was usually provided by contract, but it appears that the cellar was Newcastle's own or that the beverages had been purchased especially for the occasion. Since these cellar costs were so high, it is interesting to see what £12.11s.0d. purchased for this singular dinner. Table 24 shows the number of bottles and the types of wine and liquors.[51]

The traditional hospitality and high spirits of the duke's entertainment for his Sussex friends did not abate with debt, age or loss of teeth, for Walpole described him early in 1761 as 'old Newcastle, whose teeth are tumbled out and his mouth tumbled in.'[52] He had been entertaining Sussex people for nearly fifty years.

Thus 1761 began expensively for the duke, but this Sussex dinner was reasonable when compared to the costs of dinners he gave in September. On September 8, 1761, the young George III married Charlotte of Mecklenburg-Strelitz; on Friday, September 11, Newcastle gave a grand dinner in London to celebrate the event. Evidently twenty-one tables were set for this 'Wedding Dinner,' which was prodigiously expensive: £232.8s.8½d. The item costing the most was 'Confectionery,' perhaps a great cake for the celebration, £46.14s.0d., while the cellar costs came to a healthy, or heady, £24.9s.0d. For these grand dinners Newcastle hired much help, because his own staff could

TABLE 24

Drink purchased for the Sussex dinner, 1761

15 Claret	5 Champagne
14 Port	6 Burgundy
7 Madaira [sic]	2 Seiges
9 Caleavalla	2 Arrack
[Caracavella?]	1 Rum
5 Rhenish	1 Vin de Grave

not handle them; for this occasion ten extra cooks were hired for £26.5s.0d. It was also necessary to rent extra china at a cost of £10.19s.0d. The three great courses were meat, fish and fowl, and the dinner was brilliantly lighted, for Chandry alone came to £10.4s.0d., while the exterior illumination by a 'Bonfire' in celebration cost his grace £10.6s.11d.[53]

The second great dinner in September, 1761, came only three days after the previous one. The necessity for it was neither political, like the Sussex dinner, nor 'loyal' like the wedding dinner, but was 'academical,' for it was given by the Chancellor in honor of Cambridge University. This grand affair, for which '74 wax candles were lit,' cost the Chancellor another vast sum: £231.8s.8½d. The duke hired eleven extra cooks at over £22, hire of china cost another £22, while the confection was £43 and the wines, liquors and other beverages came to over £56.[54] Thus, in one unusual month Newcastle spent

£463.17s.5d. on special entertainment. Undoubtedly he actually spent more, for the king and queen were crowned on September 22, and, although there is no abstract of the costs in his accounts, the *Gentleman's Magazine* for that month noted an especially grand sugar confection made for the Duke of Newcastle's entertainment following the historic event. It is doubtful if the item of cost for these essentially public entertainments had an inhibiting influence on Newcastle, for they were part of what was expected of one of his rank and station.

However, it must be noted that these latter entertainments were being given at a time when his official life was becoming increasingly difficult. The duke's political situation had been uncomfortable since the new reign began. He probably should have taken this opportunity to retire at an appropriate moment, but as Horace Walpole reported, with some insight but no kindness:[55]

> Not but the Duke of Newcastle cried for his old master,
> desponded himself, protested he would retire, consulted everybody
> whose interest it was to advise him to stay, and has accepted
> today, thrusting the dregs of his ridiculous life into a young
> court, which will at least be saved from the imputation of
> childishness, by being governed by the folly of seventy years'
> growth.

Pitt resigned in September, 1761, over the refusal of the cabinet to accept his policies, and the duke's situation became more and more untenable. Both Bute and the young George III made it increasingly clear to him that he would be used at their convenience and that he carried less and less personal weight in decisions relating to matters of policy and personnel. Finally in early May, 1762, after more discussion with his friends, he decided to resign, but the formal resignation was delayed until May 26, 1762.[56] This was the end of his effective official life, although he was recognized as the elder statesman of the Whigs and his reputation as a political manager did not leave him unconsulted. A new generation of Whig leadership would have to face the uncertain future under George III.

We know that the duke needed every penny he could get to pay his current expenses, including interest on his personal debt, and that his profits of office were essential if he were to maintain his great public style of life. However, from a purely economic point of view, which his whole financial history demonstrates he never accepted, his resignation of public office may have been a blessing; when out of office for the first time in nearly fifty years, the duke could retrench and indeed might be forced to do so. The last deposit of his salary, which amounted to £588.9s.2¼d., pro-rated to the day of resignation, was made on the very day he left office, May 26. The deposit was made by his private secretary, Hugh Valence Jones, a relative of Lord Hard-wicke's, who served in the Treasury and held several sinecures as well.[57]

We have looked at the decade 1752–62 in the financial life of New-castle and its relation to his private and public life. The decade began with a grand effort to retrench, in which the duke took an active interest for about two years. After 1754, when he became head of the Treasury, no more was heard of his budget, and personal borrowing began once again. Although his estates appear to have been under better control, his household expenses and condition were chaotic and led to yet another study, this time by Charlton and Postlethwayt. This re-examination apparently resulted in a partial reorganization of the household and of the home farm at Claremont and to more effective controls over spend-ing, through the initiation of a more complete system of accounting. By 1760 it was evident to Postlethwayt that additional controls, imple-mented by a budget of £10,500, were needed to prevent the duke from undermining his financial condition once again. We have noted that his spending appears to have increased in the new reign and that his papers give no evidence of an effort to abide by the proposed budget. The period from 1760 to his resignation was one of great political turmoil and tension within the government and the demands of the war upon the Treasury were very great; Newcastle had no time for the details of his own affairs, perhaps legitimately this time.[58] Thus, from the beginning of his official life in 1717 to his resignation in 1762, a period of forty-five years, Newcastle had lived beyond the income provided by estates and salary and had been perpetually in debt. As we have seen, his style of life was paid for only by great sales of land, which represented his inherited capital, the product of generations of savings and investment by his Holles and Pelham ancestors.

NOTES

1 Add. MSS. 32731, f. 39, Murray Minute to Newcastle, January 13, 1753.
2 *Ibid.*, ff. 43v–4.
3 *Ibid.*

4 Add. MSS. 33138, f. 399v, Newcastle's Instructions to Postlethwayt, October 12, 1753; see Add. MSS. 33066, f. 433, Sharpe to Postlethwayt, March 9, 1755.

5 Add. MSS. 32731, ff. 490–1v, Newcastle to duchess, Claremont, May 27, 1753.

6 Add. MSS. 32732, f. 483v, Newcastle House, August 16, 1753.

7 *Ibid.*

8 Add. MSS. 33074, ff. 186–6v, Newcastle to duchess, October 3, 1753.

9 Sir Lewis Namier and John Brooke, *The History of Parliament, The House of Commons, 1754–1790* (London, 1964), II, 209.

10 Add. MSS. 33066, f. 396, Charlton's instructions to Stewards, October 8, 1753.

11 Add. MSS. 33074, f. 179v, Newcastle to duchess, Newcastle House, October 17, 1753.

12 Add. MSS. 33321, Waller Accounts, 1737–54; Add. MSS. 33074, ff. 184–4v, Newcastle to Waller, Newcastle House, October 25, 1753 (not sent).

13 Add. MSS. 33138, f. 399, Newcastle's Instructions to Postlethwayt, October 12, 1753.

14 *Ibid.*, f. 399v.

15 *Ibid.*, f. 400v.

16 Add. MSS. 33074, f. 181, Newcastle House, October 23, 1753.

17 Add. MSS. 32733, ff. 217–17v, Newcastle to John Dobbs, Newcastle House, November 8, 1753.

18 Add. MSS. 33075, f. 4, Newcastle House, July 2, 1754.

19 Add. MSS. 32737, f. 471, John Sharpe to Newcastle, Sunday, December 22, 1754.

20 *Ibid.*, f. 428, Sharpe to Newcastle, December 11, 1754.

21 Add. MSS. 33066, f. 421, Sharpe to Newcastle, March, 1755.

22 East Sussex Record Office, Sayer MSS., unfolioed, John Greening to John Collier, Newcastle House, November 13, 1755.

23 Hoare, Money Ledger, 1743–73, f. 16, May 11, 1751.

24 Add. MSS. 33067, f. 11, Sharpe to Newcastle, April 6, 1756.

25 See Add. MSS. 33076, f. 44v, Newcastle to duchess, Claremont, April 1, 1759.

26 Add. MSS. 33139, ff. 24–9v, Claremont, September 16, 1758.

27 Add. MSS. 33159–60, *passim*, accounts of J. Fallowfield, Clerk of the Household.

28 Add. MSS. 33324, Claremont Farm Accounts, *passim*.

29 Add. MSS. 33076, f. 44, Newcastle to duchess, Claremont, April 1, 1759.

30 *Ibid.*, f. 45.

31 *Ibid.*, f. 45v.

32 Hoare's Bank MSS., Edward Woodcock to Henry Hoare, unfolioed, July 18, 1759.

33 Add. MSS. 33076, f. 63v, Newcastle House, August 15, 1759.

34 Hoare's Bank MSS., Edward Woodcock to Henry Hoare, Lincoln's Inn, September 6, 1759.

35 India Office Library, Powis papers, Film, 552/7/59, Joseph Vere, Sir Richard Glynn and Thomas Halifax to Col. Clive, September 29, 1759.

36 India Office Library, MSS., Eur. g 37m, Box 5, No. 1.
37 Hoare, Money Ledger, 1743–73, f. 64.
38 *Ibid.*, 1696–1718, 1718–43, 1743–73, *passim.*
39 Florence Turner (ed.), *The Diary of Thomas Turner of East Hoathly, Sussex, 1754–1765* (London, 1925), pp. 18–19.
40 *Ibid.*, pp. 43–4.
41 *Ibid.*, p. 39, June 30, 1759.
42 *Ibid.*, pp. 53–4.
43 *Ibid.*, p. 65.
44 Add. MSS. 33139, f. 44, Postlethwayt to Newcastle, Claremont, January 1, 1760.
45 *Ibid.*, f. 45.
46 Add. MSS. 33056, f. 9, March 25, 1762.
47 Add. MSS. 33067, f. 309, Anne Postlethwayt to Duchess of Newcastle, September 9, 1761.
48 Add. MSS. 33325–31.
49 Add. MSS. 33326, *passim.*
50 Add. MSS. 33325, f. 7v, Register of Bills of Fares and Prices.
51 *Ibid.*, f. 6.
52 W. S. Lewis and Ralph S. Brown, Jr., *Horace Walpole's Correspondence with George Montagu* (New Haven, 1941), I, 363, April 28, 1761.
53 Add. MSS. 33325, f. 127, Abstract of the Wedding Dinner.
54 *Ibid.*, f. 130, Abstract of the University of Cambridge Dinner, London, September 14, 1761.
55 *Walpole-Montagu Correspondence*, I, 316, Friday, October 31, 1760.
56 See Namier, *England in the Age of the American Revolution*, chapters 2 and 5, and Sedgwick (ed.), *Letters from George III to Lord Bute, 1756–1766, passim.*
57 Hoare, Current Accounts, vol. B, f. 279.
58 See Reed Browning, 'The Duke of Newcastle and the financing of the Seven Years' War,' *Journal of Economic History*, 31 (June, 1971), 344–77.

CHAPTER 6

THE FINAL YEARS: 1762-8

It cannot be doubted that after a lifetime of office-holding Newcastle, and his friends as well, felt themselves nearly indispensable to the functioning of government. The duke had filled dozens of offices with his dependents, and the Pelham connection was a power in the land. No doubt the duke, although sixty-nine years of age, felt that the king would recall him to a position of influence, and, in fact, Bute did make some overtures towards gaining his support. However, as a politician, Newcastle knew the reality of power: he was excluded. On Christmas, 1762, those who had depended upon his patronage were dismissed or forced to resign. This 'slaughter of the Pelhamite innocents' could have left no doubt in anyone's mind of the determination of the new leadership to chart a new course. Newcastle knew exactly what was happening and felt for those who were suffering simply (as he saw it) for their loyalty to him—especially those who were dismissed from minor offices.[1] It was difficult for the old duke to accept the fact that he was actually out of the center of affairs; he found his levees literally without important people in attendance. Alone, he could neither hold his former dependents together nor protect them; many of them looked to the new court and to the new dispenser of patronage, Henry Fox. The duke spent much of his time at Claremont and, as time passed, came up to Newcastle House more and more rarely.

At nearly seventy years of age Newcastle had, for the first time in his adult life, to depend solely upon the income from his estates for his maintenance. What was his income after retirement, and what were the resources remaining at his disposal? The second part of the question is the easier to answer, for his unrestricted resources consisted of his Sussex estates, the Clare Market estate, Claremont, and Newcastle House. All of these were or had been mortgaged save the Clare Market estate, which must have been restricted in some manner or perhaps was unacceptable as mortgage collateral.

It was the Clare Market estate which provided the duke's largest single source of income. This property had been in trust only briefly, from 1738 to 1741, and the duke had enjoyed the income at all other times. In 1762, and for some years earlier, the management and collection of the market had been in the hands of Bartholomew Hammond, but in March, 1764, the responsibility for it had been given to the last, and one of the best, of the duke's agents, Abraham Baley. Baley was a Sussex man who had had long connections with the Pelhams. He had earlier lived at Halland, had been a receiver of part of the duke's Sussex estate at a salary of £50,[2] and had made a full study of the duke's affairs there in an effort to increase income. It was undoubtedly Baley's careful attention to detail and his proven ability which led the duke to employ him on the Clare Market estate. In his first accounts Baley noted that the duke had allowed a stationer's bill for new books and the 'new Moddelling the Accounts of this Estate,' which came to £11.10s.6½d. The duke showed his appreciation to Baley for his complete survey of the market and for all of his trouble by giving him £100.[3]

The carefully prepared and beautifully written accounts of the Clare Market estate give us clear evidence of the duke's income from this source, as well as the use to which it was put. The first full accounting period for the estate, under Baley's direction, was from November, 1765, to November, 1766. The gross produce was £4,865.19s.10d. The estate netted the duke £3,800: the duke's personal account at Hoare's Bank received £3,200, while the duchess's annual pin money took £600. The costs of the estate used up the remainder of the income: Baley's new salary of £115 p.a., and the land tax, window tax, legal costs and repairs, £945.[4] The account was prepared expeditiously; presented on February 24, 1767, to Mr Twells to be checked; and examined, passed and signed by Newcastle himself on March 30, 1767. Finally we see business-like proceedings in this profitable estate at almost the very end of Newcastle's life. This may indicate a general improvement, nation-wide, in the management of estates or a more bourgeois attitude on the part of noble owners of city property. It can be doubted that the change was a personal one on Newcastle's part, for he represented a former, aristocratic attitude toward wealth, as his whole life had demonstrated, and he was far too old to change. Furthermore he had hated change all of his life.

We have no specific information on the produce of the ancestral Sussex estates but we know that it was small. Baley made a study of the estate in an effort to increase the yield and entitled one part of this report, 'Parcells kept in his Grace's Hands for his own Use and from which no Profit arises.' He gave the annual value of the house and gardens at Bishopstone Place as £50. For Halland he was more specific, and gave acreages as well as total value. The house and gardens covered 10 acres, the park consisted of 880 acres, and the pond, 8 acres, all of which he valued at £300 p.a. Evidently he was looking also for areas in which to reduce costs and noted the benefactions which had gone on for many years to schools in Sussex: the master of the Cuckfield School received £20 p.a., the school at Lewes for the education of eighteen boys received £12 p.a., while the school at Seaford received £17 p.a. for the education of twenty-four children. Baley noted that he was to cease to pay the Seaford sum after Lady Day, 1765.[5]

Newcastle loved Claremont, and he spent much of his time there following his retirement. During his first retirement in 1762 the duke relaxed there, entertained friends and was in generally high spirits, no doubt expecting to be recalled to court. During this period he even mentioned farming in a letter to an old friend and political ally, Lord Kinnoull:[6]

> The weather is very hot, & fine; and this place is very pleasant;
> But we have had no rain: Notwithstanding which I have as Fine
> Hay, & Corn, as ever was seen. I can be a Farmer as well as your
> Lordship. I have not, I own, the Secret of Improving my Estate,
> as you have.

This remark about farming was perhaps intended for humor; his friend probably knew the truth of Newcastle's financial problems and that he had reduced his estate during his years in public office.

Perhaps Newcastle was being a bit unfair to himself and to his staff, who were managing his affairs quite efficiently at this time. In the next to last year of the duke's life, the home farm at Claremont even made a profit (see Table 25).[7] These accounts were very carefully done and were passed by Mr Twells, who had been in the family for years and who now served as the duke's principal assistant in the management of his affairs.

The last cabinet office held by Newcastle in his long ministerial career was that of Lord Privy Seal in Rockingham's first administration, where he acted as elder statesman or, to use Winstanley's phrase, served as 'patriarch of the Whig party.'[8] He was asked by the king to make ecclesiastical recommendations to him, an activity which he had greatly enjoyed in the height of his power. Newcastle divided his time between Claremont and Newcastle House; presented in the closet names for clerical nomination, advancement or translation; attended court and Whig gatherings; and continued his active correspondence. The ministry held office for only one year, beginning on July 15, 1765. The salary of the Lord Privy Seal was £4 per diem in lieu of 'ancient diet,' and the sum of £1,175 p.a., which in all would total scarcely more than £2,600 p.a.[9] There is no indication in the duke's personal account at Hoare's Bank that salary payments were deposited during that year,[10] as had been the practice when he was in the Secretary of State's office and in the Treasury. This small salary could not have been very

TABLE 25

Income from the home farm at Claremont

Claremont Farm			
	£	s.	d.
1767—Year Totall Neat money Rec'd:	1332	7	7½
Totall paid:	942	5	5
Totall proffitt clear of all Exp.es	390	2	2½

important to Newcastle in comparison to the joy of being back in the center of affairs once again.[11]

Although the young George III had no love for the old duke, who represented to him the thralldom he imagined his grandfather had suffered, he was not unmindful of the aged royal servant's contributions. When he decided to dismiss Lord Rockingham's first ministry in July, 1766, and to call Pitt, he granted the traditional audience to the departing ministers. The cabinet was told by the king that they were being dismissed because of their weakness, and he was very pleasant to them. Newcastle related how gracious the king had been to him when he spoke with him during the audience, 'by telling me... that I had done more *Service to his Family* than any man in England.'[12] This declaration must have brought infinite pleasure to the old statesman, for he longed for such marks of respect. It was widely reported that Newcastle was offered an annual pension of £4,000 but that he refused it. The only surprising thing would have been for him to have accepted it, for we know that he refused financial aid in 1723 from the young king's great-grandfather and indicated his distaste for such payments.[13]

Although there may be more, I have found only one instance in which Newcastle mentioned his financial loss during his years in office. In August, 1761, he was in the midst of his struggle with Lord Bute and sought Lord Hardwicke's advice on whether to resign or not. In his letter, Newcastle asked Hardwicke to 'consider what I owe to myself, my figure, and reputation in the world, after having sacrificed my time, my fortune etc. for such a number of years for the service of this Royal Family.'[14] Of course this statement was made to his most intimate political associate and personal friend who had had first-hand knowledge of his financial situation for a quarter of a century; Newcastle himself never mentioned the matter publicly.

We have stated many times that Newcastle's official income was essential if he were to maintain his style of life. His great salary stopped on May 26, 1762, and no doubt some of his costs also lessened when he was no longer head of the Treasury. However, the requirements for his rank and for political influence remained fairly constant. It must also be remembered that he had a large personal mortgage debt which had to be serviced. Lord Clive's mortgage on Claremont required £600 annually. A mortgage debt of £20,000 was secured by property in Hastings, Lewes and other parts of Sussex. It had been made in 1758 and was held by Francis, Lord Middleton, but parts of it had been released and reassigned to various individuals. In 1764 this mortgage debt was consolidated and the various claims were assigned to the Sun Fire Insurance Office, who in turn lent the duke £20,000 at 5 per cent for a term of seven years.[15] The interest on this mortgage of £500 each half-year was regularly paid from funds provided by Mr William Mitchell, Newcastle's Sussex steward and political agent.[16] Thus Newcastle's landed income was reduced each year by at least £1,600 for interest payments. If his personal debt stood at £35,000 in 1762 he had apparently been able to pay off some £9,000 since Murray's study in 1752; however, we have noted the mention of new debt in the late 1750s, leading to Postlethwayt's budget of 1760.

The existence of Newcastle's personal account at Hoare's Bank enables us to calculate his net income fairly exactly. In the last calendar year of his life, November, 1767, to November, 1768, the duke's account received a total of £8,688: the land stewards paid in £6,599; his trustees transferred in £2,000; and he received £89 interest on his own funds in the trust.[17] To this net income of £8,688 should be added the annual interest payments of £1,600 made directly by the stewards, to give a gross annual income for this year of £10,288.

The old duke in the mid-1760s was living in a world in many ways markedly different from that of his youth and middle years. The political world created and symbolized by Walpole and the Pelhams had been challenged and bested by the young king and his advisers. Newcastle had witnessed the beginning of the Hanoverian dynasty, and his primary political purpose had been in its support and protection, albeit under Whig direction, throughout his career. The length of his political service in high office was unparalleled in England; and by this period Newcastle, alone, remained of those who had held high station in each Hanoverian reign.

The duke could not easily give up the habits of authority and recognition which he had been accustomed to during his active political life. The isolation from the center of decision-making aggravated the natural loneliness of old age, and his emotional malaise was not aided by his deteriorating physical health. The old statesman was, in fact, not regularly consulted; young men did look to young leaders; family and relations were not as grateful as they might have been; and Newcastle was unhappy.

In this frame of mind, Newcastle unburdened and justified himself in an almost compulsive manner to an old friend, John Hume, Bishop of Salisbury, whose career in the church he had forwarded. His long statement was a real *apologia pro vita sua* and revealed his self-image:[18]

One, who have [sic] never designedly done Injury, to any Man in the World. Who, during the course of half a century, has had opportunities, to have served Many. To have raised some from Obscurity to the Highest Situations; and, to have shew'd the greatest Marks of attention & affection to all his own Relations, who, by their behaviour, have suffered him to do it and who flatters himself, has, for above half a Century, held an Irreproachable Conduct, If not a very Meritorious one, towards his Country, & the present Royal Family; and which is, & has been most gratefully acknowledged by every Prince, who has been upon the Throne, during that time; I say, to see me deserted, and abandoned by almost everybody, by my own Family particularly, & my Enemies, by that alone, encouraged, & enabled to Treat me, with the greatest Marks of Indignity and Contempt;—when all I expect is Common Decency, & Common Respect.

I have now told my short History, in a few words, and have done.

Even in his advanced years, Newcastle could not gracefully retire to the quietness and comfort of Claremont, where he might have ignored his political enemies and thereby quieted the associated fears. However, what is most significant for our purposes is what the duke left unsaid in his litany of a lifetime: not once did he mention or allude to politically motivated expenditures as praiseworthy factors in his half-century of service. Yet Newcastle was looking for every justification for himself, and he was addressing an old and intimate friend, a priest and bishop who served as his spiritual adviser, to whom he could unburden himself without fear. If in retirement he had felt that he had consciously expended his great fortune and had reduced his estate income by two-thirds for purely political or state-service ends, he would have stated it plainly. The fact is that Newcastle did not consider politically related expenditures as the major cause of his reduced financial position or even as a significant reason for praise or justification. Such expenditures were simply a part of the role of the politically guiding, aristocratic class in his lifetime.

The duke left Claremont only when it was necessary for him to come to London for social or political reasons. However much he might love his country seat near London, he was often lonely there and sought guests to relieve his tedium and as sources of news or gossip. Now that he was old and out of power, persons were not as eager to accept his invitations as they had been earlier in his lifetime. He was willing to come to town to carry out a promise he had made to George III that he would support an income for the king's brothers. 'For I promised the King, when I was in his Service, to be for a Moderate Provision for them, viz., £8000 pr. ann. for each, I will never give myself the Lie, & so far, & no farther, will I go; . . . I told his Majesty, & it is my opinion; I am neither for a Starving Prince of the Blood, nor an Independent one; £8000 pr. an. *only*, is the Medium between both.'[19] The duke apparently regretted having made the promise in the first place and covered his promise with a pure-Whig rationalization; as it turned out, the brothers were not as handsomely provided for as the duke was willing to go. According to Horace Walpole, Newcastle's last appearance at a political meeting took place July 20, 1767. 'Age and feebleness at length wore out that busy passion for intrigue, which power had not been able to satiate, nor disgrace correct. He lingered about a year, but was heard of no more on the scene of affairs.'[20]

The duke was a member of the Established Church all of his life and had been surrounded by clerics from his infancy. He took a lively interest in the Church of England as an institution, and he had helped to make it reflect faithfully the political realities of the day.[21] Newcastle's personal religious convictions are unknown, but he probably reflected the current attitudes of his class towards religious practices and beliefs. However, during his retirement Newcastle began to think seriously about his Christian faith and it should not be surprising to find that here, as in other areas of life, he had manifold fears and insecurities about his spiritual health. In December, 1766, he asked his friend Bishop Hume to come to Claremont the week before Christmas to help him to prepare to celebrate that feast. He said that the bishop knew his fears and doubts but that he had 'the best way in removing both, by carefully avoiding to encrease [sic] either.'[22] In speaking of his retirement Robert Drummond, Archbishop of York, had told him that he now had the comfort of reading, 'which should sometimes be upon *serious subjects*, but not to go *too deep*' and that was why he requested Hume to recommend books and sermons which might answer his purpose. Newcastle informed him that he had begun to read Addison and was at that time reading Tillotson's sermons, preparatory to Christmas day. He also read regularly the Lesson of the Day.[23]

Following a serious illness late in 1767, which was evidently a stroke, the duke confessed that his recovery had fixed in him a just sense of duty and gratitude to God 'for this Mark of [the] Goodness of Divine Providence, & a most Lively and Unfeigned Belief of the Truth of the Holy Gospel; and that our Saviour laid down his Life to save Sinners, by Faith and Repentance.'[24] He asked the bishop to prepare a prayer of thanksgiving for his recovery from the dangerous illness. Perhaps it was the spiritual guidance of Bishop Hume which gave Newcastle the assurance he craved.

The duke was never to recover fully from this illness. He may have been warned of its serious nature, for he made his will on February 29, 1768, and it was a very simple instrument. First it was ordered that his just debts be paid, and thereby the item which had plagued him all of his life was to receive its quietus. He confirmed the settlement of his Sussex estates on Thomas Pelham; the remainder, which was not covered by the family settlement, was to go to the duchess, who would also serve as administratrix. Finally, she was given power to see to the sorting of his papers, some of which could be destroyed upon advice, and what remained was to go to his heir at law.[25]

Newcastle was attended at this time by Dr Messenger Monsey and he did not cease to hope for health. Monsey was exactly Newcastle's age, being born in 1693, but lived on until 1788 to die at the age of ninety-five. He was a Pembroke College man and may have been at Cambridge at the time Newcastle was at Clare Hall. He was known for his rough manner and for his easy familiarity with the Whig great, for he had attended Godolphin, Walpole, Chesterfield and Newcastle, as well as many others. Newcastle continued to correspond with friends through the early fall of 1768, but his condition precluded political activity of a serious nature. The duke was living now at Newcastle House, perhaps so that he could be close to Dr Monsey, and was surrounded by his servants. Newcastle's last public appearance was apparently made on October 18, 1768 (and less than a month before his death), when he was taken to Richmond Park in his carriage and there, by chance, saluted the young king and queen for the last time. The event was described by Daniel Wray in his memoirs:[26]

> Just now, in my ride, I saw in the *Park* their Majesties in their chaise and pair of cream-colours; and the *Duke of Newcastle* with his four greys, and *Andrew Stone*. The carriages met; but according to the most authentic information of two fern-cutters— no conference.

Although Newcastle's health was precarious, the duchess went to Bath to take the waters for her health. The duke was kept constantly informed of her condition by her servants, but he himself was stricken while she was gone. Horace Walpole, who had said so many unkind things about the old duke, reported to Montagu on Tuesday, November 15, 1768, 'Your old cousin Newcastle is going: he had a stroke of palsy and they think he will not last two days.'[27] Walpole's informant was exactly correct, for the duke died two days later, November 17, 1768, at Newcastle House in Lincoln's Inn Fields, having received the Holy Sacrament from Bishop Hume shortly before. The duchess had not been informed of her husband's final stroke for fear of impairing her own health; but at his death she began her return journey to London.

Certainly no contemporary expressed a more tortuous and contrived sentiment than Mrs Montagu, when she wrote on learning of his death:[28]

> The Duke of Newcastle this morning finished his course. I
> believe time will be a Friend to his Fame, and future Ministrys a
> foil to his administration, which if not glorious was not infamous
> and if not wise was however discreet.

The Cambridge *Journal* praised him and recalled for its readers the grandeur and solemnity of his installation as Chancellor years before. It also reported that a certain great man, on hearing of Newcastle's death, remarked, 'There died the Prince of English Whigs, & the most staunch Enemy of the Tories.'[29] The paper also noted that Newcastle had reduced his estate in the service of king and country. It erroneously reported that he had had an income of £50,000 per annum; but added that he left an estate worth only £9,000, which is substantially correct. The paper also noted that the duchess had £3,000 as her jointure, and that the Sussex estate which came to Lord Pelham was worth £3,000, while Lord Lincoln and his sons received the residue.

We know nothing of the public or private obsequies for the duke, but it was not until November 23 that his remains began their journey from Newcastle House to the family vault at Laughton in Sussex, where they were interred on November 27, 1768.[30] The procession, suitable to the rank of the deceased, left Lincoln's Inn Fields at eight o'clock in the morning. Two porters mounted on milk-white horses led the van; next came eight domestics in mourning cloaks, riding grey horses; then a gentleman on horseback, uncovered, bearing the gilt ducal coronet laid on a crimson cushion, who had two men leading his horse; then the corpse in a hearse drawn by six horses. Next came four mourning coaches, each drawn by four horses, which carried the duke's principal gentlemen. A gentleman, followed by six livery servants in mourning cloaks, all on horseback, closed the procession.[31]

Dying and being fittingly buried was a costly affair for one of rank in the eighteenth century. The duke's faithful Abraham Baley kept careful account of the costs. He paid charges directly amounting to £119.9s.3d. for the funeral, which probably went for mourning cloaks, liveries, hangings and travel. Mr Parran, the undertaker, received for his work £332.15s.0d. Mr Goodison, a cabinet maker, received through Mr Parran £170.0s.0¼d., probably for the coffin and other necessary work. In all, the costs for the duke's final trip to Sussex totaled £622.4s.3¼d.[32] The duchess paid £26.6s.0d. from her own funds for the mourning apparel for herself and for her servants, which she duly noted in her account book.[33]

Less than a month after the duke's death 'the family' began to be dissolved. On December 2 eighteen servants were paid in full and discharged.[34] Soon the appraisers were busy determining a value for furniture, household goods, linen, etc. which were not entailed and which the duchess did not desire to retain (see Table 26).[35] The

TABLE 26

Valuation of household effects at the duke's death

	£	s.	d.
Newcastle House	4,405	7	9
Claremont	3,087	0	7
Bishopstone	701	7	0
Halland	579	4	0
Nottingham Castle	1,040	13	6
Plate and Wine, Sussex	40	16	0
	9,854	8	10

actual sale of the goods did not produce the appraised value overall (see Table 27).

Lord Clive purchased Claremont, upon which he held a mortgage, for £25,000 and also agreed to purchase 'all live and dead stock, corn & hay, Implements of Husbandry and Gardening, Furniture and Household goods, as Her Grace may not chuse to remove from thence, at a fair appraisement.'[36] The Claremont, upon which Newcastle had spent such great sums of money and which had been so close to his heart, was demolished by Clive; and a new mansion house arose in its place, costing him £43,000. Claremont was more than just the great home itself; it had a park of 330 acres; a kitchen garden of six acres which was walled and which also contained fruit trees; it had hothouses, stables, coach-house, offices, a farmhouse, laundry and brewhouse. Clive had little time to enjoy his fine new mansion, for he died in 1774,

and his Claremont was on the market by May, 1775.[37] The new Lord
Pelham, formerly Thomas Pelham of Stanmer, purchased the contents
of Bishopstone. A Mr Russell bought the contents of Halland, while
the new Duke of Newcastle, formerly Lord Lincoln, purchased the
furniture of Nottingham Castle.[38] The libraries of Newcastle House
and Claremont, purchased by a Mr Robson, brought a large sum,
£1,134.[39]

It appears that although Mr Russell purchased the furniture at
Halland, other items were sold at auction, for which a catalogue was
printed. Some of the items contained in the sale must have been in the

TABLE 27

Proceeds from the sale of household effects

	£	s.	d.
Newcastle House	2,313	0	0
Claremont	2,902	1	8
Bishopstone	581	7	0
Halland	603	0	0
Nottingham Castle	1,051	3	6
	7,450	12	2

family since Halland was built as a manor house in the days of Eliza-
beth. For example:

Large parcel of steel caps & sundry armour	15s
In the Long Gallery—Eight family pictures	14s

The hangings and tapestry in the duke's bed chamber and in the
State Room each brought £2.13s.0d. The very names of the rooms,
including the Spinning Room, evoke an earlier age.[40] It should be
repeated that the money received by sale and auction did not actually
represent the value of the contents of the various seats, for most of the
plate was entailed and could not have been sold, and perhaps other
items were so restricted. The duchess also had her rights to personal
property.

In a sense Newcastle's death marked the end not only of a long
political career but also of a political and personal way of life which

stretched back into the seventeenth century and beyond. It was a mode founded on deference to great and extensive landed wealth, to extended family connections and interconnections, to open and expensive hospitality to persons of quality and to dependents and tenants alike. Public acceptance of political leadership from this class was being challenged, or at least questioned. New forces were arising, perhaps symbolized by Wilkes in Newcastle's own day, which would not accept political tutelage.

The passing of Newcastle from the scene was a reminder of mortality to a person of a very different mold, one who had withdrawn from political strife many years before, Lord Chesterfield:[41]

> My old kinsman and contemporary is at last dead, and for the first time quiet. He had a start of me at his birth by one year and two months, and I think we shall observe the same distance at our burial. I own I feel for his death, not because it will be my turn next; but because I knew him to be very good-natured, and his hands extremely clean, and even too clean if that were possible, for, after all the great offices he held for fifty years, he died three hundred thousands pounds poorer than he was when he first came into them. A very unministerial proceeding!

Lord Chesterfield was impressed by his old kinsman's kindness and by his honesty in a corrupt age. None of Newcastle's contemporaries accused him of personal financial dishonesty and his rectitude in this area presented some problems for those who disliked him. His honesty earned him no rewards from his critics and his losses were looked upon with apparent scorn by his enemies. Items about the financial condition of contemporaries made a constant appearance in the correspondence of the day. Aristocratic ladies and gentlemen eagerly retailed news or gossip about inheritances, portions, jointures, debts and the worth of heiresses. Often such gossip was near the mark. Newcastle's financial condition appears to have been widely known, and Horace Walpole summed up in his sarcastic way the reasons for the duke's economic difficulty: 'There was no expense to which he was not addicted, but generosity. His houses, gardens, table, and equippage, swallowed immense treasures: the sums he owed were only exceeded by those he wasted.'[42] It will be noted that political expenditure did not enter Walpole's list of expenditures.

In speaking of the duke's financial life, Chesterfield used the term 'poorer' in describing Newcastle's loss while in state service. In the quotation above the earl gave the sum as £300,000; but when he came to write his *Characters* of men of his time, he gave this evaluation of his relative, whom he knew well:[43]

> He was exceedingly disinterested, very profuse of his own fortune, and abhorring all those means, too often used by persons in his station, either to gratify their avarice, or to supply their prodigality; for he retired from business in the year 1762, above four hundred thousand pounds poorer than when he first engaged in it.

Horace Walpole in writing of Newcastle's loss does not use a gross figure but rather computes it upon the basis of how much the duke had 'sunk his estate' in his lifetime:[44]

> It was assiduously propagated in all the public papers, that he departed [from office] without place or pension; and his enormous estate, which he had sunk from thirty to thirteen thousand pounds a year, by every ostentatious vanity, and on every womanish panic, between cooks, mobs, and apothecaries, was represented by his tools as wasted in the cause of Government.

Walpole always believed that Newcastle's annual income was larger than it was but he was remarkably close to being correct about Newcastle's actual condition, for we know that he had but approximately £9,000 per annum income in the last years of his life. Where these men secured their information it is difficult to tell. It is possible that the duke spoke unguardedly of his own financial problems to his kinsmen and to others, and that this information became common knowledge among persons of his class. However, it may be possible to calculate the duke's actual loss by using the data we have presented in the study to test the statements of both Chesterfield and Walpole.

First, what did Chesterfield understand by his concept that Newcastle was 'poorer' by his years of public service? Clearly, one of his aristocratic class would think in terms of the loss of landed wealth, i.e. capital investment, for this was the economic basis of the class, when considering the situation of an individual or family. How much land had to be sold in order to pay off the debts of the Duke of Newcastle? If we take land sales made by the trustees, plus the income from the lands while they held them, in the thirty-year period 1738–68, we find that they paid off encumbrances of £207,500. The trust left an indebtedness of £79,000 at the duke's death, and the duke himself left a mortgage debt of £35,000, both of which obligations had to be liquidated. In all, these figures total £321,000 which is close enough for either of Chesterfield's figures and which would indicate either that some financial gossip was fairly reliable or that some one actually had factual data relating to the duke's condition.

Second, let us use Walpole's yardstick for stating the duke's loss, that he had reduced his rental income from £30,000 to £13,000, i.e. by £17,000 per annum. It is immaterial for our purposes that the figures given by Walpole inflate the duke's annual rental loss by about £2,000. It was probably only with the signing of the permanent trust in 1738 that it became public knowledge among the upper classes that the Duke of Newcastle's resources had been limited or restricted. In fact, it would have been to the advantage of the estate to have it known that all of the duke's debts were to be paid, for it would have tended to restore his credit. It is a safe assumption that Walpole, who had an almost morbid interest in the duke, knew of the trust and perhaps picked up a rumor or two about its provisions.

His statement that the duke had reduced the annual value of his estate by £17,000 Walpole wrote in 1756, that is, eighteen years after the trust's establishment. Interestingly, if we use Walpole's annual rental loss figure and multiply it by the number of years the trust had been in existence, we find that this 'sinking' of the estate totaled £306,000. This sum is remarkably close to that used by Chesterfield, writing in 1762, the year of the duke's resignation.

Thus, by using either method of computation (that is, by determining the land sales and debts remaining, on the one hand; or by figuring from the annual reduction in the rental value of the estate, on the other hand), we arrive at approximately the same sum. This result may be coincidental, for we do not, in fact, know the method, if there was one, used by either man. However, we can be fairly certain that Chesterfield and Walpole would not have agreed on the cause of Newcastle's financial difficulties. Although Chesterfield never named causes, he implied that it was due to political expenditures on behalf of government; Walpole was closer to the facts when he saw the cause in the duke's style of life. He rightly pointed out that many of the duke's family, friends and dependents had been amply rewarded by means of the duke's influence. However, Walpole was never generous when writing of the Duke of Newcastle and he did not see, or else failed to state, that the duke's high position in the government of the nation necessitated a style of life which was costly. To this dilettante reporter of the actions of men of affairs, Newcastle, whose only passion was the work and business of government, was little above a fool whose spending was wasted 'on every ostentatious vanity.'

Even though Newcastle had greatly reduced his estate and income, he was able to live on his own resources after he left public office and his goodly salary ceased. At seventy years of age and over, his needs or desires were few; a lifetime of spending had provided nearly all of the material things he could want or need; his personal debt was stabilized and the interest regularly and promptly paid; and he could at last retrench in the area related to politics, for his political base had been destroyed in 1762–3 and his effective political career had ended.

NOTES

1 L. B. Namier, *England in the Age of the American Revolution* (London, 1930), pp. 468–83.
2 Add. MSS. 33338, f. 84.
3 Add. MSS. 33169, f. 18.
4 *Ibid.*, f. 34.
5 Add. MSS. 33338, ff. 64, 72, 76.
6 Add. MSS. 32939, ff. 353–4, Newcastle to Kinnoull, Claremont, June 15, 1762.
7 Add. MSS. 33324, *passim*, Farm Accounts.
8 D. A. Winstanley, *Lord Chatham and the Whig Opposition* (London, 1966), vii.
9 Add. MSS. 33056, f. 46, Treasury Warrant.
10 Hoare, Current Accounts, vol. D, f. 116.
11 For a description of his political activities during this period see Mary Bateson (ed.), *A Narrative of the Changes in Ministry, 1765–1767*, ... (London, 1898), *passim*.
12 Add. MSS. 34728, f. 116v, Newcastle to James West, July 12, 1766.
13 Add. MSS. 32686, ff. 254v–5.
14 Add. MSS. 32926, ff. 284–5.
15 *Sussex Archaeological Society Collections*, XXXVII (1890), pp. 82–3, Indentures No. 242, 246, 254; Add. MSS. 33339, f. 70, Baley's Accounts.
16 Add. MSS. 33166, f. 73.
17 Hoare, Current Accounts, vol. D, f. 120.
18 Add. MSS. 33071, ff. 17–18, Newcastle to Bishop of Salisbury, Claremont, November 7, 1766.
19 *Ibid.*, ff. 39–40, Newcastle to Robert Drummond, Archbishop of York, Claremont, November 17, 1766.
20 Horace Walpole, *Memoirs of the Reign of King George III* (London, 1845), III, 82.

21 See Norman Sykes, 'The Duke of Newcastle as ecclesiastical minister,' *English Historical Review*, LVII (1942), p. 59 ff., and L. P. Curtis, *Chichester Towers* (New Haven, 1966).
22 Add. MSS. 33071, f. 71, Newcastle to Bishop of Salisbury, Claremont, December 4, 1766.
23 *Ibid.*, f. 72.
24 Add. MSS. 33072, f. 93v, Newcastle to Bishop of Salisbury, Claremont, January 31, 1768.
25 Sussex Archaeological Society MSS., Lewes, P., 261, Newcastle's Will.
26 John B. Nichols, *Illustrations of the Literary History of the Eighteenth Century* (London, 1858), 'Memoirs of Daniel Wray, Esq.,' I, 137.
27 W. S. Lewis (ed.), *Horace Walpole's Correspondence with George Montagu* (New Haven, 1941), II, 269.
28 Reginald Hunt (ed.), *Mrs. Montagu 'Queen of the Blues'* (London, 1923), I, 180, Mrs Montagu to Mrs Carter, November 17, 1768.
29 Add. MSS. 5832, f. 114 *et seq.*, Cambridge *Journal* reports for November 19 and November 26, 1768.
30 Add. MSS. 33610, A–T, ff. 102–3, Laughton Burials, 1554–1797.
31 *The Annual Register*, 1769, pp. 187–8.
32 Add. MSS. 33377, ff. 31 and 55v.
33 Add. MSS. 33628, f. 27v.
34 Add. MSS. 33337, ff. 28–9.
35 *Ibid.*, ff. 22–3.
36 India Office Library, Clive papers, MSS., Eur. g37, Box 13, No. 25, June 15, 1769.
37 India Office Library, Ormathwaite Collection, MSS., Eur. D 546/14.
38 Add. MSS. 33377, f. 23.
39 *Ibid.*, f. 5.
40 *Sussex Archaeological Society Collections*, VII (1854), 232.
41 Philip Dormer Stanhope, *The Letters of Philip Dormer Stanhope* (ed. Bonamy Dobrée) (London, 1932), VI, 2872–3, to Lieutenant General Irvine, Bath, November 21, 1768.
42 Horace Walpole, *Memoirs of the Reign of King George the Second* (London, 1847), I, 165–6.
43 [Philip Dormer Stanhope, fourth Earl of Chesterfield], *Characters by Lord Chesterfield* ... (London, 1778), p. 49.
44 Horace Walpole, *Memoirs of the Reign of King George the Second* (London, 1847), II, 272.

CHAPTER 7

RECAPITULATIONS AND CONCLUSIONS

The late seventeenth and early eighteenth centuries saw the return to power of the aristocratic classes in English society and the final consolidation of their authority in the amalgam which was the Whig party or connection. The aristocratic landed class directed but did not dictate; it held the reins of power but reflected the interests of other social, economic and religious sectors of the community. The conjunction brought with it fairly rapidly a political stability which replaced the bitter conflicts of the earlier seventeenth century.[1]

In the Duke of Newcastle we see an example of the class and of the individuals who helped to make this stability possible; who did not devise anything new in the way of government but who used the institutions and practices of the past to establish the rule of wealth and birth. He was unusual in that his whole life was devoted to maintaining the new balance in a way unmatched by any of his contemporaries. He did not create the system of influence, he simply used it in a more methodical way than any had before him. He and his Whig brethren employed the power of the crown to cement the rule of their class; at times they explained their policy on the basis of high principle but often on the more honest basis of individual or class interest.

The Pelhams had been in parliament for generations, as had the Holleses. However, it was the factor of chance in history which made the landed estates of both families devolve on young Pelham; his uncle might just as well have made his Vane nephews his heirs. This landed wealth was basic to Newcastle's career but did not necessarily determine that it would take the form it did. The young aristocrat of great means was essentially free to do as he pleased with his life. What roles were open to the rich, young noble? He could be a traditional landlord, manage and improve his estates, and live largely as a private person, except perhaps for a few local or county responsibilities and occasional attendance in the House of Lords. He could be a patron of individuals, causes or endeavors which he felt worthy of encouragement. He could be a man of the world and fritter away his time and substance in the great life of London and the continent. Then, too, he could follow the role traditional for his class and help to govern by taking an active part in local and national political and public affairs. Newcastle was a young aristocrat of great energy and drive who chose the path of public life; he probably never considered any other, for he inherited political influence in the north from his uncle and in the south from his father. It was the factor of family and class tradition which provided the womb in which his career could develop. He was in the public eye from an early age, for he was active in the election of 1713[2] and probably won recognition, reward and praise through this activity. The excitement, the festivities and the recognition made him love the labor involved in political life for the remainder of his days. The die was cast before he reached his majority; he never looked back or questioned his role as a public official.

Newcastle began his political activity on a local level through the influence he had inherited; this influence he continued to enlarge, for it was one foundation of his political power. His energy and activity, his drive and ambition in the career he had chosen, plus his willingness to spend his own resources, soon led to recognition and reward through offices at court and in the government. Thus by the age of twenty-four he was involved at the center of public affairs and he really never left it.

Although always active at the center of affairs, Newcastle basically held the position of a great landed magnate, a role which was fairly well defined in itself. The landed gentleman of whatever rank was ordinarily expected to live on his estates. He should take a personal interest in the welfare of the estates and of his tenants, he should seek to conserve, improve and perhaps enlarge his patrimony. He should be concerned in local activities of all sorts—in a word, participate actively in the management of his own estate affairs and in local county business and pleasures. Newcastle never led the traditional rural life on his estates for any extended period of time, but we know that he maintained a keen interest from a distance and looked forward to his visits to Sussex. He was always conscious, however, that he was slighting his responsibilities in the country.

Thus, we see that Newcastle, in reality, had two basic roles to play: the role of a great noble landholder, which he could not escape, and that of a political leader and public official, which he followed by choice.

These two roles, *per se*, were not necessarily in conflict, or even contradictory; but in Newcastle's case, they frequently proved to be so. There was no way of resolution which did not endanger something which was of great importance to him. If he had to choose, it seemed better to endanger his estates and the welfare of his heirs, than to endanger his public life, which gave meaning to his existence and where success was supremely necessary.

Newcastle was not obliged to spend excessively nor to establish the high life style he did. He had rank and status; given his energy and interests, he could have maintained himself in office. The duke, himself, created in part the tensions between the two roles. He may have been over-compensating for his real or imagined inadequacies, for we know that he did not feel himself especially well qualified for high office. The necessary and the unnecessary expenditures which went with his roles ate up the profits of both. Paradoxically, it was the very success of the consolidation of Whig power, for which Newcastle was partly responsible, which made possible his long tenure in public office, from 1717 to 1762, and contributed directly to his financial difficulties. He over-played his roles in both style and time. When there were conflicts between his private role and his public one, the public always 'won' and the private 'lost,' as his financial history amply demonstrated. He, personally, may have won psychologically, but in the end it meant relative ruin for him economically.

INCOME

We have determined with fair exactness in the preceding pages Newcastle's landed income at various stages of his life. He never had a net landed income approaching that which his contemporaries believed he had, if evidence from his stewards' accounts, from his account at Hoare's Bank and from the various studies made of his affairs, is to be credited, as it must. The most obvious error, made by contemporaries and by many historians subsequently, has been to confuse the gross rent roll with the net landed income, ignoring the manifold charges upon an estate. It must again be noted that Newcastle had the full income of his great estate available to him only until the trust of 1738, and that the estate itself was permanently reduced following the family settlement of 1741.

Beyond any doubt Newcastle's income from office was essential to supplement his landed income, for without it he could have sustained neither his style of life nor his full political influence, especially after 1738. Without it his credit structure would probably have collapsed as well. The duke held high offices which carried great salaries almost uninterruptedly from 1724 to 1762. The salaries were roughly £5,600 p.a.; if we assume a net of £5,000 and multiply by the thirty-eight years of service in these offices, we arrive at an approximate net lifetime income of £190,000. His private and public life more than consumed both this and his landed income as well. At no time in his long life did he have any appreciable capital resources available for investment in securities or ventures which might have given him additional income.

Finally, our study of his doleful financial history demonstrates fully that Newcastle's hands were indeed clean, as Lord Chesterfield stated. He took no specific personal financial advantage from his many offices, above rewarding some personal staff or dependents with small sinecures. His financial honesty may well have been based on a strongly held moral or religious belief. It may have reflected also his fear and insecurity, since the easiest way for parliamentary enemies to attack a minister or official was on the ground of personal peculation. No doubt he remembered both those who lost all from unclean hands at the time of the South Sea Bubble and those who were saved solely through Walpole's nerve and skill.

EXPENDITURE

The study has demonstrated throughout that Newcastle spent on a grand scale in every area of his interest and with small regard to the resources available at any given time. The fact that his total expenditures during his lifetime exceeded his total income by a very large sum is evidenced by the liquidation of a sizeable portion of his estate and the considerable indebtedness remaining at his death. It has been conjectured, based on little or no research in the available records, that Newcastle practically beggared himself through expenditures in politics, in borough or county electoral 'corruption,' or 'in service to the public,' as some of his more friendly contemporaries termed it. It has been one of the purposes of this study to attempt to determine the relative truth or falseness of this conjecture.

After reaching his majority Newcastle never had a day in which he was free of debt or when his financial affairs were without pressure. In a sense it was his doing on a grand scale the expected things for one of his class, in both the private and public areas of his life, which led to his trouble. Extraordinary pressures for spending came early in his life, first for building and improving his seats, and, second, for the elections of 1715 and 1722, which taken together made his financial structure creak and then led to crisis, which was resolved in part by the temporary trust of 1723. Without unusual expenditure he could have sustained his great household, which was the major drain on his resources. Newcastle attempted time and again, with expert help, to analyze his costs or expenditures and it was the household or family which in every case was considered the locus of his problems. We noted budget after budget and each represented an attempt to reduce, or at least control, expenses in the areas of his personal or family life as distinct from his political one. However, household or family budgets for Sussex would have included, as a matter of course, normal costs for public entertaining at Halland.

A study of Robert Burnett's Sussex accounts, which survive for the period 1735–42,[3] demonstrate that election costs were seldom noted. But taking those that are mentioned, plus any which might be related to an election interest, such items, for example, as 'Purchases at Lewes, Buildings and Repairs' and all 'Extraordinaries,' we get just over £7,300 for the seven-year period, roughly £1,000 per annum. Even if my conjectures are correct (and these items do actually relate to indirect costs of an election interest), the sum could easily have been sustained by the duke. Detailed studies of the elections of 1727, 1734, 1741 and 1761 have been made by Nulle, Williams, Perkins and Namier, respectively, but they were principally interested, naturally enough, in the political process. Rarely did these historians give specific examples of actual costs in these elections because few exist in the Newcastle papers, but each contended nevertheless that such expenditures were of major importance in causing his financial difficulties.[4] Nulle contended that the duke went deeper into debt with each year and that he 'devoted his fortune and life' to politics,[5] and Williams estimated that he spent at least £6,000 on the elections in 1734, an estimate based solely on what money might have been available to Burnett for the 1741 election, data which make the estimate very suspect.[6]

Williams must be far wide of the mark for he based his estimate on very dubious premises. First, he was reading backward, i.e. from the election of 1741 to that of 1734, and the duke's situation was quite different at the two dates. Second, he apparently failed to realize that Burnett was not an election paymaster-in-chief for Newcastle but was concerned only with Sussex and even there largely for constituencies where the duke's personal and family influence, not the government's, was paramount. Indeed, Burnett's actual notations in his accounts of 'Election Extraordinaries' for Sussex to October, 1741, total £788.7s.3d.[7] Burnett had much money available each year, but it was available not for political expenses but rather to pay bills for house-keeping expenses, debts and interest, wages, pensions and charities, tradespeople, building and a host of other things. After all, Burnett was his Grace's Steward of the Household.

No one would argue or contend that political expenditures did not add color to the duke's financial picture but the evidence is lacking to help us determine their actual depth. Negative historical evidence can be helpful or suggestive in attempting to analyze a situation or problem. It seems significant to me that never once in any of the memoranda written by Newcastle himself during anxious periods of financial crisis did he mention or allude to electoral costs of any kind. Perhaps he could not distinguish them, but others could have. We have noted that extant accounts and correspondence contain few references to direct political expenditures. Although it would take a bold man to hold the opinion, it is at least possible that such references are rare because they were, in fact, unusual.

We have seen clearly that there is insufficient evidence to indicate that direct political expenditure was a decisive factor in causing Newcastle's financial problems. Areas where the duke's political influence was great required constant nursing, and such expenditures were normal for one of his status at that time; but evidence is not in existence which would demonstrate that this electoral care or indirect political expenditure was the primary cause for his financial embarrassment throughout his life. It was the expense of maintaining the ducal life style and beneficence for nearly fifty years, rendered greater by the demands of his high offices, which was the primary cause of his financial anxiety; contributory but secondary were expenditures in political activity.

DEBTS

The Duke of Newcastle deserves full credit for one achievement in his long life: he alone built his great debt. We have demonstrated beyond any doubt that he inherited his estates debt-free from both his father and his uncle. The creation of debt is dependent upon the existence of credit. Newcastle had credit available in plenty from the age of eighteen, when he inherited his uncle's estates, and more at nineteen, after he inherited his paternal estate. Although he did not have full control of his paternal inheritance until he came of age in 1714 and of his uncle's until the Act of Parliament received the royal assent early in 1719, he was a fine credit risk for such careful bankers as Messrs Hoare. Newcastle's debt appeared so quickly after 1714 that, although no hard evidence exists to substantiate it, there is reason to conjecture that he anticipated his full inheritance by borrowing upon it, perhaps in part to support his early political activity in 1713. His landed estates, his great homes in Sussex, London and Claremont, as well as his plate, served at one time or another as collateral for loans.

It is necessary to ask why the duke became indebted in the first place and why he was never able to stop adding to his debt. The simplest answer to the query is that he continually spent more than his total annual income. He was never out of office long enough to actually retrench his expenses and he was unable to accumulate a surplus from current income to pay off his obligations. He carried a large debt in the form of personal bonds and notes whose only collateral was his name and credit. When pressures for payment of current short-term obligations became too great, he re-financed his indebtedness by borrowing on mortgage and the total long-term debt kept growing. Mortgage and other forms of debt carried interest at current rates, which fortunately for Newcastle, were quite low, but even so, interest on notes and bonds was often seriously in arrears. Debt in the form of unpaid bills of tradesmen and of arrears of wages and board-wages and liveries of servants carried no interest. All these forms of indebtedness were cumulative.

We have noted carefully the state of his indebtedness at various stages of his career and have seen that he was able by various means to continue spending in spite of it. He cleared at least partially the debt on his Sussex estate at the time of his marriage in 1717 and it was available as mortgage collateral once again. The temporary trust of 1721–3 evidently cleared additional indebtedness. No doubt his appointment as Secretary of State in 1724 with that office's great salary aided him in meeting current charges and made him more credit-worthy. However, it was in the period following the appointment that his indebtedness grew very rapidly, as we saw in Chapter 2.

The well of credit had dried up by 1738 and a trust had to be established to save the improvident Newcastle from bankruptcy. This instrument provided a legal guarantee that the resources provided under it would be used strictly for the purposes set forth in its preface. Legal title to lands was placed in the hands of trustees to hold for a certain period and the trustees were given power to use the annual income, or money derived from mortgage upon terms specified, to carry out the terms of their trust. The trust's resources were inadequate to service the debt and this necessitated the family settlement of 1741. The trustees were directed to sell specified estates or manors in order to carry out the provisions of the original trust, as well as added obligations, such as the costs arising from the settlement. This is why the settlement was at times referred to as 'the New Trust,' although it was basically that of 1738, which had only received additional obligations and directions and to which the name of Henry Pelham had been added as a result of the new agreement.

We must note here that Newcastle had full personal control of his financial affairs only from 1714 to 1738–41, during which period he benefited from both the income and credit resources of his estate. Since the duke was as traditional in the area of agricultural economics as he was in the political and diplomatic spheres, it was probably a weakness, but perhaps a necessary one, to make rent increases and other major lease changes dependent upon his approval.

Newcastle was to remain a power in the land for an additional twenty-one years, from 1741 to 1762, during which time the demands on him remained very great but his resources were much reduced. There was no lessening of spending, for he spent as if he had his old resources, and, of course, debt-building necessarily followed, which led to the financial crisis of 1752. New credit which became available from friends and private persons made it possible for Newcastle to continue to borrow, and the interest on the new loans was regularly and promptly paid by individual estate stewards. This personal debt survived at his death as well as a greatly reduced trust debt. Newcastle was fortunate that his inheritance was only reduced and his estate not bankrupted by his vast expenditures. It is the more amazing, considering the pressures and the opportunities, that his personal financial rectitude survived unsullied.

The trust of 1738–41 was on one level a grand success in that it consolidated and paid off vast debts, paid interest regularly on the debt which could not be liquidated, and saved the duke from bankruptcy. Much of the remaining trust debt was held over long periods of time by individuals, which meant that the trust was a secure place for profitable investment. The trust also partially restored the duke's credit and made Hoare's Bank and individuals willing to lend him money once again. Of course, owing to the necessity of liquidating much of his patrimony to pay off long-term debt, the settlement and trust were destructive of the very foundation upon which Newcastle's world rested. The changes of 1738–41 did in fact make Newcastle 'easy for the rest of [his] life,' for he continued to live on his accustomed level and never really retrenched; that his heirs received a much reduced inheritance could not have been a great concern of his.

MANAGEMENT

The management of Newcastle's affairs falls naturally into three distinct, yet often over-lapping, areas: his estates, his finances, and his household. In each area the duke employed separate sets of officials, advisers or servants, yet their roles often intertwined to make the whole establishment function. Each area involved a sizeable number of individuals who, taken together, would have populated a small village. The central direction of the whole would, in the normal course of events, have come from the duke, but we have seen that this supervision was lacking much of the time. Even if he had had the inclination, as well as the necessary knowledge and ability, it is questionable if he could have provided this function and yet have performed the duties of his offices and kept up his political activities. As his hurried manner and his harried demeanor testified, there were not enough hours in the day for all of his interests.

Newcastle retained administrative or management control of all of his estates at all times: those in his own name, those in the hands of the trustees, and those prepared for sale by the barring of the entails. His attention to the administration of his estates, as well as of his finances and household, was fitful at best. In the volumes of the Newcastle papers dealing with his personal or family life, I have uncovered not a single letter in which he offered any opinion or advice on purely agricultural matters; when he found time to write or to have conferences with his estate servants, his concern was usually financial, and at times administrative.

The diversity of his estates was great; they were, like those of the

Russells, scattered over London, Middlesex and many other counties. Surprisingly few letters have survived of stewards or collectors of the separate estates; letters from estate officials below the level of steward are extremely rare. Although the estate accounts must have been massive after so many years, and all would have been carefully preserved, relatively few have survived to become a part of the Newcastle papers. Perhaps all of the records, surveys of estates, all of the rentals and the stewards' accounts, went with the separate estates when they were sold by the trustees; others went to those who inherited them upon Newcastle's death or that of the duchess in 1776. Regardless of the correct explanation, no complete run of records exists for any of Newcastle's estates from the time of his inheritance of them, or before, to his death.

The layers of administration between the duke on one level, and a bailiff on a separate estate or manor on the other, were many and the distance great. The question must be raised of where and how decisions were made in the management of the estates. We can be certain that the duke was rarely involved directly in routine estate matters; it is probable that he was informed of areas in which decisions had to be made by the man of business, who was in direct contact with the stewards and receivers. We know that conferences were held, probably fairly regularly, between the man of business and the duke or, when he was too busy, with the duchess. The absence of correspondence does not prove that the duke took no part in estate management. It is probable that the duke gave general, or at times specific, directions, which were transmitted by the man of business to the stewards concerned. Upon occasions stewards came to London or Claremont for conferences with the duke, but these conferences may well have dealt more with political matters close to Newcastle's heart than with estate affairs. There are only two or three examples in the correspondence where the duke wrote directly to the stewards giving specific orders for actions, and those deal with financial or administrative matters. We need not assume that new, strange or complex problems arose very frequently, most matters being fairly routine in the agricultural area and the solutions largely traditional ones. Even in a matter such as the collection of arrears of rent, I have found no case in which suit was brought by the duke's agents or where a distraint was made on the chattels of a tenant. It would be just to conclude that Newcastle's higher employees actually managed his estates for him and that he was personally only peripherally concerned, although he may have set the mood. In routine matters decisions were made by the man of business or by the steward, or by the two together, as some correspondence would lead us to believe. There is no evidence that these men were creative or imaginative in the management of his affairs. They suggested no changes and trod the well-worn path of custom, which was probably in the mood set by Newcastle. When suggestions for change came in the management of the affairs of the estate, they always came from someone outside the system, from an expert hired because of one crisis or another.

The management of the finances of a holder of large estates was necessarily complex and usually or always involved a fair number of persons besides the actual holder. Newcastle never attempted to manage the financial side of his affairs or even pretended to. When he needed additional money for immediate projects or to pay pressing debts, he simply asked someone, as he stated it, 'to help him to the money,' that is, to procure it for him. He did at times suggest methods but always left the final decision dependent on expert advice, as we have noted throughout. Newcastle used his financial advisers on two levels, first in finding methods to meet current financial exigencies and, second, to analyze his overall financial situation, usually involving indebtedness, and to suggest a remedy through budgets for his whole establishment. The duke's advisers came from every area of his interest, from the family in the person of Henry Pelham and other relations, from the church in Bishop Bowers, from his political associates and personal friends in Hardwicke, Murray and Stone, and from what we might call a professional management class in Peter Forbes, Peter Walter, James Waller and James Postlethwayt. All, save the purely professional financial advisers, were intimates of Newcastle, and their own welfare was to one degree or another involved in the duke's reputation and solvency.

A word must be said of the role of Hoare's Bank. There is no indication that the duke was in any way personally intimate with the Hoare family, but perhaps his father had been, since the bank was used by many of the family. Thus it was a purely business arrangement useful to both; the bank played a central role and a nearly continuous one in the duke's financial life through his drawing account and through the many loans made to him. It is fortunate and surprising that the bank's ledgers have survived complete, but it is regrettable that very little of the bank's correspondence with its clients has been preserved for this period. Perhaps that correspondence might have given us more specific information on some areas of his expenditure, for example, building, and have enabled us to see his needs more clearly through the years.

Although many attempts were made to control the financial situation by keeping running balances of expenditures weekly, monthly or quarterly to see that budgets were being followed, they were never successful. Why? Certainly servants were under strict orders to abide by the budgets in their separate areas of responsibility. Either the orders were countermanded directly or the budgets were by-passed by using the category of 'extraordinary expenditures,' that is, those outside the current budget, or, by a completely separate category simply called 'unpaid bills,' which ran alongside, but completely separate from, the formal budget, idiotic as this practice was. In either case the directions to spend came from above.

The management of the duke's finances was an obvious failure, at least until he was an old man and out of office, and the failure must be blamed on Newcastle himself. He could never keep his resolve to stop excessive spending; Waller personalized it perfectly in 1741, when he told the duke that the virtue he lacked was 'a little Self Denyal.' He wanted immediate gratification of his wants or needs in an almost child-like way, and most categories of expenditure took precedence over his need to retrench or to live within a budget. Again we must note that Newcastle's attention to his overall financial situation was only fitful, and when he did give it some of his time he was always greatly shocked to discover its sorry state. The shock led him to take a resolution to change his ways, a resolution which always turned out to be temporary; he was an expert in fooling himself.

We have held that a probable key to Newcastle's constant over-spending and consequent perilous financial state was a conflict in his roles brought about by his psychological needs and insecurities. Even admitting these tensions and insecurities, the decisions in his financial life may have been made openly and knowingly, even calculatedly. He may well have felt that beneath it all, it was unlikely that he would bankrupt himself, considering his resources in land and his annual landed and official income. Besides, he had no heir of his own body and one descended through the line of Marlborough, which he had contemplated with joy when a young man, to inherit his vast estates and other property, so he could spend according to his needs and with little thought of the future. Newcastle had little real sense of history above that which touched his own life and experience, and then it was largely political. He left no memoir, no review of his own childhood and youth, no impressions or accounts of influences which molded him, not even so much as a note of regret at the sale of lands which might have remained in his family for years to come.

The failure of the financial management of the duke's affairs can be attributed to actions taken by him either compulsively and innocently or callously and calculatedly. In either case the result was the same: an additional area of turmoil and uncertainty in his life.

The management of the Newcastle household was central and critical, for this area consumed thousands of pounds each year. The costs included those for staffing, feeding the family, for clothing many of them, for building and repairs, for gardens and parks and for the stables, which at times had a separate budget but which was an integral part of the whole. The household servants, high and low, were all a part of 'the Family,' which in 1752 included nearly forty persons at London and Claremont. Perhaps the body servants of the duke and duchess should also be included in the family, even though they were never included in lists of servants and received their salaries from the duke's pocket money and the duchess's pin money and no doubt received board at the duke's table as well.

The major and continuing cause for Newcastle's financial embarrassment and disarray was expenditure for the household and the family. In each instance, when Newcastle found himself in a financial crisis, the expert advisers who examined and analyzed his affairs recommended control on expenditure for these areas and prepared budgets to provide it. In a normal household it would appear that the wife would have the greater responsibility for supervision and control. It is not at all clear who really managed or had an over-view of the Newcastle establishment. The duchess was evidently at home much of the time and could well have kept an eye on domestic affairs, but the records are largely silent on this point. We know that the duke frequently asked her to look into their affairs but such requests were above and beyond day-to-day household concerns. We can assume that both were concerned in their own domestic welfare and comfort, but it is certain that it was the duke and not the duchess who was responsible for initiating major domestic expenditures. Under their direction the Steward of the Household and the Clerk of the Kitchen had direct authority for expending the great sums necessary.

Neither the duke nor the duchess, singly or together, gave effective supervision of the household and the family. The staff was large and so fragmented into virtually separate jurisdictions that supervision would have been difficult under ideal circumstances. The servants, although departmentalized, formed a practical community in maintaining their own interests, for many had long tenure with the duke, even from father to son, and many set practices and perquisites existed, as was indicated by Murray, which needed to be changed. It can be safely assumed that these time-honored perquisites were an aid to the servants and not to the duke's budgets. It is to be noted that there were two examples in which both husband and wife were salaried by the duke: John Greening as Steward of the Household at £200 p.a., while Mrs Greening as Housekeeper at Claremont received £20 p.a.; John Twells received £100 p.a. as apothecary, and later as a general aide, while Mrs Twells received £20 p.a. as Housekeeper at Newcastle House. The staff was separated into those resident at Claremont and those at Newcastle House, and we are ignoring the resident housekeepers in Sussex and necessary staffs there because we know little of them save the names of those in charge. Since the duke moved constantly between Claremont and Newcastle House, each had to be fully staffed; Sussex homes had only to be put in readiness for ducal visits and he brought additional staff with him and hired local help as well.

There can be no doubt at all that the management or control in the household and family areas was inadequate to the needs of the whole establishment. What caused the problems throughout the decades? Was it size? Was it the fact that separate establishments had to be maintained at two or more locations? Was it entrenched customs and practices among the servants, high and low? Was it the cost of wages, board-wages and livery? It may well have been due to one or all, but the principal one was not that of error in the traditional structure of the great household and family, but the fact that no structure of management, no control, could provide financial stability with a man like Newcastle at its head, who was either incapable or unwilling when it came to limiting his expenditures in living, in entertaining and in all extraordinaries. Newcastle attempted to keep his affairs 'in a proper Method' so that they could be supervised; but this was all to no avail, for he would not play by the budgetary rules that he himself caused to be established.

THE EXIT

Newcastle's attitude to income and expenditure was aristocratic: wealth should be used to provide for a full life in the areas of one's interests or concerns. For Newcastle the full life meant a style of life befitting his position as a holder of the highest rank in the peerage, as a chief minister of the crown, and as an English gentleman who helped the king to govern his realm by assisting the return of loyal Whigs to Parliament. It is possible that from his point of view he used his wealth wisely in maintaining these roles; perhaps that is why he recorded no regrets.

It is difficult to think of Newcastle as a private man. His public role so overshadowed his private life that historians have never looked at the latter in depth, although his papers have been fully available since 1886 and are the most extensive record of any public man in eighteenth-century English history. Statements written about the man himself appear to be conclusions which are usually descriptive, often judgmental and seldom analytical. This study of his whole life from the viewpoint of his financial history is the first effort to see the person of Newcastle; we have in essence been inside, seeing highly intimate aspects of his personal and family life which were a constant concern to him, and only upon occasion looking outward at his public activity.

Yet it was his life, a great and lengthy play: Claremont, Newcastle House, the Court, the House of Lords, counties and boroughs, the stage; and the actors and audience, those entitled to play parts, great or small, in the political life of the nation. Behind the scenes were a host of lesser folk—from stewards of estates and of households, scriveners and bankers, men of business and accountants, chefs and butlers, down to maids and footmen—who made it all possible. And as after the last performance the stage is struck, and nothing remains of the performance but memories, so it was with Newcastle's lifetime of spending. Even before he finally left the stage, part of the county and borough scenery had disappeared, along with many of the actors; and within months of Newcastle's exit the world of Claremont and Newcastle House was gone and only silence remained: no united party to perpetuate his labor, no children to carry on his name, and no imposing monument in Westminster Abbey, like Duke John's, to fix the memory of his services—in fact, no monument at all except in the Manuscript Room of the British Museum.

NOTES

1 J. H. Plumb, *The Growth of Political Stability in England* (London, 1967), p. 187.
2 S. H. Nulle, *Thomas Pelham-Holles, Duke of Newcastle: His Early Political Career, 1693-1724* (Philadelphia, 1931), p. 18.
3 Add. MSS. 33157, *passim*.
4 S. H. Nulle, 'The Duke of Newcastle and the election of 1727,' *Journal of Modern History*, IX (1937); Basil Williams, 'The Duke of Newcastle and the elections of 1734,' *English Historical Review*, XII (1897); Clarence Perkins, 'Electioneering in eighteenth-century England,' *Quarterly Journal*, University of North Dakota, 13 (1923); L. B. Namier, *Structure of Politics at the Accession of George III* (London, 1929).
5 Nulle, 'The Duke of Newcastle and the election of 1727,' p. 2.
6 Williams, 'The Duke of Newcastle and the elections of 1734,' p. 477.
7 Add. MSS. 33157, f. 72.

SELECT BIBLIOGRAPHY

MANUSCRIPT SOURCES

British Museum:
Additional Manuscripts
  5832, 5852, 9149
Newcastle papers—Pelham papers
  32686–7, 32690, 32731, 32734, 32737, 32902, 32939, 32946, 33044, 33054–33056, 33058–61, 33064–78, 33084, 33137–9, 33157–66, 33168–9, 33184, 33320–2, 33324–8, 33330, 33337–8, 33442, 33584, 33610, 33691, 33728 33732
West papers
  34728
Hardwicke papers
  35406–7
British Museum Loan: Cavendish papers, 29/238
Public Record Office
  Close Rolls: C 34–5668
East Sussex Record Office, Pelham House, Lewes
  The Sayer Manuscripts
Sussex Archaeological Society, Barbican House, Lewes
  MSS.: Deeds, indentures, Newcastle marriage contract and mortgages on
      land and other property located in the Gatehouse of Lewes Castle
Hoare's Bank, 37 Fleet St, London
  Bank Ledgers, Current Accounts:
    Thomas, Lord Pelham, 1696–1712
    Duke of Newcastle, 1714–70
    Trustees for the Duke of Newcastle's Estates, 1738–70
  Money Ledgers [Loans]:
    I–1696–1718; II–1718–43; III–1743–73
    Duke of Newcastle
    Duke of Newcastle's Trustees
  Bank MSS.:
    Correspondence, as cited
India Office Library
  Clive papers
  Ormathwaite Collection
  Powis papers, film

Lincolnshire Archives Office, The Castle, Lincoln
    The Monson papers: Accounts of the Trustees of the Duke of Newcastle,
    1738–70
Nottingham University Library
    Newcastle papers
Bank of England
    Records of the holders of South Sea Company and East India Company
    Stock and the records of the holders of government annuities and other
    securities
Child's Bank (Glynn Mills)
    Ledgers, Current Accounts (incomplete)

PRINTED PRIMARY SOURCES

Bateson, Mary (ed.), *A Narrative of the Changes in the Ministry, 1765–1767,
    told by the Duke of Newcastle in a series of letters to John White, M.P.,*
    Longmans, London, 1898.
Blanchard, Rae (ed.), *The Correspondence of Richard Steele,* Oxford University
    Press, London, 1941.
Calendar of State Papers: Treasury Books, vol. 32 (1–2).
Carswell, John, and Dralle, Lewis A. (eds), *The Political Journal of George
    Bubb Doddington,* Clarendon Press, Oxford, 1965.
Cobbett, William (ed.), *The Parliamentary History of England from the Earliest
    Period to the year 1803,* Longmans, London, 1912.
Dobrée, Bonamy, and Webb, Geoffrey (eds), *The Complete Works of Sir
    John Vanbrugh,* Nonesuch Press, London, 1928.
[Glover, Richard], *Memoirs by a Celebrated Literary and Political Character,
    from the Resignation of Sir Robert Walpole in 1742, to the Establishment of
    Lord Chatham's Second Administration in 1757; containing Strictures on some
    of the most distinguished Men of that time,* John Murray, London, 1814.
Halsband, Robert (ed.), *The Complete Letters of Lady Mary Wortley Montagu,*
    Clarendon Press, Oxford, 1965–7.
Hervey, Lord John, *Some Materials towards Memoirs of the Reign of King
    George II* (ed. Romney Sedgwick), King's Printers, London, 1931.
Historical Manuscripts Commission:
    Thirteenth Report, Appendix 1–2, Portland Manuscripts
    Fifteenth Report, Appendix Part 4, Portland Manuscripts
    *Manuscripts of the Earl of Egmont. Diary of the First Earl of Egmont
        (Viscount Percival),* His Majesty's Stationery Office, London, 1923.
    Report on Manuscripts in Various Collections, vol. VIII (Manuscripts of
        M. L. S. Clements, Esq.), His Majesty's Stationery Office, London, 1909.
Lewis, W. S., and Brown, Ralph S., Jr, *Horace Walpole's Correspondence with
    George Montagu,* Yale University Press, New Haven, 1941.
Lodge, Sir Richard (ed.), *The Private Correspondence of Sir Benjamin Keene,
    K.B.,* Cambridge University Press, 1933.
Newton, Lady E., *Lyme Letters: 1660–1760,* Heinemann, London, 1925.

Phillimore, Robert (ed.), *Memoirs and Correspondence of George, Lord Lyttleton, from 1734 to 1773*, Ridgeway, London, 1845.

Russell, Lord John (ed.), *Correspondence of John, Fourth Duke of Bedford Selected from the Originals at Woburn Abbey*, Longman, Brown, Green and Longmans, London, 1842.

Saussure, Cesar de, *A Foreign View of England in the Reigns of George I and George II*, John Murray, London, 1902.

Sedgwick, Romney (ed.), *Letters from George III to Lord Bute, 1756–1766*, Macmillan, London, 1939.

[Stanhope, Philip Dormer, 4th Earl of Chesterfield], *Characters by Lord Chesterfield contrasted with characters of the same Great Personages by other respectable Writers*, Edward and Charles Dilly, London, 1778.

——, *The Letters of Philip Dormer Stanhope* (ed. Bonamy Dobrée), Eyre & Spottiswoode, London, 1932.

Suffolk, Henrietta, Countess of, *Letters to and from Henrietta Countess of Suffolk, and her second husband, the Hon. George Berkeley; from 1712 to 1767*, John Murray, London, 1824.

Swift, Jonathan, *Journal to Stella* (ed. Harrold Williams), Clarendon Press, Oxford, 1949.

Toynbee, Paget, and Whibley, Leonard (eds), *The Correspondence of Thomas Gray*, Clarendon Press, Oxford, 1935.

Turner, Florence M., *The Diary of Thomas Turner of East Hoathly, Sussex (1754–1765)*, John Lane, London, 1925.

Walpole, Horace, *Memoirs of the Reign of King George the Second* (ed. Lord Holland), Colburn, London, 1847.

——, *Memoirs of the Reign of King George III* (ed. Sir Denis LeMarchant), Richard Bentley, London, 1845.

—— (ed.), *The Works of the Right Honourable Sir Charles Hanbury-Williams, K.B.*, Edward Jeffrey, London, 1822.

Wyndam, Henry P. (ed.), *The Diary of the late George Bubb Doddington, Baron of Melcombe Regis: from March 8, 1748 to February 6, 1761*, Salisbury, London, 1828.

Yorke, Philip C., *The Life and Correspondence of Philip Yorke, Earl of Hardwicke, Lord High Chancellor of Great Britain*, Cambridge University Press, 1913.

PRINTED PRIMARY SOURCES: NEWSPAPERS

The Annual Register
Gentleman's Magazine and Historical Chronicle
Historical Register

SECONDARY WORKS: BOOKS

Almon, John, *The History of the Late Ministry. Exhibiting the Conduct, Principles, and views, of that party, during the years 1762–1764, 1765*, London, 1766.

Ashton, John, *Social Life in the Reign of Queen Anne*, Scribners, New York, 1925.

Baker, C. H. Collins and Muriel I., *The Life and Circumstances of James Brydges, First Duke of Chandos, Patron of the Liberal Arts*, Clarendon Press, Oxford, 1949.

Beattie, John M., *The English Court in the Reign of George I*, Cambridge University Press, 1967.

Chambers, J. D., *Nottinghamshire in the Eighteenth Century: A Study of Life and Labour under the Squirearchy*, Cass, London, 1966 (originally published 1932).

Clark, John W., *Endowments of the University of Cambridge*, Cambridge University Press, 1904.

Coxe, William, *Memoirs of the Administration of the Right Honourable Henry Pelham*, Longman, Reese, Orme, Brown, and Green, London, 1829.

Cranfield, G. A., *The Development of the Provincial Newspaper, 1700–1760*, Clarendon Press, Oxford, 1962.

Cronne, H. A. *et al.* (eds), *Essays in British and Irish History in honour of J. E. Todd*, F. Muller, London [1949].

Curling, Jonathan, *Edward Wortley Montagu, 1713–1776*, Andrew Melrose London, 1954.

Fussell, G. E., *Village Life in the Eighteenth Century*, Worcester Press, Worcester [1948].

Goodwin, A. (ed.), *The European Nobility in the Eighteenth Century*, Adam and Charles Black, London, 1953.

Gray, Arthur, *Cambridge University. An Episodal History*, Houghton-Mifflin, London, 1927.

Handover, P. M., *A History of the London Gazette, 1665–1965*, Her Majesty's Stationery Office, London, 1965.

Harsfield, Thomas H., *The History, Antiquities and Topography of the County of Sussex*, Lewes and London, 1835.

Hasbach, W., *A History of the English Agricultural Labourer*, Cass, London, 1966 [first English edition, 1908].

Hill, Sir Francis, *Georgian Lincoln*, Cambridge University Press, 1966.

[Hoare, H. P. R.], *Hoare's Bank: A Record 1672–1955. The Story of a Private Bank*, Collins, London, 1955.

Horn, D. B., *The British Diplomatic Service, 1689–1789*, Clarendon Press, Oxford, 1961.

Hunt, Reginald (ed.), *Mrs. Montagu 'Queen of the Blues,' her letters and friendships from 1762 to 1800*, Constable, London, 1923.

Ilchester, Earl of, and Longford-Brooke, Mrs, *The Life of Sir Charles Hanbury-Williams, Poet, Wit, and Diplomatist*, Thornton and Butterworth, London, 1928.

Jones, E. L., and Mingay, G. E., *Land, Labour and Population in the Industrial Revolution, Essays in Honour of J. D. Chambers*, Edward Arnold, London, 1967.

Kennedy, William, *English Taxation, 1640–1799. An Essay on Policy and Opinion*, Bell, London, 1913.

Laprade, William T., *Public Opinion and Politics in Eighteenth Century England to the Fall of Walpole*, Macmillan, New York, 1936.

Lever, Sir Tresham, *Godolphin, his Life and Times*, John Murray, London, 1952.

Lodge, Sir Richard, *Studies in Eighteenth-Century Diplomacy, 1740–1748*, John Murray, London, 1930.

Mair, John, *Book-keeping Methodiʒ'd; or a Methodical Treatise of Merchant-accompts, according to the Italian Form*, Edinburgh, 1741.

Mingay, Gordon E., *English Landed Society in the Eighteenth Century*, Routledge & Kegan Paul, London, 1963.

Namier, Sir Lewis B., *England in the Age of the American Revolution*, Macmillan, London, 1930.

——, *The Structure of Politics at the Accession of George III*, Macmillan, London, 1929.

——, and Brooke, John, *The History of Parliament. The House of Commons 1754–1790*, Her Majesty's Stationery Office, London, 1964.

Nichols, John B., *Illustrations of the Literary History of the Eighteenth Century*, Nichols, London, 1858.

Nulle, Stebelton H., *Thomas Pelham-Holles, Duke of Newcastle: His Early Political Career, 1693–1724*, University of Pennsylvania Press, Philadelphia, 1931.

Owen, John B., *The Rise of the Pelhams*, Methuen, London, 1957.

Plumb, J. H., *Sir Robert Walpole*, The Cresset Press, London, 1956–60.

——, *The Growth of Political Stability in England, 1675–1725*, Macmillan London, 1967.

—— (ed.), *Studies in Social History, A Tribute to G. M. Trevelyan*, Longmans, Green and Co., London, 1955.

Robson, Robert, *The Attorney in Eighteenth Century England*, Cambridge University Press, 1959.

Smollett, Tobias, *The Adventures of Sir Launcelot Greaves together with The History and Adventures of an Atom*, Blackwell, Oxford, 1926.

——, *The Expedition of Humphry Clinker*, Modern Library, New York, 1929.

Sykes, Norman, *Church and State in England in the Eighteenth Century*, Cambridge University Press, 1934.

Thomson, Mark A., *Secretaries of State, 1681–1782*, Clarendon Press, Oxford, 1932.

Torrens, W. M., *History of Cabinets: From the Union with Scotland to the Acquisition of Canada and Bengal*, Allen, London, 1894.

Turberville, A. S., *A History of Welbeck Abbey and its Owners*, Faber, London, 1938.

——, *The House of Lords in the XVIIIth Century*, Clarendon Press, Oxford, 1927.

Walford, Edward, *Old and New London: A Narrative of its History, its People, and its Places*, Cassell, London, n.d.

Ward, William R., *The English Land Tax in the Eighteenth Century*, Oxford University Press, London, 1953.

Watson, J. Steven, *The Reign of George III, 1760–1815*, Clarendon Press, Oxford, 1960.

Wilkes, J. W., *A Whig in Power: The Political Career of Henry Pelham*, Northwestern University Press, Evanston, 1964.

Williams, Basil, *The Life of William Pitt, Earl of Chatham*, Cass, London, 1966 [first published 1913].

——, *The Whig Supremacy*, Clarendon Press, Oxford, 1936.

——, *Carteret and Newcastle: A Contrast in Contemporaries*, Cambridge University Press, 1943.

Winstanley, D. A., *Lord Chatham and the Whig Opposition*, Cass, London, 1966 [first published 1912].

——, *The University of Cambridge in the Eighteenth Century*, Cambridge University Press, 1922.

——, *Unreformed Cambridge*, Cambridge University Press, 1935.

Wright, Thomas, *Caricature History of the Georges*, John Hatten, London, 1867.

SECONDARY WORKS: ARTICLES

Barnes, D. G., 'The Duke of Newcastle, ecclesiastical minister, 1724–1754,' *Pacific Historical Review*, III (1934), pp. 164–91.

——, 'Henry Pelham and the Duke of Newcastle,' *Journal of British Studies*, no. 2 (1962), pp. 62–77.

Beattie, J. M., 'The court of George I and English politics, 1717–1720,' *English Historical Review*, LXXXI (1966), pp. 26–37.

Browning, Reed, 'The Duke of Newcastle and the imperial election plan, 1749–1754,' *Journal of British Studies*, VII (1967), p. 28 ff.

Hess, Robert L., 'The Sackville family and Sussex politics: the campaign for the by-election, 1741,' *Sussex Archaeological Collections*, XCIX (1961), pp. 20–37.

Joslin, D. M., 'London private bankers, 1720–1785,' *Economic History Review*, 2nd series, VII, 2 (1954), pp. 167–86.

Nulle, Stebelton H., 'Duke of Newcastle and the election of 1727,' *Journal of Modern History*, IX (1937), pp. 1–22.

Reitan, E. A., 'The Civil List in eighteenth-century British politics: Parliamentary supremacy versus the independence of the crown,' *Historical Journal*, IX, 3 (1966), pp. 318–37.

Sykes, Norman, 'The Duke of Newcastle as an ecclesiastical minister,' *English Historical Review*, LVII (1942), p. 59 ff.

Williams, Basil, 'The Duke of Newcastle and the elections of 1734,' *English Historical Review*, XII (1897), pp. 448–88.

INDEX

In this index the Duke of Newcastle is referred to as N.